THE CONCISE BIBLE
Christian Community Bible
Catholic Pastoral Edition

THE CONCISE BIBLE

Christian Community Bible

CATHOLIC PASTORAL EDITION

Claretian Publications

THE CONCISE BIBLE
Christian Community Bible
Catholic Pastoral Edition

A division of Claretian Communications, Inc.
U.P. P.O. Box 4, diliman 1101 Quezon City, Philippines
TE: 921-3984 • FAX: 921-6502
Email: cci@claret.org
Website: www.bible.claret.org

Claretian Publications is a pastoral endeavor of the Claretian Missionaries in the Philippines. It aims to promote a renewed spirituality rooted in the process of total liberation and solidarity in response to the needs, challenges and pastoral demands of the Church today.

Originally published by
Ediciones Mensajero, Spain

ISBN 971-501-939-0

TABLE OF CONTENTS

Old Testament

Introduction 9
Pentateuch 11
Genesis 13
Exodus 63
Deuteronomy 87
Historical Books 93
Joshua 95
Judges 101
1 Samuel 111
2 Samuel 125
1 Kings 135
2 Kings 153
Ezra 159
Nehemiah 160
1 Maccabees 163
2 Maccabees 167
Stories 173
Ruth 175
Prophets 183
Isaiah 185
Jeremiah 199
Ezekiel 209
Daniel 215

Psalms 227
Sapiential Books 245
Proverbs 247
Job 249
Sirach 259
Other Books 263
Jonah 265

New Testament

Gospels 277
Matthew 279
Mark 307
Luke 311
John 335
Acts of the Apostles 359
Letters 385
Letters of St. Paul 387
Romans 387
1 Corinthians 389
2 Corinthians 393
Galatians 397
Philippians 399
Colossians 401
2 Timothy 403
Other Letters 405
James 407
1 John 409
Revelation 413

OLD TESTAMENT

Introduction

Oftentimes the Bible becomes a book too bulky and we even find some of its narratives uninteresting. This CONCISE BIBLE presents a collection of the most important moments of the Bible, with concise introductions and notes for better understanding and easy reading.

What we call "The Bible" is a complete library, gathering 74 books, with all imaginable styles: poetry, fiction, novels, laws, history, moral treatises, theological reflections... a bit of everything. These books were written in the course of many centuries. The oldest fragment possibly dates from 1800 before Christ. The most recent book is from 95-100 after Christ.

Along this path, the styles, traditions, literary modes, even religion and the idea of God, keep changing. Israel begins with a very primitive, very tribal faith, and little by little grows in the understanding of God... until we arrive at Jesus, in whom the Plenitude of Revelation dwells.

All along these centuries, the people are sometimes faithful to the Lord, but sometimes they are not. The Bible does not hide the sins, the abuses, the deviations of Israel. Precisely because of this, we can read "the chronicle about the discovery of God, the chronicle about sin and forgiveness throughout History."

In a book with so many different topics, its "truth" depends also in its genre. What is the truth of poetry? What is the truth of a novel? All these genres are present in the Bible: every passage has to be understood in its own genre.

We are used to reading the Bible as Word of God, and rightly so. But this does not mean that every sentence is a definitive and untouchable Word. We know how Jesus himself completed and even changed the Old Testament. Therefore, each text has its "own truth," frequently provisional, as a discovery that is better than the previous one but worse than the future. That is how we can understand things of the Old Testament that today appear wrong: these are steps in the long ladder that bring us to the summit: Jesus. And sometimes the steps are very far from the summit.

— — — — —

To select the text of the different books of the Bible for the compilation of this CONCISE BIBLE, we have chosen passages from some books, paying attention to particular chapters, and within the chapters to some concrete verses or versicles (the small number preceding the sentence). It is not our purpose to hide anything, since the Christian Community Bible upon which this selection is based, can be consulted at any time. The purpose is to summarize or, rather, adapt a book, the Bible that is extremely long and that many people, children, youth, women and men, do not dare to read because it is too long.

We have kept the paragraphs of the chosen texts with their own numbering in chapters and versicles, giving the impression that some text is lacking. That is not so. Through the continuous reading of the text the reader still finds its complete meaning and it is perfectly well adjusted to the intention that has guided us in the preparation of this CONCISE BIBLE.

Pentateuch

Introduction

"Pentateuch" means "five books." It is called this way because it is composed of Genesis, Exodus, Leviticus, Numbers and Deuteronomy. These are very different books: we find in them stories, legends, legislations, traditions, theology... Its origin is also varied: to put it in writing old traditions were compiled, some of them very old written and oral traditions that were retouched and re-written... We are not making references to these sources in the present exposition. We have only chosen the most interesting texts of Genesis, Exodus and Deuteronomy. These are famous writings for the universal literature and history (or rather pre-history) of our faith.

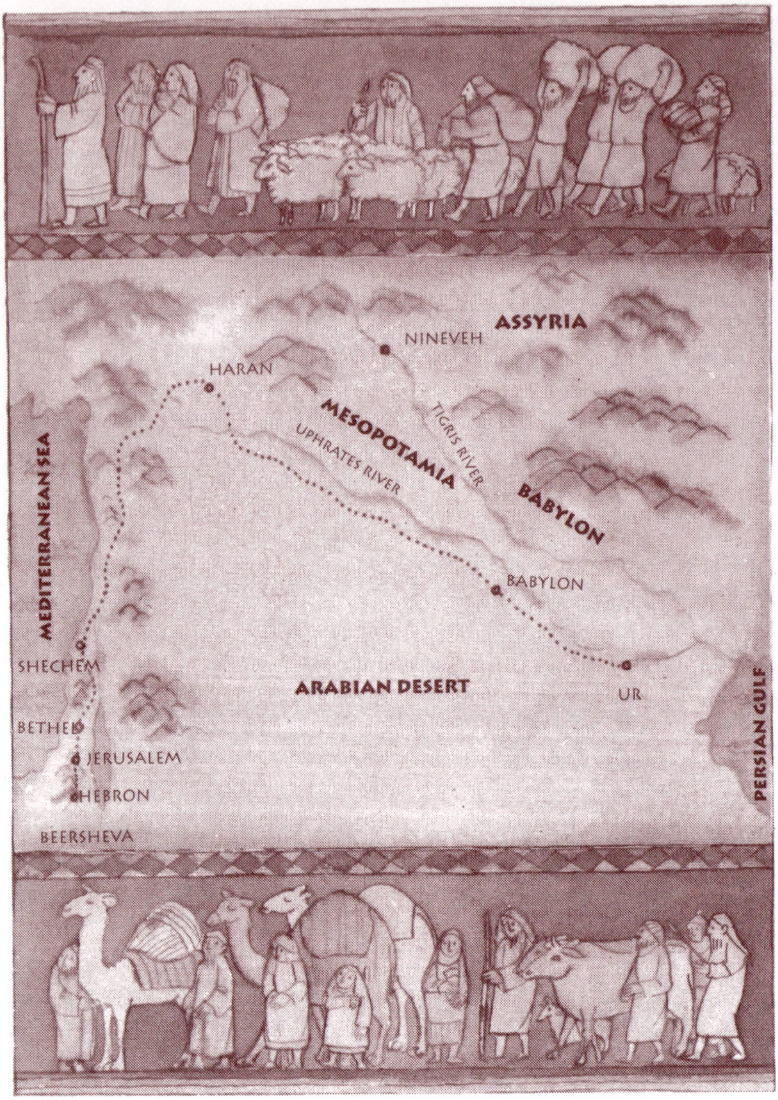
ASSYRIA
NINEVEH
HARAN
MESOPOTAMIA
TIGRIS RIVER
UPHRATES RIVER
BABYLON
MEDITERRANEAN SEA
BABYLON
SHECHEM
ARABIAN DESERT
UR
PERSIAN GULF
BETHEL
JERUSALEM
HEBRON
BEERSHEVA

Genesis

Introduction

Its name derives from the book's first words: "In the beginning...". We can distinguish three important divisions in the book:

Theological writings. *They refer to the Creation of the world, Paradise, and the First Sin. These are stories, they are not history but theology. They do not relate events that happened, but are fundamental messages about human beings, their relationship with God, and sin.*

Very old traditions. *The famous stories about Cain and Abel, the Flood, the Tower of Babel. These are very old traditions, previous even to the history of Israel. The great history compilers of Israel found them, and they included them as a "history of the origins", more legendary than historic, giving them a strong religious meaning.*

The history of the Patriarchs. *Abraham, Isaac and Jacob are the "fathers of the people". The origin of these stories is also rooted in legend. They have for us a symbolic value and the authors were more interested in their religious messages than in the historical events in themselves. This "history" ends with the marvelous "history of Joseph", one of the most beautiful stories of the whole Bible.*

Creation

1 1 In the beginning, God began to create the heavens and
the earth.

[2] The earth had no form and was void; darkness was over the deep and the Spirit of God hovered over the waters.

[3] God said:

—Let there be light.

And there was light.

[4] God saw that the light was good and he separated the light from the darkness. [5] God called the light 'Day' and the darkness 'Night'.

There was evening and there was morning: the first day.

[6] God said:

—Let there be a firm ceiling between the waters and let it separate waters from waters. [7] So God made the ceiling and separated the waters below it from the waters above it. And so it was.

[8] God called the firm ceiling 'Sky'.

There was evening and there was morning: the second day.

[9] God said:

—Let the waters below the sky be gathered together in one place and let dry land appear."

And so it was.

[10] God called the dry land 'Earth', and the waters gathered together he called 'Seas'.

God saw that it was good.

[11] God said:

—Let the earth produce vegetation, seed-bearing plants,

fruittrees bearing fruit with seed, each according to its kind,
upon the earth.

And so it was.

12 The earth produced vegetation: plants bearing seed
according to their kind and trees producing fruit which has
seed, according to their kind.

God saw that it was good.

13 There was evening and there was morning: the third day.

14 God said:

—Let there be lights in the ceiling of the sky to separate day
from night and to serve as signs for the seasons, days and
years; 15 and let these lights in the sky shine above the earth.

And so it was.

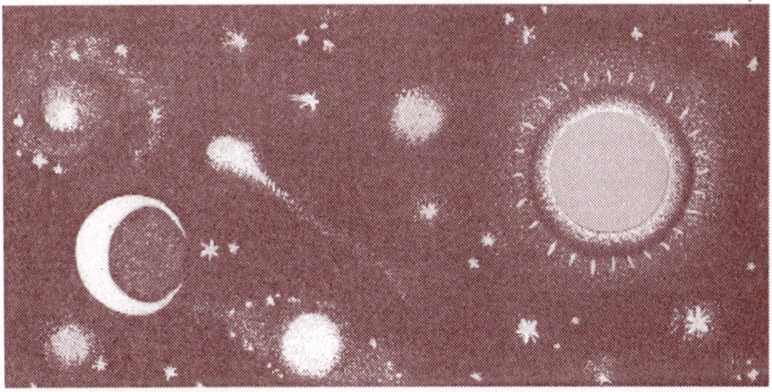

16 God therefore made two great lights, the greater light to
govern the day and the smaller light to govern the night; and
God made the stars as well. 17 God placed them in the ceiling
of the sky to give light on the earth 18 and to separate the light
from the darkness.

God saw that it was good.

19 There was evening and there was morning: the fourth
day.

20 God said:

—Let the water teem with an abundance of living creatures, and let birds fly above the earth under the ceiling of the
sky.

[21] God created the great monsters of the sea and all living animals, those that teem in the waters, according to their kind, and every winged bird, according to its kind.

God saw that it was good.

[22] God blessed them saying:

—Be fruitful and increase in number, fill the waters of the sea, and let the birds increase on the earth.

[23] There was evening and there was morning: the fifth day.

[24] God said:

—Let the earth produce living animals according to their kind: cattle, creatures that move along the ground, wild animals according to their kind.

So it was.

[25] God created the wild animals according to their kind, and everything that creeps along the ground according to its kind.

God saw that it was good.

[26] God said:

—Let us make man in our image, to our likeness. Let them rule over the fish of the sea, over the birds of the air, over the cattle, over the wild animals, and over all creeping things that crawl along the ground.

[27] So God created man in his image; in the image of God he created him; male and female he created them.

[28] God blessed them and said to them:

—Be fruitful and increase in number, fill the earth and subdue it, rule over the fish of the sea and the birds of the sky, over every living creature that moves on the ground.

[29] God said:

—I have given you every seed-bearing plant which is on
the face of all the earth, and every tree that bears fruit with
seed. It will be for your food. [30] To every wild animal, to every
bird of the sky, to everything that creeps along the ground, to
everything that has the breath of life, I give every green plant
for food.

So it was.

[31] God saw all that he had made, and it was very good.

There was evening and there was morning: the sixth day.

2 [1] That was the way the sky and earth were created and all their vast array.

[2] By the seventh day the work God had done was completed, and he rested on the seventh day from all the work he had done.

[3] And God blessed the seventh day and made it holy, because on that day he rested from all the work he had done in his creation.

[4a] These are the successive steps in the creation of the heavens and the earth.

In these two chapters we see two different stories about the creation of the world and of human beings that, evidently, contradict each other. The explanation is that the intention is not to try to explain how things happened (this was unknown to the authors, and even to us), but explain who God is (the Ruler, the Lord) and how humans relate to Him. These are also a beautiful hymn to the wisdom and power of God.

You can also read:

Proverbs 8:11,23-32. Good sense is the first of the creative tasks of God.

Ecclesiasticus 43:1-33. It is a great hymn to nature that is presented as a commentary to Psalm 148.

Job 38and 39. God answers Job, who blames Him for the evil in his life.

And making use of lyrical genre addresses God in prayer of praise and thanksgiving in the Psalms. Psalms are the prayer of Israel. They are the expression of human experience turned towards God. They are the expression of the life of a people dragged along by God.

Psalms were composed for repeated use: they are not to become exhaust by the first person who composes or orders it, nor by the first historical experience of the people.

You can also see:

Psalms 8, 24, 104, 136, 148. All of them talk about the creation of God.

Paradise and Sin

4b On the day that Yahweh God made the earth and the
heavens, 5 there was not yet on the earth any shrub of the
fields, nor had any plant yet sprung up, for Yahweh God had
not made it rain on the earth, and there was no man to till the
earth, 6 but a mist went up from the earth and watered the surface of the earth.

7 Then Yahweh God formed Man, dust drawn from the clay, and breathed into his nostrils a breath of life and Man became alive with breath.

8 God planted a garden in Eden in the east and there he placed Man whom he had created.

9 Yahweh God caused to grow from the ground every kind of tree that is pleasing to see and good to eat, also the tree of Life in the middle of the garden and the tree of the Knowledge of Good and Evil.

15 Yahweh God took Man and placed him in the garden of

Eden to till it and take care of it. 16 Then Yahweh God gave an order to Man saying:

—You may eat of every tree in the garden, 17 but of the tree of the Knowledge of Good and Evil, you will not eat, for on the day you eat of it, you will die.

18 Yahweh God said:

It is not good for Man to be alone; I will give him a helper who will be like him.

19 Then Yahweh God formed from the earth all the beasts of the field and all the birds of the air and brought them to Man to see what he would call them; and whatever Man called every living creature, that was its name. 20 So Man gave names to all the cattle, the birds of the air and to every beast of the field. But he did not find among them a helper like himself.

21 Then Yahweh God caused a deep sleep to come over Man and he fell asleep. He took one of his ribs and filled its place with flesh.

22 The rib which Yahweh God had taken from Man he formed into a woman and brought her to the man.

23 The man then said:

—Now this is bone of my bone and flesh of my flesh. She shall be called woman because she was taken from man.

24 That is why man leaves his father and mother and is attached to his wife, and with her becomes one flesh.

25 Both the man and his wife were naked and were not ashamed.

God has created everything good, innocent, perfect. But humanity is not like that: there is pain, work, death. In what follows the author of the book explains why there is so much evil in the world. Once again, the intention is not to tell what happened. The characters and actions are symbolic. It is a presentation, marvelously described, about the essence of temptation. Human beings prefer a small and immediate good to friendship with God. That is in the origin of humanity's problems. This tendency, ignorant and slaving, origin of all evils, is what we call "original sin". Not because it happened at the historical origin of humanity, but because it is at the deep root of all our mistakes, of all our sins.

3 [1]Now the serpent was the craftiest of all the wild creatures that Yahweh God had made.

He said to the woman:

—Did God really say: You must not eat from any tree in the garden?

[2]The woman said to the serpent:

[3]—We may eat the fruit of the trees in the garden, but of the fruit of the tree that is in the middle of the garden God said:

—You must not eat, and you must not touch it or you will die.

[4]The serpent said to the woman:

[5]—You will not die, but God knows that the day you eat it, your eyes will be opened and you will be like gods, knowing good and evil.

[6]The woman saw that the fruit was good to eat, and pleasant to the eyes, and ideal for gaining knowledge. She took its fruit and ate it and gave some to her husband who was with her. He ate it.

[7]Then their eyes were opened and both of them knew they

were naked. So they sewed leaves of a fig tree together and made themselves loincloths. 8 They heard the voice of Yahweh God walking in the garden, in the cool of the day, and they, the man and his wife, hid from Yahweh God among the trees of the garden.

9 Yahweh God called the man saying to him:

—Where are you?

10 He said:

—I heard your voice in the garden and I was afraid because I was naked, so I hid.

11 God said:

—Who told you that you were naked? Have you eaten of the tree I ordered you not to eat?

12 The man answered:

—The woman you put with me gave me fruit from the tree and I ate it.

13 God said to the woman:

—What have you done?

The woman said:

—The serpent deceived me and I ate.

14 Yahweh God said to the serpent:

—Since you have done that, be cursed among all the cattle and wild beasts! You will crawl on your belly and eat dust all the days of your life.

15 I will make you enemies, you and the woman, your offspring and her offspring. He will crush your head and you will strike his heel.

17 To the man, He said:

—Because you have listened to your wife, and have eaten from the tree of which I forbade you to eat, cursed be the soil because of you! In suffering you will provide food for yourself from it, all the days of your life.

20 The man called his wife by the name of Eve, because she was the mother of all the living.

21 Yahweh God made garments of skin for the man and his wife, and with these he clothed them.

Cain and Abel

It is a very, very old legend about grudges between farmers and cattlemen, represented by two typical personages. But the author has used it to portray what is perhaps the most important message of the whole book: YOU SHALL NOT KILL. Not even the killer. Pay special attention to the final passage, versicle 15.

4 1 Adam had intercourse with Eve his wife; she became
pregnant and gave birth to a child. She named him Cain, for
she said:

—I have got a man with help from Yahweh.

2 She later gave birth to Abel, his brother. Abel was a shepherd and kept flocks, and Cain tilled the soil. Cain was downcast. 6 Then Yahweh said to Cain:

—Why are you angry and downcast? 7 If you do right, why
do you not look up? But if you are not doing what is right, sin
is lurking at the door. It is striving to get you, but you must
control it.

8 Cain said to his brother Abel:

—Let's go to the fields.

Once there, Cain turned on his brother Abel and killed him.

9 Yahweh said to Cain:

—Where is your brother, Abel?

He answered:

—I don't know; am I my brother's keeper?

10 Yahweh asked:

—What have you done? Your brother's blood cries out to
me from the ground. 11 Now be cursed and driven from the
ground that has opened its mouth to receive your brother's
blood that your hand has shed. 12 When you till the soil, it will
no longer yield you its produce. You will be a fugitive wandering on the earth."

13 Cain said to Yahweh:

—My punishment is greater than I can bear. 14 See! Today
you drive me from this land. I must hide from you and be a
wanderer and a fugitive on the earth, and it will so happen
that whoever meets me will kill me.

15 Yahweh said to him:

—Well then, whoever kills Cain, will suffer vengeance seven times.

And Yahweh put a mark on Cain to prevent anyone who met him from killing him.

16 Cain then went from Yahweh's presence and settled in the land of Nod, to the east of Eden.

Sin: Flood

Historical data of terrible past floods, made bigger by legends, is used by the author to make an important penitential sermon, showing the graveness of sin and its consequences.

6 4 At that time there were giants on the earth, and afterwards as well, when the sons of God went to the daughters of men and had children by them. These were the heroes of old, men of renown.

5 Yahweh saw how great was the wickedness of man on the
earth and that evil was always the only thought of his heart.
6 Yahweh regretted having created man on the earth and his
heart grieved. 7 He said:

—I will destroy man whom I created and blot him out from the face of the earth, as well as the beasts, creeping creatures and birds, for I am sorry I made them.

8 But Noah was pleasing to God.

Noah and the ark

9b Noah was a just man, blameless among the people of his
time, a man who walked with God. 10 Noah became the father
of three sons: Shem, Ham and Japheth.

11 The earth became corrupt in God's sight and was full of
violence. 12 God saw the earth and saw it was corrupt, for corrupt, indeed, was the way of all mortals.

13 Yahweh said to Noah:

—I have in mind to destroy all people, for the earth is filled with violence because of them. This is why I will destroy them and with them the earth. 14 As for you, build an ark of cypress wood. You will make rooms in the ark and coat it with pitch inside and outside. 17 I am about to bring floodwaters on the earth to destroy the earth, to destroy all life under the heavens, every creature that has the breath of life. Everything on earth will perish, 18 but I will establish my covenant with you. You shall come into the ark, you, your wife, your sons and your sons' wives with you. 19 You shall bring into the ark two of every kind of living thing, male and female, to keep them alive with you. 20 Of the birds, the animals and all creeping things on the ground, according to their kind, two of every sort shall come in to be kept alive with you. 21 Take with you every sort of food that is eaten. Make a store of it and it will be food for you and them.

22 And Noah did all as God had commanded him.

Noah enters the ark

7 7 So Noah went into the ark with his children, his wife and his sons' wives to escape the waters of the flood. 8 Clean animals and also unclean, birds, and all that crawls on the earth went into the ark with Noah; 9 they went two and two, male and female, as God had commanded Noah.

10 And after seven days the waters of the flood were over the earth. 11 In the six hundredth year of Noah's life, in the second month and on the seventeenth day of the month, all the fountains of the great deep burst forth.

12 And there was a downpour on the earth lasting forty days and forty nights.

24 The waters flooded the earth for one hundred and fifty days.

End of the flood

8 1 Then God remembered Noah and all the animals and cattle that were with him in the ark. God made a wind blow over the earth and the waters subsided. [4]In the seventh month, in the seventeenth day of the month, the ark rested on Mount Ararat.

[6]At the end of the forty days Noah opened the window of the ark that he had built [7]and let the raven out. This went off and kept flying to and fro until the waters had dried up from the earth. [8]Then Noah let out the dove to see if the waters were receding from the earth. [9]But the dove could not find a place to set its foot and flew back to him in the ark for the waters still covered the surface of the whole earth. So Noah stretched out his hand, took hold of it and brought it back to himself in the ark. [10]He waited some more days and again sent the dove out from the ark. [11]This time the dove came back to him in the evening with a fresh olive branch in its beak. [12]He waited seven more days and let the dove loose, but it did not return to him any more.

Noah goes out of the ark

[15]Then God said to Noah:

[16]—Come out of the ark, you and your wife, your sons and their wives with you. [17]Bring out with you all flesh, that is, all the animals who are with you, all things of flesh; birds, cattle and all that crawls on the earth. Let them abound on the earth, be fruitful and increase in number.

18 So Noah went out, with his sons, his wife and his sons'
wives with him. 19 All the animals, all the birds, all that creeps
on the earth, came out of the ark, one kind after another.

20 Noah built an altar to Yahweh and, taking some of all the
clean animals and all the clean birds, he offered burnt offerings on it.

21 Yahweh smelled the pleasing aroma and said to himself:

—Never again will I curse the earth because of man, even
though his heart is set on evil from childhood; never again
will I strike down every living creature as I have done.

Covenant between God and Noah

9 1 God blessed Noah and his sons and he said to them:
—Be fruitful, multiply and fill the earth.
3 Everything that moves and lives
shall be food for you;
as I gave you the green plants.
5 And from man I will demand a reckoning
for the life of his fellow man.
6 For in the image of God has God made man.
7 As for you, be fruitful and increase.
Abound on the earth and be master of it.
8 God spoke to Noah and his son:

—This is the sign of the covenant I make between me and
you, and every animal living with you for all future generations. 13 I set my bow in the clouds and it will be a sign of the
covenant between me and the earth. 14 When I bring clouds
over the earth, 16 when the rainbow is in the clouds, I will see
it and remember the everlasting covenant between God and
every living creature of every kind that exists on the earth.

17 God said to Noah:

—This is the sign of the covenant I have made between me
and all that has life on the earth.

We have seen in this text a very deep and valid religious conception: God, the Lord, gives the earth to humans, as their house, and humans will have to render account of it. God is an Ally of humans: if they behave bad, He will punish them so they can change, but never looking for death but for their conversion. The rainbow is God's arch of war, hanging in the firmament for ever, as a sign of peace. This will be a permanently present throughout the Old Testament.

The Babel Tower

The tower of Babel gets its inspiration in the pyramidal constructions of Babylon and its imperialists pretensions.

11 [1] The whole world had one language and a common
speech. [2] As people moved from east, they found a plain in the
country of Shinar where they settled.

[3] They said to one another:

—Come, let us make bricks and bake them in fire.

They used brick for stone and bitumen for mortar.

[4] They said also:

—Come, let us build ourselves a city and a tower with its top reaching heaven; so that we may become a great people and not be scattered over the face of the earth!

[5] Yahweh came down to see the city and the tower that the
sons of man were building, [6] and Yahweh said:

—They are one people and they have one language. If they
carry this through, nothing they decide to do from now on
will be impossible. [7] Come! Let us go down and confuse their
language so that they will no longer understand each other.

[8] So Yahweh scattered them over all the earth and they
stopped building the city. [9] That is why it was called Babel,
because there Yahweh confused the language of the whole
earth and from there Yahweh scattered them over the whole
face of the earth.

PATRIARCHAL CYCLE: ABRAHAM

We now shift from the "history" of all humanity to the history of the people of Israel. Their great ancestors are presented, figures aggrandized by legends, who became religious types.

God intervenes in history and He always does it to call humans to a better destiny, although apparently more demanding and unknown. Abraham will be, first of all, "the one who trusted in God", thus he left his land, trusting in God's promise: "I will give you this land, I will make you father of a great people."

His descendants were more mediocre. There are many dark stops in their lives. The author does not hide them; he also chronicles their sins, showing that God uses human frailty to carry on with his plan of salvation.

Vocation of Abram

12 1 Yahweh said to Abram:
—Leave your country,
your family and your father's house,
for the land I will show you.
2 I will make you a great nation.
I will bless you and make your name great,
and you will be a blessing.
3 I will bless those who bless you,
and whoever curses you,
I will curse, and in you
all peoples of the earth will be blessed.
4 So Abram went as Yahweh had told him, and Lot went
with him.

Abram was seventy-five years old when he left Haran.

5 Abram took Sarai, his wife, his nephew Lot, all the possessions they had accumulated and the people they had acquired in Haran. They set out for the land of Canaan.

6 Abram traveled through the country as far as Shechem, to the oak of Moreh. At that time the Canaanites were in the land.

7 Yahweh appeared to Abram and said:

—To your descendants I will give this land.

There he built an altar to Yahweh who had appeared to him.

8 From there he went on to the mountains east of Bethel and pitched his tent, with Bethel to the west and Ai to the east. There also he built an altar to Yahweh and called on the name of Yahweh.

Abram and Lot

13 1 Abram went up from Egypt to the Negeb, he and his wife, with all he had and Lot with him.

12 Abram settled in the country of Canaan while Lot lived among the towns of the plain and moved his tent as far as Sodom.

14 Yahweh said to Abram after Lot had left him:

—Raise your eyes and look from where you are, towards the north, the south, the east and the west; [15] all the land you see I will give to you and your descendants forever. [16] I will make your descendants as the dust of the earth; if the grains of the dust can be counted, then your descendants may be counted.

Covenant of the Lord with Abram

15 [1] After this the word of Yahweh was spoken to Abram in a vision:

—Do not be afraid, Abram, I am your shield; your reward will be very great!

[5] Then Yahweh brought him outside and said to him:

—Look up at the sky and count the stars if you can. Your descendants will be like that.

[6] Abram believed Yahweh who, because of this, held him to be an upright man.

[7] And he said:

—I am Yahweh who brought you from Ur of the Chaldeans to give you this land as your possession.

17 [1] When Abram was ninety-nine years old, Yahweh appeared to him and said:

—I am God Almighty. Walk in my presence and be without blame! [2] I will make a covenant between myself and you, and I will multiply your race.

[3] Abram fell face down and God said to him:

[4] —This is my covenant with you: you will be the father of
a multitude of nations. [5] No longer will you be called Abram,
but Abraham, because I will make you the father of a multitude of nations. [7] And I will establish a covenant, an everlasting covenant between myself and you and your descendants
after you; from now on I will be your God and the God of your
descendants after you, for generations to come. [8] I will give to
you and your descendants after you the land you are living in,

all the land of Canaan, as an everlasting possession and I will be the God of your race.

15 God said to Abraham:

—As for Sarai, your wife, no longer are you to call her Sarai, but Sarah. 16 I will bless her, and I will give you a son by her.

Intercession of Abraham

18 17 Yahweh said:

—Can I conceal from Abraham what I am about to do?
18 Abraham, in fact, is going to become a great and powerful nation and through him all the nations of the earth will be
blessed, 19 for I have chosen him to command his sons and his household after him to keep the way of the Lord by doing what is right and just, so that Yahweh may bring about for Abraham what he has promised him.

20 Then Yahweh said:

—How great is the cry for justice against Sodom and
Gomorrah! And how grievous is their sin! 21 I am going down to see if they have done all that they are charged with in the outcry that has reached me. If it is not so, I will know.

23 Abraham went forward and said:

—Will you really let the just perish with the wicked?
24 Perhaps there are fifty good people in the town. Are you really going to let them perish? Would you not spare the place
for the sake of these fifty righteous people? 25 It would not be at all like you to do such a thing and you can't let the good perish with the wicked, nor treat the good and the wicked alike. Far be it from you! Will not the judge of all the earth be just?

26 Yahweh said:

—If I find fifty good people in Sodom, I will spare the whole place for their sake.

27 Abraham spoke up again:

—I know that I am very bold to speak like this to my Lord,

I who am only dust and ashes! 28 But perhaps the number of the good is five less than fifty. Will you destroy the town because of five?

Yahweh replied:

—I will not destroy the town if I find forty-five good people there.

29 Again Abraham said to him:

—Perhaps there will be only forty.

He answered:

—For the sake of forty I will not do it.

30 Abraham went on, saying:

—May my Lord not be angry, but let me speak. Maybe only thirty good people will be found in the town.

Yahweh answered:

—I will not destroy it if I find thirty there.

31 Abraham said:

—Now that I have been so bold as to speak to my Lord, what if only twenty can be found?

He said:

—For the sake of twenty I will not destroy the place.

32 But Abraham insisted:

—May my Lord not be angry, but let me speak just once more. What if only ten can be found?

And Yahweh answered:

—For the sake of ten good people, I will not destroy Sodom.

33 When Yahweh had finished speaking with Abraham, he left and Abraham went home.

Israel's tradition has always seen Abraham as "the friend of God". In its ingenuity and deepness, it is moving the image of Abraham bargaining with God to save the just of Sodoma.

19 29 So when God destroyed the towns of the plain he remembered Abraham and made Lot escape from the catastrophe while he destroyed the cities where Lot had lived.

Birth of Isaac

21 [2] Sarah became pregnant and bore a son to Abraham in his old age, at the very time Yahweh had promised. [3] Abraham gave the name Isaac to the son that Sarah bore him [4] and circumcised him when he was eight days old, as Yahweh had commanded.

[34] And Abraham stayed in the land of the Philistines for a long time.

The Sacrifice of Isaac

This story is confusing. It seems a cruel actuation of God. In reality, the writer has taken a very old story, previous to Israel, of human sacrifices, and cancelled it by substituting children with animals. As a result a kind of fable is created that magnifies the great obedience of Abraham. The happy ending shows that even in the worst scenarios one can still trust in God.

22 [1] Some time later God tested Abraham and said to him:

—Abraham!

And he answered:

—Here I am.

[2] Then God said:

—Take your son, your only son, Isaac, whom you love, and go to the land of Moriah and offer him there as a burnt offering on one of the mountains I shall point out to you.

[3] Abraham rose early next morning and saddled his donkey and took with him two of his young men and his son Isaac. He chopped wood for the burnt offering and set out for the place to which God had directed him. [4] On the third day Abraham looked up and saw the place in the distance, [5] and he said to the young men:

—Stay here with the donkey. The boy and I will go over there to worship and then we will come back to you.

[6] Abraham took the wood for the burnt offering and laid it on Isaac his son. He carried in his hand the fire and the knife. As the two of them went on together,

7 Isaac spoke to Abraham, his father:

—Father!

8 And Abraham replied:

—Yes, my son?

Isaac said:

—The fire and the wood are here, but where is the lamb for the sacrifice?

Abraham replied:

—God himself will provide the lamb for the sacrifice.

They went on, the two of them together, 9 until they came
to the place to which God had directed them. When Abraham
had built the altar and set the wood on it, he bound his son
Isaac and laid him on the wood placed on the altar. 10 He then
stretched out his hand to seize the knife and slay his son. 11 But
the Angel of Yahweh called to him from heaven:

—Abraham! Abraham!

And he said:

—Here I am.

12 Yahweh told him:

—Do not lay your hand on the boy; do not harm him, for now I know that you fear God, and you have not held back from me your only son.

13 Abraham looked around and saw behind him a ram
caught by its horns in a bush. He offered it as a burnt offering
in place of his son. 14 Abraham named the place 'The Lord will
provide.' And the saying has lasted to this day.

15 And the Angel of Yahweh called from heaven a second
time:

16 —By myself I have sworn, it is Yahweh who speaks,
because you have done this and not held back your son, your
only son, 17 I will surely bless you and make your descendants
as numerous as the stars in the sky and the sand on the
seashore. Your descendants will take possession of the lands
of their enemies. 18 All the nations of the earth will be blessed
through your descendants because you have obeyed me.

19 So Abraham returned to his servants, and they set off
together for Beersheba and it was there that Abraham stayed.

PATRIARCHAL CYCLE: ISAAC

In the following passages little we will find about important religious messages. These are old stories, present in the tradition on the origin of these people as well as other neighbor peoples; the authors try to give a certain religious meaning.

25 19 This is the story of Isaac, son of Abraham.

20 Isaac was forty when he married Rebekah, daughter of
Bethuel, the Aramean from Paddan-aram, the sister of Laban
the Aramean. 21 Isaac prayed to Yahweh for his wife, because
she could not have children. Yahweh heard Isaac's prayer and
Rebecca, his wife, conceived. 22 As the children struggled
together within her, she said:

—If it is like this, why do I continue to live?

She went to consult Yahweh, [23]and Yahweh said to her:

—Two nations are in your womb, and two peoples will be born of you; one nation will be stronger than the other, and the elder shall serve the younger.

[24]When the time came for her to give birth, there were twins in her womb.

[25]The first to be born was red and his whole body was like a hairy garment, so they called him Esau. [26]Then his brother was born and his hand had gripped Esau's heel so he was named Jacob. Isaac was sixty at the time of their birth.

[27]When the boys grew up, Esau became a skillful hunter, a man of the open country; Jacob was a quiet man living in tents. [28]Isaac who had a liking for game loved Esau, but Rebecca loved Jacob.

[29]Once when Jacob was making a stew, Esau came back from the country and he was famished; [30]and he said to Jacob:

—Let me have some of that red stew, for I am famished. That is why he was also called Edom.

[31]Jacob said:

—First sell me your right as the firstborn.

[32]Esau said:

—Since I am to die soon, what good is my right as the firstborn to me?

[33]Then Jacob said:

—Give me your oath first.

So he swore to him and sold his firstborn right to Jacob. [34]Then Jacob gave him bread and the lentil stew. Esau ate and drank and then got up and went his way. So it was that Esau thought nothing of his right as the firstborn.

Isaac blesses Jacob

27 [1]When Isaac was old and his eyes so weak that he could no longer see, he called Esau, his older son, and said to him:

—My son!

He answered:

—Here I am.

2 Isaac continued:

—You see I am old and I don't know when I shall die; 3 so
take your weapons, your bow and arrow, go out into the country and hunt some game for me. 4 Then prepare some of the
savory food I like and bring it to me so that I may eat and give
you my blessing before I die.

5 Now Rebecca was listening when Isaac spoke to his son
Esau. When Esau went into the country to hunt game and
bring it back, 6 Rebecca said to her son Jacob:

—I heard your father saying to your brother Esau: 7 'Bring
me some game and prepare food for me that I may eat and
bless you before Yahweh before I die.' 8 Now my son, listen
and do what I command you. 9 Go to the flock and bring me
two fine kids so that I can prepare for your father the food that
he likes. 10 You will bring it to your father and he will eat it and
give you his blessing before he dies.

11 Jacob said to Rebecca:

—My brother Esau is a hairy man and I am smooth-
skinned. 12 Perhaps my father will feel me and I will seem to
be tricking him and so bring a curse on myself instead of a
blessing.

13 But his mother said:

—Let the curse fall on me, my son! Only do what I tell you;
go and get the kids for me.

14 So he went and got them and took them to his mother to
prepare food that his father liked. 15 Then Rebecca took the
best clothes of her elder son Esau that she had in the house
and put them on Jacob, her younger son. 16 With the goatskin
she covered his hands and the smooth part of his neck, 17 and
she handed to him the bread and food she had prepared.

18 He went to his father and said:

—Father!

He answered:

—Yes, my son, who is it?

19 and Jacob said to his father:

—It is Esau, your firstborn; I have done what you told me to do. Come, sit up and eat my game so that you may give me your blessing.

20 Isaac said:

—How quick you have been my son!

Jacob said:

—Yahweh, your God, guided me.

21 Isaac said to Jacob:

—Come near and let me feel you, my son, and know that it is you, Esau my son, or not.

22 When Jacob drew near to Isaac, his father felt him and said:

—The voice is the voice of Jacob but the hands are the hands of Esau.

23 He did not recognize him, for his hands were hairy like the hands of Esau his brother and so he blessed him. 24 He asked:

—Are you really my son Esau?

And Jacob answered:

—I am.

25 Isaac said:

—Bring me some of your game, my son, so that I may eat and give you my blessing.

So Jacob brought it to him and he ate. And he brought him
wine and he drank. 26 Then his father Isaac said to him:

—Come near and kiss me, my son.

27 So Jacob came near and kissed him.

Isaac then caught the smell of his clothes and blessed him, saying:

—The smell of my son
is like the smell of a field
which the Lord has blessed.
28 May God give you of the dew of heaven;
and of the richness of the earth;
and abundance of grain and wine.
29 Let peoples serve you
and nations bow down before you.
Be lord over your brothers,
and let your mother's sons bow down to you.
Cursed be everyone that curses you
and blessed be everyone
that blesses you!

30 When Isaac had finished blessing him and Jacob
had just left Isaac's room, Esau came in from hunting. 31 He

also prepared food and brought it to his father and said to him:

—Father, sit up and eat the game your son has prepared, so that you may give me your blessing.

32 Isaac said:

—Who are you?

—I am your son, your firstborn, Esau.

33 Isaac trembled violently and said:

—Who was it then that hunted game and brought it to me? I ate it all before you came and I blessed him and he will be blessed.

34 On hearing his father's words, Esau gave a loud and bitter cry and said:

—Bless me, too, father.

35 But Isaac said:

—Your brother came deceitfully and took your blessing.

36 Esau said:

—Is it because he is called Jacob that he has supplanted me twice? First he took my birthright and now he has taken my blessing.

Then he asked:

—Haven't you kept a blessing for me?

37 Isaac answered Esau:

—I have made him your lord. I have given him all his brothers as servants; I have provided him with grain and wine. What can I do for you, my son?

38 Esau said to his father:

—Have you only one blessing? Father, bless me, too. Then Esau wept aloud.

39 Isaac then gave him this answer:

—Your dwelling place shall be far away
from the richness of the earth,
away from the dew of heaven above.
40 You shall live by your sword,
and you shall serve your brother;
but when you win your freedom
you will throw off his yoke from your neck.

41 Now Esau continued to hate his brother because of the
blessing his father had given him and he thought to himself:

—The time of mourning for my father is near; I shall then
kill my brother Jacob.

42 When Rebecca was told what her elder son had said, she
sent and called her younger son, Jacob, and said to him:

—Your brother Esau is consoling himself with the thought
of killing you. 43 Now my son, listen to me and flee to Laban,
my brother, in Haran. 44 You will stay with him for a time
45 until your brother's fury has cooled; and when he has forgotten his anger and what you did to him, I will send someone to bring you back. Why should I lose both of you on the
same day?

PATRIARCHAL CYCLE: JACOB

Jacob a Pilgrim

28 1 Isaac summoned Jacob and blessed him and commanded him:

—Do not marry a Canaanite woman. 2 Go to Paddan-aram,
to the house of Bethuel, your mother's father, and choose a
wife for yourself from the daughters of Laban, your mother's
brother. 3 May God Almighty bless you and make you increase
to become a group of nations.

Jacob at Bethel

10 Jacob left Beersheba and set out for Haran. 11 When he
reached a certain place the sun had set and he spent the night
there. He took one of the stones that were there and using it as
a pillow, he lay down to sleep.

12 While Jacob was sleeping, he had a dream in which a ladder stood on the earth with its top reaching to heaven and on
it were angels of God going up and coming down. 13 And
Yahweh was standing there near him and said:

—I am Yahweh, the God of your father, Abraham, and the
God of Isaac. The land on which you sleep, I give to you and
your descendants. 14 Your descendants will be numerous like
the specks of dust of the earth and you will spread out to the
west and the east, to the north and the south. Through you
and your descendants all the nations of the earth will be
blessed. 15 See, I am with you and I will keep you safe wherever you go. I will bring you back to this land and not leave
you until I have done what I promised.

16 Jacob woke from his dream and said:

—Truly, Yahweh was in this place and I was not aware of it.

17 He was afraid and said:

—How full of awe is this place! It is nothing less than a
House of God; it is the Gate to Heaven!

18 Then Jacob rose early and took the stone he had put
under his head and set it up as a pillar and poured oil on the
top of it.

Death of Isaac

35 22 Jacob had twelve sons. 23 By Leah: Reuben, Jacob's
eldest son, then Simeon, Levi, Judah, Issachar and Zebulun.
24 The sons by Rachel: Joseph and Benjamin. 25 The sons by Bilhah, Rachel's slave girl: Dan and Naphtali. 26 The sons by
Zilpah, Leah's slave girl: Gad and Asher. These were the sons
born to Jacob in Paddanaram.

27 Jacob came home to his father Isaac at Mamre or
Kiriatharba (that is, Hebron) where Abraham and Isaac had
lived. 28 After living a hundred and eighty years 29 Isaac
breathed his last and was gathered to his people at a good old
age. His sons Esau and Jacob buried him.

CYCLE OF JOSEPH

The history of Joseph is one of the most beautiful and known of the whole Old Testament. It is doubtful that it is historical, or even a legend. It seems rather a historical novel with a moralizing intention.

The message is heartbreaking: the fidelity of God that never fails the just person who remains faithful. In spite of all the calamities, God is there and the patience and fidelity of man will come back as blessing for him and his brothers.

This issue about the misfortunes of the just will occur many times, but not always with a "happy ending." The deepest expression of misfortunes will be found in the Book of Job.

Joseph's dreams

37 1 Jacob lived in the land where his father had settled,
in the land of Canaan. 2 This is the history of Jacob's family.

2 Joseph, a young man of seventeen, was shepherding the
flock with his brothers, the sons of Bilhah and the sons of
Zilpah, his father's wives. Joseph informed his father of the
bad reputation they had. 3 Now Israel loved Joseph more than
any of his other children, for he was the son of his old age and
he had a coat with long sleeves made for him. 4 His brothers
who saw that their father loved him more than he loved them,
hated him and could no longer speak to him in a friendly way.

5 Joseph had a dream which, when he told it to his brothers, made them hate him the more:

6 —Listen to the dream I had. 7 We were binding sheaves in
the field when my sheaf rose and stood up and your sheaves
gathered round and bowed down to my sheaf.

8 His brothers said to him:

—So you want to rule us or lord it over us!

They hated him even more because of his dreams and what he said.

9 Joseph had another dream which he told to his brothers:

—I saw the sun, the moon and seven stars bowing down before me.

10 When he told this to his father and brothers, his father rebuked him:

—What is this dream of yours? Are all of us, myself, your mother and your brothers to bow to the ground before you?

11 His brothers were jealous of him but his father kept in mind what he had said.

[12] His brothers had gone to pasture their father's flock at Shechem, [13] and Israel said to Joseph:

—Your brothers are pasturing the flock at Shechem; come along, I'll send you to them.

Joseph replied:

—Here I am.

[14] Then his father said:

—Go and see if all is well with your brothers and with the flock; then come back and tell me.

Jacob sent him from the valley of Hebron and Joseph arrived at Shechem.

[18] They saw him in the distance and before he reached them, they plotted to kill him. [19] They said to one another:

—Here comes the specialist in dreams! [20] Now's the time! Let's kill him and throw him into a well. We'll say a wild animal devoured him. Then we'll see what his dreams were all about!

[21] But Reuben heard this and tried to save him from their hands [22] saying:

—Let us not kill him; shed no blood! Throw him in this well in the wilderness, but do him no violence.

This he said to save him from them and take him back to his father.

Joseph sold by his brothers

[23] So as soon as Joseph arrived, they stripped him of his long-sleeved coat that he wore [24] and then took him and threw him in the well. Now the well was empty, without water. [25] They were sitting for a meal when they looked up and saw a caravan of Ishmaelites coming from Gilead, their camels laden with spices, balm and myrrh, which they were taking down to Egypt. [26] Judah then said to his brothers:

—What do we gain by killing our brother and hiding his blood? [27] Come! We'll sell him to the Ishmaelites and not lay our hands on him, for he is our brother and our own flesh!"

His brothers agreed to this. [28] So when the Midianite mer-

chants came along they pulled Joseph up and lifted him out of
the well. For twenty pieces of silver they sold Joseph to the
Midianites, who took him with them to Egypt. [29] When
Reuben went back to the well, Joseph was no longer there. He
tore his clothes [30] and returned to his brothers and said:

—The boy has disappeared, and what am I to do?

[31] They then took Joseph's coat, killed a goat and dipped
the coat in its blood. [32] They sent the long-sleeved coat and had
it taken to their father, saying:

—This we have found; see if it is your son's coat or not.

[33] He recognized it and said:

—It is my son's coat. Joseph has been attacked by a wild animal and torn to pieces.

[34] Jacob then tore his garments, put on sackcloth and
mourned his son for a long time. [35] All his sons and daughters
came to comfort him but he refused to be consoled saying:

—No, I shall go down to the land of Shadows, mourning for my son.

Thus his father wept for him.

[36] Meanwhile the Midianites sold Joseph in Egypt to Potiphar, an officer of Pharaoh and the commander of the guard.

Joseph, steward of Potiphar

39 [1] Now Joseph was taken down to Egypt, and Potiphar, an officer of Pharaoh, commander of the guard, an Egyptian, bought him from the Ishmaelites who had brought him there.

[2] Yahweh blessed Joseph while he lived in the house of his
master, the Egyptian, and everything went right for him. [3] The
Egyptian could see that God was with him and everything
worked well for him. [4] So Joseph pleased his master who
made him overseer of his house and of all that he owned, [5] and
from that time God blessed the Egyptian's house because of
Joseph; he blessed all that the Egyptian owned, his household
and his land. [6] The Egyptian left all he had to the care of
Joseph and, with Joseph fully in charge, he concerned himself

with nothing except the food that he ate. Joseph was a handsome man and well-built.

Temptation, calumny and jail

[7] After some time his master's wife kept noticing him and said:

—Sleep with me.

[8] But he refused and said to her:

[9] —How can I do such an evil thing and sin against God?

[10] Although day after day she spoke to Joseph, he would not agree to sleep with her or give himself to her.

[11] It happened that one day, when he entered the house to attend to his duties, none of the servants were in the house. [12] Then Potiphar's wife caught hold of Joseph by his cloak. But Joseph left his cloak in her hands and ran out of the house.

[13] As soon as he had run out of the house, [14] she called her servants and said:

—Look, a Hebrew has been brought here to make fun of us; he came here to lie with me, so I screamed [15] and he left his cloak with me and run out of the house.

[16] Then she kept the cloak by her until the master came home. [17] She then told her story

[19] When his master heard what his wife told him, "This is how your servant treated me," he blazed with anger. [20] He took Joseph and put him in the Royal Prison where the king's prisoners were kept.

But while Joseph was in prison [21] Yahweh was with him and showed him kindness so that he was well-liked by the warden of the prison.

40 [1] Some time after this, it happened that the cupbearer of the king of Egypt, who prepared the drinks for Pharaoh, and his chief baker offended their lord. [2] Pharaoh was angry with his two officers [3] and put them in custody in

the house of the captain of the guard, in the prison where
Joseph was kept. 4 So the captain of the guard appointed
Joseph to attend to their needs, for they were under arrest for
some time.

20 It so happened that on the third day, Pharaoh's birthday,
he made a feast for all his officers and remembered the chief
cupbearer and the chief baker. 21 The cupbearer was restored
to his office and placed the cup in Pharaoh's hand; 22 but the
chief baker was hanged, as Joseph had interpreted to them.
23 Yet the chief cupbearer did not remember Joseph, but forgot
him.

The dreams of Pharaoh

41 1 After two whole years Pharaoh dreamed that he was
standing by the Nile 2 when seven cows, sleek and fat, were
coming up from the Nile and beginning to feed among the
rushes. 3 Behind them came seven other cows, lean and scraggy that stood beside the cows already there. 4 These devoured
the sleek and fat cows. Then Pharaoh awoke.

5 He fell asleep again and had a second dream. He saw
growing on one stalk seven ears of corn that were full and
ripe. 6 And after these, there sprouted seven more ears of corn
that were small and scorched by the east wind. 7 Now the
small ears of corn swallowed the plump and ripe ones. Then
Pharaoh awoke.

8 In the morning he was uneasy and called all the magicians
and wise men in Egypt. He told his dreams to them but not
one among them was able to interpret his dreams. 9 Then the
chief cupbearer spoke to Pharaoh:

—This reminds me of my wrongs. 10 Pharaoh was angry
with his servants and had me put in custody in the house of
the captain of the guard and with me the chief baker. 11 Once
on the same night we both had a dream, each with its own
meaning. 12 With us was a young Hebrew, a servant of the captain of the guard. When we told him our dreams he interpreted them giving to each one its own meaning. 13 What he interpreted for us happened. I was restored to my office and the
chief baker was hanged.

Joseph interprets the dreams

14 Pharaoh then had Joseph summoned. They took him
quickly from the prison, shaved him, changed his clothes and
he presented himself to Pharaoh.

15 Then Pharaoh addressed him:

—I have had a dream which no one can explain; now I
have heard that when you hear a dream you are able to interpret it.

16 Joseph replied:

—It's not I but God who will give Pharaoh a favorable
answer.

17 Pharaoh then began telling his dream.

—I was beside the Nile 18 when seven fine cows, sleek and
fat, came up from the river and began to feed in the rushes.
19 Then seven other cows came up behind them. These were
poor, scraggy and lean. I had never seen any so ugly in all the
land of Egypt. 20 The thin, gaunt cows ate up the seven fat
cows, 21 but after eating them, it was as if they had not eaten
them at all because they remained as lean and scraggy as they
were before. And then I woke. 22 I also saw in my dream seven
ears of corn growing on one stalk, full and ripe. 23 Then, after
them, there sprouted seven ears of corn that were hard and
small and withered by the east wind. 24 The withered ears of
corn swallowed the good ears. I told this to the magicians but
none of them could explain its meaning.

25 Then Joseph said:

—Pharaoh's dream is one and the same. Yahweh has just
revealed to Pharaoh what he will do. 26 The seven fat cows are
seven years and the seven good ears as well. It's one dream!
27 The seven lean cows coming after them are seven years as
are the seven withered ears of corn scorched by the east wind,
and they are seven years of famine. 28 As I said to Pharaoh,
God is revealing to him what he is about to do. 29 There will be
seven years of plenty throughout the land of Egypt, 30 but they
will be followed by seven years of famine. Then the time of
abundance will be forgotten and famine will exhaust the land.
31 So severe will the famine be that no one will remember the
time of plenty.

32 If the dream has been repeated twice for Pharaoh it is
because God has so determined and will soon make it happen.
33 Now it is for Pharaoh to choose an intelligent and wise man
and set him over the land of Egypt. 34 Pharaoh could have
supervisors in the land and could levy a tax of one fifth of the
produce of the land during the seven years of plenty. 35 They
must gather all the food of these productive years that are
coming and, by the authority of Pharaoh, store grain for food
in the towns and keep it. 36 This food will be a reserve for the
seven years of famine coming to the land of Egypt so that the
people will not die of hunger.

Joseph, the head minister

37 The proposal of Joseph pleased Pharaoh and his ministers, and Pharaoh asked them:

38 —Where shall we find such a man possessed with the spirit of God?

39 And to Joseph he said:

40 —You shall be over my house, and all my people will obey your orders.

46 Joseph was thirty years old when he was summoned to
the presence of Pharaoh, King of Egypt. After taking his leave
of Pharaoh he journeyed through the entire land of Egypt.
47 During the seven years of plenty the land produced abun-
dantly. 48 So Joseph gathered up all the food that was produced during these years, storing in each town the food from
the fields around it. 49 Joseph stored huge quantities of wheat,
like the sand from the sea, so much that they lost count of the
amount.

53 When the seven years of plenty throughout the land of
Egypt came to an end, 54 the seven years of famine began as
Joseph had foretold. There was famine in all the countries but
in every part of Egypt there was bread. 55 When the land of
Egypt began to suffer from the famine, the people came to
Pharaoh for bread. But Pharaoh told all the Egyptians:

—Go to Joseph and do as he tells you.

57 As the famine had worsened throughout the whole

world, people came from other countries to buy grain from Joseph.

Joseph's brothers: First encounter

42 [1] When Jacob heard there was wheat in Egypt he said to his sons:

—Why do you stand looking at one another? [2] I've heard there is grain in Egypt, so go down and buy some for us so that we may stay alive and not die!

[3] Joseph's brothers—ten of them—went down to Egypt to buy wheat. [7] Joseph recognized his brothers but did not make himself known and, instead, said harshly to them:

—Where do you come from?

And they answered:

—We come from the land of Canaan to buy grain for food.

[8] Joseph recognized his brothers but they did not recognize him. [9] And he remembered the dreams he once had concerning them. He told them:

—You are spies, and it is to discover the weak points of the land that you have come.

[10] They said:

—No, my lord, your servants have come to buy grain for food. [11] We are all sons of the same man. We are honest men; your servants are not spies.

[12] Joseph replied:

—No, it is to find out the weak points of the country that you have come.

[13] They said:

—Your servants are twelve brothers, the sons of one man in the land of Canaan; the youngest is today with our father and the other is no more.

[14] But Joseph insisted:

—It's just as I said, you are spies! [15] And this will be proved. By the life of Pharaoh you will not leave this place unless your youngest brother comes here. [16] One of you is to go and fetch your brother. The others will be imprisoned while I verify whether you are telling the truth. If not, then as true as Pharaoh lives, you are spies.

17 And so he put them all in prison for three days.

18 On the third day Joseph said to them:

—I will help you to save yourselves, for I am a man who
fears God. 19 If you are sincere, let one of your brothers remain
prisoner in the house of the guard where you now are, and the
rest of you take the grain to save your families from famine.
20 Then you will bring back your youngest brother, so the truth
of what you say will be proved and your lives spared.

They did as they were ordered 21 and said among themselves:

—Alas! We are guilty because of the way we treated our brother when he pleaded with us for mercy, but we didn't listen. That is why this trouble has come upon us.

22 Reuben answered them:

—Didn't I tell you not to sin against the boy. But you did not listen and now we are brought to account for his blood.

23 Now they did not know that Joseph understood them as there was an interpreter between them.

24 As for Joseph, he withdrew and wept. When he came back, he spoke to them and took Simeon and had him bound and put in prison while they looked on.

Return to Canaan

25 Joseph ordered their sacks to be filled with wheat and
their money replaced in the sack of each one and provisions be
given them for the journey. All this was done; 26 they loaded
the grain on their donkeys and set off.

27 But in the evening one of them emptied his sack to feed his donkey at the lodging place, and he saw his money at the mouth of the sack, so he said:

28 —My money has been put back: here it is in my sack! Their hearts failed them and they trembled and turned to each other and said:

—What is this that God has done to us!

29 When they came back to Jacob in the land of Canaan, they told him about all their adventures:

30 —The man who is governor of the country spoke harshly to us and treated us as spies.

31 But we said:

—We are honest men, not spies. 32 We were twelve brothers, sons of the same father; one is no more and the youngest is with our father in the land of Canaan.

33 Then the man who is lord of the land said: By this I will know if you are honest. Leave one of your brothers here; take grain to save your families from the famine and go. 34 Bring back your youngest brother and let me see you are not spies but honest men. Then I shall release your brother and you can trade in the land.

35 Now, when they emptied their sacks, each one found his money bag in his sack. When they saw this, they were afraid and their father as well. 36 Jacob their father said to them:

—You are taking my children from me. Joseph has gone; Simeon has gone and now you are taking Benjamin. I have all this to bear!

37 Then Reuben said to his father:

—You may have the lives of my two sons if I do not bring him back to you. Entrust him to me and I shall see that he comes back.

38 But Jacob said:

—My son will not go with you, for his brother is dead and he alone is left. If he were to meet with some misfortune on the way, you would send my gray head to the land of Shadows in sorrow.

Second encounter

43 1 The lack of food was severe in the land, 2 and when they had eaten the grain they brought from Egypt, their father said to them:

—Go down again and buy us a little food.

3 But Judah said to him:

—The man solemnly warned us that our brother had to
come with us. 4 If you send our brother with us, we will go
down and buy food for you; 5 but if you don't send him, we
will not go, for the man said: You will not be admitted to my
presence if your brother is not with you.

6 Israel then said:

—Why did you bring this misery on me by letting the man
know you have another brother?

7 They replied:

—The man questioned us carefully about ourselves and
our kinsfolk saying: 'Is your father still alive? Have you another brother?' And so we answered these questions. Could we
have known that he would tell us to bring our brother?

8 Judah then said to Israel his father:

—Send the boy with me. Let us go so that we, you and our
children may live and not die. 9 I will guarantee his safety. If I
do not bring him back and set him here before you, I will bear
the blame forever. 10 If we hadn't delayed for so long we could
have been there and back twice over.

11 Israel their father said to them:

—If it must be so, then do this: take some choice products
of the land in your bags and a gift for the man-some balm, a
little honey, gum, myrrh, pistachio nuts and almonds. 12 Take
double the money with you and you will repay what was put
in your sacks; it may have been a mistake. 13 Take your brother and go back to the man. 14 May God Almighty grant you
mercy in his presence, so that he will allow you to bring back
your other brother and Benjamin. As for myself if I am
bereaved of my children, then bereaved I shall have to be.

15 Taking Benjamin, they set off and went down to Egypt
and were admitted to the presence of Joseph. 16 When Joseph
saw that Benjamin was with them, he said to his steward:

—Bring these men to my house. Have an animal slaughtered and a meal prepared, for these men will eat with me at
noon.

17 The steward did as Joseph directed and brought the men
to Joseph's house. 18 They were afraid and said to each other:

—It's because of the money that was placed in our sacks the last time, that we are brought in. He wants to attack and overpower us and have us as slaves and take our donkeys.

19 So they approached Joseph's steward and spoke to him at the door of the house:

20 —Oh my Lord, we came down here the first time to buy
food, 21 and when we reached a lodging place and opened our
sacks, we found in the mouth of the sacks each one's money
to the full weight. We have brought it back with us 22 as well
as additional money to buy food. We don't know who put the
money in our sacks.

23 The steward said:

—Be at peace! Don't be afraid. Your God, the God of your father, put a treasure in your grain sacks. Your money reached me safely.

He then brought Simeon out to them. 24 The steward took
them into Joseph's house, gave them water to wash their feet
and fodder for their donkeys. 25 They prepared their present
and waited for Joseph's arrival at midday, for they heard they
were to dine there.

26 When Joseph came into the house, they offered him the
gift they had with them and bowed to the ground before him.
27 He asked them how they were and said:

—Is your father well, the old man you spoke about? Is he still alive?

28 They answered:

—Your servant our father is well and is still alive. 29 He
looked up and saw his brother Benjamin, the son of his own
mother, and said:

—Is this your youngest brother, the one you told me about?

And he added:

—God be good to you, my son!

30 So deeply moved was Joseph, on seeing his brother that
he wanted to cry and went out quickly and wept in his own
private room. 31 After he had washed his face and come out,
controlling himself, he said:

—Serve the meal.

32 He was served separately and so were they, and the

Egyptians as well, for the Egyptians cannot share a meal with Hebrews; for the Egyptians this would be a shame. 33 They were seated opposite him in the order of their ages from the eldest to the youngest and they looked at each other in astonishment. 34 Joseph had portions from his own dish taken to them and Benjamin's portion was five times more than that of the others. So they drank freely with him.

Benjamin guilty

44 1 Now Joseph gave this order to his steward:

—Fill the men's sacks with as much food as they can carry and put back each man's silver in the mouth of his sack, 2 and put my cup, the silver cup with the money for the grain in the sack of the youngest.

The steward did as Joseph had directed.

3 As soon as it was light next morning the men were sent away with their donkeys. 4 When they had gone but were still not far from the city, Joseph said to his steward:

—Go quickly after those men and when you have caught up with them, say this: 'Why have you repaid good with evil? 5 Isn't this the cup my master drinks from and uses for divination? You have done a wicked thing.'

6 When he caught up with them he repeated these words. 7 They said to him:

—Why does my lord speak like that? Far be it from your servants to do such a thing. 8 The money we found in the mouths of our sacks, we brought back to you from the land of Canaan! How then could we have stolen silver or gold from your lord's house? 9 If one of your servants is found with the object, he will die and we too will become my lord's slaves.

10 —Very well then, he said, it will be as you say. The one who is found to have the cup will become my master's slave; the rest of you will go free.

11 Then each one quickly lowered his sack to the ground and opened it. 12 And he searched, beginning with the eldest and ending with the youngest. And the cup was found in Ben-

jamin's sack. [13]Then they tore their clothes and, reloading their donkeys, they returned to the city.

Third encounter

[14]Joseph was still in the house when Judah and his brothers returned and they threw themselves on the ground before him. [15]Joseph said to them:

—What have you done? Didn't you know that a man such as I am is able to practice divination?

[16]Then Judah said:

—What shall we say to my lord? How can we prove our innocence? God has uncovered your servant's guilt; we are my lord's slaves, we and the one who has been found with the cup.

[17]But Joseph said:

—Far be it from me to do that. Only the man found to have the cup will be my slave. As for the rest, go back in peace to your father.

[18]Judah then went forward and said:

—My lord, allow your servant to speak. Do not be angry with your servant, although you are equal to Pharaoh himself.
[19]The last time you questioned your servants saying: 'Have you a father or a brother?' [20]We said to my lord: 'We have an aged father who had a child in his old age. His brother is dead and he is the only one left of his mother's children. And his father loves him.' [21]Then you said to us: 'Bring him down so that I can see him for myself.' [22]We told my lord that the boy could not leave his father, for if he did, his father would die.

[23]You then told us that if our youngest brother did not come with us, we would not be admitted to your presence.
[24]All this we said to our father on returning there. [25]So when he told us to come back and buy a little food, [26]we said: 'We cannot go down again unless our youngest brother is with us. We shall not be admitted to the lord's presence unless our brother is with us.' [27]Then my father said: 'You know that my wife had two children. [28]One went away from me and has surely been torn to pieces since I have not seen him anymore.

[29] If you take this one from me and something happens to him
you will bring my gray hair in sorrow to the grave.' [30] Now I
can't return to my father without the boy, for my father loves
him very much. If he sees that the boy is not there, [31] he will
die and we will have sent the gray hairs of our father in sorrow to the grave.

[32] Now I, your servant, guaranteed the boy's safety and said
to my father: 'If I do not bring him back, I will bear the blame
before you all my life.' [33] So now let me take the place of the
boy and stay here as slave and let the boy go with his brothers,
[34] for I can't return to my father without the boy. Do not let me
see the misery that would be too much for my father.

Joseph reveals himself

45 [1] Now Joseph could no longer control his feelings in
the presence of all those standing by and he called out:

—Leave my presence, everyone!

And only his brothers were with him when Joseph made
himself known to them. [2] He wept so loudly that the Egyptians
heard and the news spread through Pharaoh's house.

[3] Joseph said to his brothers:

—I am Joseph. Is my father still alive?

And his brothers could not answer because they were terrified at seeing him.

[4] Joseph said:

—Come closer.

And they drew nearer.

—I am Joseph your brother, yes, it's me, the one you sold to
the Egyptians. [5] Now don't grieve and reproach yourselves for
selling me, because God has sent me before you to save your
lives. [6] It's two years since famine has been in the land and
there will be another five years without tilling and without
harvest. [7] God has sent me ahead of you to make our race sur-
vive there and to save many of you. [8] So it was not you but
God who sent me here, and made me a father to Pharaoh and
lord of his household, and ruler also of all the land of Egypt.

9 Go back quickly to my father and say to him: 'Joseph your
son sends you this message: God has made me lord of all
Egypt; so come down to me without delay; 10 you shall live in
the land of Goshen and you shall be near me, you, your children and grandchildren, your flocks and your herds, all that
you have. 11 And there I will provide for you (for there will be
five more years of famine) lest you and your household and
all who belong to you, be in need. 12 Now you can see for yourselves, and your brother Benjamin can see that it is I myself
who speak to you. 13 You will tell my father of the glory I have
in Egypt and of all that you have seen. Go quickly and bring
my father down here.

14 Joseph then threw his arms around Benjamin and wept.
15 Then weeping he kissed and embraced his brothers and they
began to talk with him.

24 Then he sent his brothers away and as they left he said:

—Don't quarrel on the way.

25 They returned from Egypt and came back to Jacob their
father in Canaan. 26 They told him:

—Joseph is alive and he is the ruler of all Egypt!

Jacob was stunned for he could not believe them. 27 But
they told him all that Joseph had said and showed him the
wagons that Joseph sent to carry him. Then Jacob's spirit
revived and he said:

[28]—It's enough, my son Joseph is alive; I will go and see him before I die.

Jacob goes down to Egypt

46 [1]Israel left with all he owned and reached Beersheba where he offered sacrifices to the God of his father Isaac. [2]God spoke to Israel in visions that he had during the night:

—Jacob! Jacob!

He said:

—Here I am.

[3]—I am God, the God of your father. Do not be afraid to go to Egypt, for there I will make you into a great nation. [4]I will go with you to Egypt and I will bring you back again and Joseph's hand will close your eyes.

[5]Jacob left Beersheba and the sons of Israel carried Jacob their father with their little children and their wives in the wagons that Joseph had sent to fetch him.

[6]They also took their flocks and all that they had acquired in Canaan. And so it was that Jacob came to Egypt and with him all his family, [7]his sons and his grandsons, his daughters and his granddaughters, in short all his children he took with him to Egypt.

Jacob meets Joseph

[28]Jacob sent Judah ahead to let Joseph know he was coming and that he would soon arrive in the land of Goshen.

[29]Joseph got his chariot ready in order to meet Israel his father in Goshen. He presented himself, threw his arms around his father and wept on his shoulder for a long time.

Jacob in Egypt

47 11 So Joseph had his father and brothers settled, giving
them property in the best part of Egypt, in the land of
Rameses as Pharaoh had commanded. 12 Joseph provided his
father, his brothers and his father's entire household with
food according to the number of their dependents.

Death of Jacob: Manasseh and Ephraim

48 1 Some time later, when Joseph was told that his
father was ill, he took with him his two sons, Manasseh and
Ephraim. 2 So they told Jacob that Joseph his son had come.
Then Israel, mustering his strength, sat up in bed. 3 And he
said to Joseph:

—God Almighty appeared to me at Luz in the land of
Canaan and blessed me 4 saying, 'I will make you fruitful and
increase your number, and I will make of you a group of
nations, and I will give this land to you and to your descendants after you as an everlasting possession.' 5 From now on
your two sons who were born in Egypt, before I came to you
here, are mine! Ephraim and Manasseh shall be mine just as
Reuben and Simeon are mine. 6 Only the children born after
them will be yours and the land they inherit shall be known
by the names of Ephraim and Manasseh.

49 33 When Jacob had given these instructions to his
sons, he drew his feet up into the bed; he breathed his last and
was gathered to his people.

50 15 When Joseph's brothers realized that their father
was dead they said:

—What if Joseph turns against us in hate because of the evil
we did him?

16 So they sent word to Joseph saying:

—Before he died your father told us to say this to you:
17 Please forgive the crime and the sin of your brothers in

doing evil to you. Forgive the crime of the servants of your father's God.

When he was given the message, Joseph wept. [18] His brothers went and threw themselves down before him, and said:

—We are your slaves.

[19] But Joseph reassured them:

—Don't be afraid! Am I in the place of God? [20] You intended to do me harm, but God intended to turn it to good in order to bring about what is happening today—the survival of many people. [21] So have no fear! I will provide for you and your little ones.

In this way he touched their hearts and consoled them.

Death of Joseph

[22] Joseph remained in Egypt together with all his father's family. He lived for a hundred and ten years, [23] long enough to see Ephraim's great-grandchildren, and also to have the children of Machir, the son of Manasseh, placed on his knees after their birth.

[24] Then Joseph said to his brothers:

—I am going to die, but God will surely remember you and take you from this country to the land he promised to Abraham, Isaac and Jacob.

[25] Joseph then made the sons of Israel swear, saying:

—When God comes to bring you out from here, carry my bones with you.

[26] Joseph died at the age of one hundred and ten; they embalmed him and laid him in a coffin in Egypt.

Here ends the Book of Genesis. A "history of the origins" in which religious messages, traditions and legends, events of history are interwoven. But absolutely all these stories are written as religious messages. The Bible was never interested in telling these things as pure historical curiosities; rather it uses history, or invents it, to transmit a religious message. This religious message is the true argument of all these stories.

You can also see:
Psalm 23. It is a Psalm of trust with the image of God as a shepherd and as host. See also Psalm 105.

Exodus

Introduction

Exodus is the book about liberation and covenant with its codes, about the first steps in the desert. Those who today acknowledge the existence of a historical nucleus in these stories place the oppression and exile from Egypt between the reign of Ramses II and Mernepta (1290–1204).

EXILE FROM EGYPT

The Lord enters history by siding with an enslaved people, oppressed by one of the powers of that time. The Lord of history appears as a redeemer of slaves, as defender of the rights of those who have no rights, as a righteous deliverer. The Lord acts, in part through Moses, the great human liberator.

The final author, using diverse texts, composes a magnificent and grandiose picture, using diverse repetitions.

These chapters are anchored in people's memory, becoming a model or patron of successive liberations. It also enters in the New Testament along this line extending its influence and inspiration even to people who do not believe in that liberating God. The Lord will always be for Israel "the one who took us out of Egypt, from slavery."

1 8 A new king who had not known Joseph came to power
9 and said to his people:

—The Israelites are more numerous and stronger than we
are. 10 Let us deal warily with them lest they increase still more
and, in case of war, side with our enemy, fight against us and
escape from the land.

11 So they set taskmasters over them to oppress them with
forced labor. In that way they built the storage towns of
Pithom and Rameses. 12 But the more they oppressed the
Hebrews the more they increased and spread, until the
Egyptians dreaded the Israelites 13 and became ruthless
in making them work. 14 They made life bitter for them in
hard labor with bricks and mortar and with all kinds of work
in the fields. In all their work the Egyptians treated them
harshly.

15 Then the king of Egypt gave orders to the Hebrew midwives—one of whom was called Shiprah and the other
Puah:

16 —when they attended Hebrew women who were on the
birth stool and saw that it was a boy, they were to kill it, but if
it was a girl they were to let it live.

17 But the midwives feared God and did not do as the king
of Egypt commanded but let the children live.

22 Pharaoh then gave this order to all the people:

—Every infant boy born to the Hebrews must be thrown into the Nile, but every girl may live.

Moses' infancy

2 1 Now a man belonging to the clan of Levi married a woman of his own tribe. 2 She gave birth to a boy and, seeing that he was a beautiful child, she kept him hidden for three months. 3 As she could not conceal him any longer, she made a basket out of papyrus leaves and coated it with tar and pitch. She then laid the child in the basket and placed it among the reeds near the bank of the Nile; 4 but the sister of the child kept at a distance to see what would happen to him.

5 Now the daughter of Pharaoh came down to bathe in the Nile; her attendants meanwhile walked along the bank. When she saw the basket among the reeds, she sent her maidservant to fetch it. 6 She opened the basket and saw the child:

—A boy, and he was crying!

She felt sorry for him, for she thought:

—This is one of the Hebrew children.

7 Then the sister of the child said to Pharaoh's daughter:

—Shall I go and get one of the Hebrew women to nurse the baby for you?

8 Pharaoh's daughter agreed, and the girl went to call the
mother of the child.

9 Pharaoh's daughter said to her:

—Take the child and nurse him for me and I will pay you.

So the woman took the child and nursed him 10 and, when
the child had grown, she brought him to Pharaoh's daughter
who adopted him as her son. And she named him Moses to
recall that she had drawn him out of the water.

Moses' youth

11 After a fairly long time, Moses, by now a grown man,
wanted to meet his fellow Hebrews. He noticed how heavily
they were burdened and he saw an Egyptian striking a
Hebrew, one of his own people. 12 He looked around and seeing no one, he killed the Egyptian and hid him in the sand.

15 When Pharaoh heard about it he tried to kill Moses, but
Moses fled from Pharaoh and went to live in the land of
Midian. There he sat down by a well.

16 A priest of Midian had seven daughters. They came to
draw water and fill the troughs to water their father's sheep.
17 Some shepherds came and drove them away; but Moses
went to their help and watered the sheep.

18 When the girls returned to their father Reuel, he asked
them:

—Why have you come back so early today?

19 They said:

—An Egyptian protected us from the shepherds, and even
drew water for us and watered the sheep.

20 The man said:

—Where is he? Why did you leave him there? Call him and
offer him a meal.

21 Moses agreed to stay with the man and he gave Moses his
daughter Zipporah in marriage. 22 She had a child and Moses
named him Gershom, to recall that he had been a guest in a
strange land.

23 It happened during that long period of time that the king

of Egypt died. The sons of Israel groaned under their slavery; they cried to God for help and from their bondage their cry ascended to God. 24 God heard their sigh and remembered his covenant with Abraham, Isaac and Jacob. 25 God looked upon the Israelites and revealed himself to them.

Moses' vocation

3 1 Moses pastured the sheep of Jethro, his father-in-law, priest of Midian. One day he led the flock to the far side of the desert and came to Horeb, the Mountain of God.

2 The Angel of Yahweh appeared to him by means of a flame of fire in the middle of a bush. Moses saw that although the bush was on fire it did not burn up.

3 Moses thought:

—I will go and see this amazing sight, why is the bush not burning up?

4 Yahweh saw that Moses was drawing near to look, and God called to him from the middle of the bush:

—Moses! Moses!

He replied:

—Here I am.

5 Yahweh said to him:

—Do not come near; take off your sandals because the place where you are standing is holy ground.

6 And God continued:

—I am the God of your fathers, the God of Abraham, the God of Isaac and the God of Jacob.

Moses hid his face lest his eyes look on God.

7 Yahweh said:

—I have seen the humiliation of my people in Egypt and I hear their cry when they are cruelly treated by their taskmasters. I know their suffering. 8 I have come down to free them from the power of the Egyptians and to bring them up from that land to a beautiful spacious land, a land flowing with milk and honey, to the territory of the Canaanites, the Hittites, the Amorites, the Perizzites, the Hivites and the

Jebusites. 9 The cry of the sons of Israel has reached me and I
have seen how the Egyptians oppress them. 10 Go now! I am
sending you to Pharaoh to bring my people, the sons of Israel,
out of Egypt.

11 Moses said to God:

—Who am I that I should go to Pharaoh and bring the people of Israel out of Egypt?

12 God replied:

—I will be with you and this will be the sign that I have sent you. When you have brought the people out of Egypt, you will worship God on this mountain.

13 Moses answered God:

—If I go to the Israelites and say to them: 'The God of your fathers has sent me to you,' they will ask me: 'What is his name?' What shall I answer them?

14 God said to Moses:

—I AM WHO AM. This is what you will say to the sons of Israel: 'I AM sent me to you.'

15 God then said to Moses:

—You will say to the Israelites: 'YAHWEH, the God of your fathers, the God of Abraham, the God of Isaac and the God of Jacob, has sent me.' That will be my name forever, and by this name they shall call upon me for all generations to come.

16 Go! Call together the elders of Israel and say to them,
'Yahweh, the God of your fathers, the God of Abraham, the
God of Isaac and the God of Jacob appeared to me and said: I
have seen and taken account of how the Egyptians have treat-
ed you, 17 and I mean to bring you out of all this oppression in
Egypt and take you to the land of the Canaanites, a land flowing with milk and honey.'

Moses and Aaron in the presence of Pharaoh

5 1 After this Moses and Aaron went to Pharaoh and said:

—This is what Yahweh, the God of Israel says: 'Let my people go, that they may hold a feast for me in the desert.

2 Pharaoh replied:

—Who is Yahweh that I should listen to his voice and
let Israel go? I do not know Yahweh and I will not let Israel
go.

6 That same day Pharaoh gave the following order to the
taskmasters of the people and to the Israelite foremen:

7 —You will no longer supply the people with straw for
making bricks. Let them go and find it themselves; 8 but you
will exact from them the same number of bricks as before, not
one less. They are lazy and that is why they are crying out to
go and sacrifice to their God. 9 Make the work harder for the
people and pay no attention to their lies.

PASSOVER

12 1 Yahweh spoke to Moses and Aaron in the land of
Egypt and said:

2 —This month is to be the beginning of all months, the first
month of your year. 3 Speak to the community of Israel and
say to them:

On the tenth day of this month let each family take a lamb,
a lamb for each house. 4 If the family is too small for a lamb,
they must join with a neighbor, the nearest to the house,
according to the number of persons and to what each one can
eat.

5 You will select a perfect lamb without blemish, a male
born during the present year, taken from the sheep or goats.
6 Then you will keep it until the fourteenth day of the month.

On that evening all the people will slaughter their lambs
7 and take some of the blood to put on the doorposts and on
top of the doorframes of the houses where you eat.

8 That night you will eat the flesh roasted at the fire with
unleavened bread and bitter herbs. 11 And this is how you will
eat: with a belt round your waist, sandals on your feet and a
staff in your hand. You shall eat hastily for it is a passover in
honor of Yahweh. 12 On that night I shall go through Egypt
and strike every firstborn in Egypt, men and animals; and I
will even bring judgment on all the gods of Egypt, I, Yahweh!
13 The blood on your houses will be the sign that you are there.

I will see the blood and pass over you; and you will escape the mortal plague when I strike Egypt.

[14] This is a day you are to remember and celebrate in honor of Yahweh. It is to be kept as a festival day for all generations forever.

Exile of Israel

29 It happened that in the middle of the night Yahweh struck down all the firstborn in Egypt, from the firstborn of Pharaoh, heir to the throne, to the firstborn of the prisoner in the dungeon and the firstborn of all the animals.

31 Pharaoh called Moses and Aaron in the night and said:

—Get up and go from among my people, you and the people of Israel. Go and worship Yahweh as you have said! 32 Take
your sheep and your cattle, as you told me, and go!

Passover ritual

13 1 Yahweh spoke to Moses saying:

2 —Consecrate to me every firstborn: the first to leave the womb among the sons of Israel, whether of man or beast, is mine.

3 Moses said to the people:

—Remember the day you came out of Egypt from the
house of slavery, for it was by his power that Yahweh brought
you out; because of this you will not eat leavened bread. 4 The
day you left was in the month of Abib.

The unleavened bread

5 When Yahweh brings you to the land of the Canaanites,
the Hittites, the Amorites, the Hivites and the Jebusites—a
land flowing with milk and honey which he swore to your
fathers to give you—you will carry out this ceremony.

6 For seven days you will eat unleavened bread and on the
seventh day you will hold a feast in honor of Yahweh. 7 You
will eat unleavened bread for seven days and no leavened
bread is to be seen among you or anywhere throughout all
your territory. 8 On that day you will tell your son: 'I do this
because of what Yahweh did for me when I came out of
Egypt.'

9 This ceremony will be for you as a sign on your hand and
a reminder on your forehead, so that Yahweh's law may be
ever on your lips, for it was with great power that Yahweh
brought you out of Egypt. 10 Because of this you will observe
this ordinance at the appointed time from year to year.

Towards the Red Sea

19 Moses took with him the bones of Joseph for he had
made the Israelites swear saying, "God will surely remember
you and then you will carry my bones with you away from
here."

20 They moved on from Succoth and encamped at Etham
bordering the wilderness. 21 By day Yahweh went before them
in a pillar of cloud to guide them along the way, and by night
in a pillar of fire to give them light, enabling them to travel
day and night. 22 Neither the cloud by day nor the fire by
night, disappeared from the sight of the people.

Crossing of the Red Sea

14 5 The king of Egypt was told that the people had fled;
then Pharaoh and his ministers changed their minds with
regard to the people. 'What have we done,' they said, 'in
allowing Israel to go and be free of our service?' 6 Pharaoh

prepared his chariot and took his army with him. 7 There were
six hundred of his best chariots; indeed he took all the
Egyptian chariots, each one with his warriors.

8 Yahweh had hardened the mind of Pharaoh, king of
Egypt, who set out in pursuit of the Israelites as they marched
forth triumphantly.

9 The Egyptians—all the chariots and horses of Pharaoh,
his horsemen and his army—gave chase and caught up with
them when they had encamped by the sea near Pihahiroth,
facing Baalzephon.

10 The Israelites saw the Egyptians marching after them:
Pharaoh was drawing near. They were terrified and cried out
to Yahweh. 11 Then they said to Moses:

—Were there no tombs in Egypt? Why have you brought us
to the desert to die? 12 What have you done by bringing us out
of Egypt? Isn't this what we said when we were in Egypt: Let
us work for the Egyptians. Far better serve Egypt than to die
in the desert!

13 Moses said to the people:

—Have no fear! Stay where you are and see the work
Yahweh will do to save you today. The Egyptians whom you
see today, you will never see again! 14 Yahweh will fight for
you and all you have to do is to keep still.

15 Yahweh said to Moses:

—Why do you cry to me? Tell the people of Israel to go forward.

16 You will raise your staff and stretch your hand over the
sea and divide it to let the Israelites go dry foot through the
sea. 17 I will so harden the minds of the Egyptians that they
will follow you. 18 And I will have glory at the expense of
Pharaoh, his army, his chariots and horsemen. The Egyptians
will know that I am Yahweh when I gain glory for myself at
the cost of Pharaoh and his army!

19 The Angel of God who had gone ahead of the Israelites
now placed himself behind them. The pillar of cloud changed
its position 20 from the front to the rear, between the camps of
the Israelites and the Egyptians. For one army the cloud provided light, for the other darkness so that throughout the
night the armies drew no closer to each other.

21 Moses stretched his hand over the sea and Yahweh made a strong east wind blow all night and dry up the sea.

The waters divided 22 and the sons of Israel went on dry ground through the middle of the sea, with the waters forming a wall to their right and to their left. 23 The Egyptians followed them and all Pharaoh's horses, his chariots and horsemen moved forward in the middle of the sea.

24 It happened that in the morning watch, Yahweh in the pillar of cloud and fire, looked towards the Egyptian camp and threw it into confusion. 25 He so clogged their chariot wheels that they could hardly move. Then the Egyptians said:

—Let us flee from the Israelites for Yahweh is fighting for them against Egypt.

26 Then Yahweh said to Moses:

—Stretch your hand over the sea and let the waters come back over the Egyptians, over their chariots and horsemen.

27 Moses stretched out his hand over the sea. At daybreak the sea returned to its place. As the Egyptians tried to flee, Yahweh swept them into the sea. 28 The waters flowed back and engulfed the chariots and horsemen of the whole army of Pharaoh that had followed Israel into the sea. Not one of them escaped. 29 As for the Israelites they went forward on dry ground in the middle of the sea, the waters forming a wall on their right and their left.

30 On that day Yahweh delivered Israel from the power of the Egyptians and Israel saw the Egyptians lying dead on the seashore. 31 They understood what wonders Yahweh had done for them against Egypt, and the people feared Yahweh. They believed in Yahweh and in Moses, his servant.

The exile from Egypt will be the most important event in the history of Israel. It is the beginning of the awareness of being God's chosen people. It will always be handed down from parents to children and they will celebrate it during the yearly feast of the Passover and in the Psalms, where they sing to the mercy of God leading them through the Red Sea, and the manna, and the water in the desert.

You can also read:

Psalm 78. The theme of this Psalm is the liberation of the people of Israel until the election of King David.

FIRST STAGE IN THE DESERT

Introduction

The people are already out of Egypt but have not yet arrived to the promised land. In between these two frontiers, in between these two decisive moments emerges a time of discernment in the desert.

This stage becomes a pattern of future pilgrimages through other deserts, to conquer freedom and hope. Because of its primordial character, these events have a symbolic value of future religious experiences (water, manna), culminating in the symbolic theology of the evangelist John.

Manna and quails

16 1 The Israelites left Elim and the entire community
reached the desert of Sin, between Elim and Sinai, on the fif-
teenth day of the second month after leaving Egypt.

2 In the desert the whole community of Israel grumbled
against Moses and Aaron 3 and said to them:

—If only we had died by the hand of Yahweh in Egypt
when we sat down to caldrons of meat and ate all the bread
we wanted, whereas you have brought us to this desert to let
the whole assembly die of starvation!

4 Yahweh then said to Moses:

—Now I am going to rain down bread from heaven for
you. Each day the people are to gather what is needed for that
day. In this way I will test them to see if they will follow my
Teaching or not. 12 I have heard the complaints of Israel. Speak
to them and say: Between the two evenings you will eat meat,
and in the morning you will have bread to your heart's content; then you shall know that I am Yahweh, your God!

13 In the evening quails came up and covered the camp.
And in the morning, dew had fallen around the camp. 14 When
the dew lifted, there was on the surface of the desert a thin
crust like hoarfrost. 15 The people of Israel upon seeing it said
to one another:

—What is it?

For they didn't know what it was.

Moses told them:

—It is the bread that Yahweh has given you to eat.

16 This is what Yahweh commanded: Gather it according to the amount each one eats, about four liters a piece, and according to the number of persons each of you has in his tent.

17 This is what the people of Israel did. They gathered it,
some more, others less. 18 But when they measured it with an
omer, those who gathered more didn't have too much while those who gathered less didn't have too little. Each one had as much as he needed.

Water from the rock

17 1 The whole community of the people of Israel moved on from the desert of Sin going from place to place as Yahweh commanded, and encamped at Rephidim. But there was no water to drink.

2 The people complained to Moses and said:

—Give us water to drink.

But Moses replied:

—Why do you find fault with me? Why do you put Yahweh to the test?

3 But the people thirsted for water there and grumbled against Moses:

—Why did you make us leave Egypt to have us die of thirst with our children and our cattle?

4 So Moses cried to Yahweh:

—What shall I do with the people? They are almost ready to stone me!

5 Yahweh said to Moses:

—Go ahead of the people and take with you the elders of Israel. Take with you the staff with which you struck the Nile,
and go. 6 I will stand there before you on the rock at Horeb.
You will strike the rock and water will flow from it and the

people will drink." Moses did this in the presence of the elders of Israel.

7 The place was called Massah and Meribah because of the complaints of the Israelites, who tested Yahweh saying, 'Is Yahweh with us or not?'

COVENANT

Introduction

The great encounter of the people with God takes place in the desert. It is about a foundational encounter.

The human institution of the covenant, especially between the ruler and the vassal, is used to signify and carry out the union between God and a chosen people.

God manifests this offer through a liberating act, offers and demands conditions, sanctions with promises and threats. The ceremony is liturgical; the pact is sealed with a sacrifice.

The primary conditions of God are "ten words" and to these a "code of Covenant" is added.

As soon as the covenant is done, the people break the second commandment. Moses, as intermediary of the covenant, has to intervene, siding with his people.

19 1 Exactly two months after the Israelites had left
Egypt, they arrived at the wilderness of Sinai. 2 They arrived
there coming from Rephidim and camped in the wilderness of
Sinai.

3 The Israelites camped there in front of the mountain, but Moses went up to God and Yahweh called to him from the mountain, saying:

4 —This is what you are to say and to explain to the
Israelites: You have seen what I did to the Egyptians and how
I carried you on eagle's wings and brought you to myself.
5 Now if you listen to me and keep my covenant, you shall be
my very own possession among all the nations. For all the

earth is mine, [6] but you will be for me a kingdom of priests and a holy nation.

And he added:

—This is what you are to say to the people of Israel.

[7] So Moses went and summoned all the elders of the people and related to them all that Yahweh had commanded him to say.

[8] All the people responded with one voice:

—All that Yahweh has said, we will do.

Moses then brought back to Yahweh the people's response.

[9] Yahweh spoke to Moses:

—I am going to come to you in a dense cloud so that the people may hear me speaking with you and trust you always.

Then Moses related to Yahweh what the people had said.

The Decalogue

20 [1] God spoke all these words. [2] He said:

—I am Yahweh your God who brought you out of the land of Egypt, out of the house of slavery.

—[3] Do not have other gods before me.

—[4] Do not make yourself a carved image or any likeness of anything in heaven, or on the earth beneath, or in the waters under the earth; [5] you shall not bow down to them or serve them. For I, Yahweh your God, am a jealous God; for the sin of the fathers, when they rebel against me, I punish the sons, the grandsons and the great-grandsons; [6] but I show steadfast love until the thousandth generation for those who love me and keep my commandments.

—[7] Do not take the name of Yahweh your God in vain for Yahweh will not leave unpunished anyone who takes his name in vain.

—[8] Remember the sabbath day and keep it holy. [9] For six days you will labor and do all your work, [10] but the seventh day is a sabbath for Yahweh your God. Do not work that day, neither you, nor your son, nor your daughter nor your servants, men or women, nor your animals, nor the stranger who is staying with you. 11 For in six days Yahweh made the heavens and the earth and the sea and all that is in them, but on the seventh day he rested; that is why Yahweh has blessed the sabbath day and made it holy.

—12 Honor your father and your mother that you may have a long life in the land that Yahweh has given you.

—13 Do not kill.

—14 Do not commit adultery.

—15 Do not steal.

—16 Do not give false witness against your neighbor.

—17 Do not covet your neighbor's house. Do not covet your neighbor's wife, or his servant, man or woman, or his ox, or his donkey, or anything that is his.

18 In the meantime, all the people witnessed the thunder and lightning and heard the blast of the trumpet and saw the mountain smoking. They trembled with fear and kept at a distance.

19 Then they said to Moses:

—You yourself speak to us and we shall listen. But do not have God speak to us, lest we die.

[20] Moses answered the people:

—Do not be afraid, for God has come to test you, so that the fear of God may be with you, and that you may not sin again.

[21] So the people kept at a distance while Moses went forward to the cloud where God was.

Rite of the Covenant

24 [12] Yahweh said to Moses:

—Come up to me on the mountain and stay there. I will give you the slabs of stone, the Teaching and commandment which I have written for their instruction.

[13] So Moses arose with his servant, Joshua, and before going
up the mountain of God, [14] Moses said to the elders:

—Remain here until we come back to you.

SIN AND PARDON

The golden calf

32 [1] When the people saw that Moses was so long in coming down from the mountain they assembled around Aaron and said to him:

—Come, make us gods to walk ahead of us; as for this Moses who brought us out of Egypt, we don't know what has happened to him.

[2] And Aaron said to them:

—Take the gold earrings from your wives, your sons and daughters and bring them to me.

[3] So all the people took off their earrings and brought them
to Aaron. [4] He took what they gave him and with a graving
tool made the gold into a molten calf.

They then said:

—These are your gods, O Israel, who brought you out of Egypt.

5 Now, when Aaron saw this, he built an altar before the molten calf and cried out:

—Tomorrow will be a feast day for Yahweh.

6 So next day they rose early and sacrificed burnt offerings and brought peace offerings. They then sat down to eat and drink and got up to make merry.

7 Then Yahweh said to Moses:

—Go down at once, for your people, whom you brought up from the land of Egypt, have corrupted themselves. 8 They have quickly turned from the way I commanded them and have made for themselves a molten calf; they have bowed down before it and sacrificed to it and said: 'These are your gods, Israel, who brought you out of Egypt.'

9 And Yahweh said to Moses:

—I see that these people are a stiff-necked people. 10 Now just leave me that my anger may blaze against them. I will destroy them, but of you I will make a great nation.

11 But Moses calmed the anger of Yahweh, his God, and said:

—Why, O Yahweh, should your anger burst against your people whom you brought out of the land of Egypt with such great power and with a mighty hand? 12 Let not the Egyptians say: 'Yahweh brought them out with evil intent, for he wanted to kill them in the mountains and wipe them from the face of the earth.' Turn away from the heat of your anger and do not bring disaster on your people. 13 Remember your servants, Abraham, Isaac and Jacob, and the promise you yourself swore: I will multiply your descendants like the stars of heaven, and all this land I spoke about I will give to them as an everlasting inheritance.

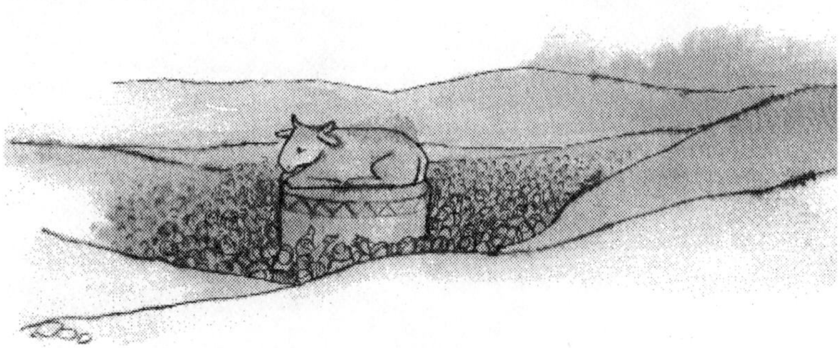

14 Yahweh then changed his mind and would not yet harm his people.

Punishment

15 Moses then returned and came down from the mountain
carrying in his hand the two slabs of the Statement, slabs written on both sides, back and front. 16 These slabs were the work
of God and the writing graven on the slabs was the writing of
God.

17 When Joshua heard the noise of the people who were shouting he said to Moses:

—There is a sound of war in the camp.

18 But Moses answered:

—It is not a victory song, nor the cry of defeat that I hear, but the sound of singing.

19 When he drew near to the camp and saw the calf and the dancing, his anger burst forth and he threw the slabs from his hands and shattered them against the base of the mountain.
20 Then he seized the calf they had made and burned it in the fire, grinding it into a powder that he scattered over the surface of the water, and this he made the Israelites drink.

Intercession

[30] The next day Moses said to the people:

—You have committed a very grave sin, but now I am going up to Yahweh; perhaps I will obtain pardon for your sin.

[31] So Moses went towards Yahweh and said:

—Ah! This people has committed a very great sin; they
made a god out of gold. [32] And now please forgive their sin…
if not, blot me out of the book you have written.

[33] Yahweh said to Moses:

—Whoever has sinned against me, I will blot him out from
my book. [34] Go now! Lead the people where I told you. My
Angel will walk before you and on the day of punishment I will punish them for their sin.

The glory of the Lord

33 [18] Moses said:

—Then let me see your Glory.

[19] And He said:

—I will make all my goodness pass before you and proclaim the name of Yahweh before you. For I am gracious to whom I want to be gracious and I am merciful to whom I want to be merciful.

[20] Then Yahweh said:

—You cannot see my face because man cannot see me and live.

[21] And he added:

—See this place near me; you shall stand on the rock [22] and
when my Glory passes I will put you in a hollow of the rock
and cover you with my hand until I have passed by. [23] Then I
will take away my hand and you shall see my back, but my face shall not be seen.

New covenant. The passing of glory

34 1 Yahweh said to Moses:
—Cut two slabs of stone like the first, and I will write on
the slabs the words that were on the former slabs that you
broke.
2 Be ready in the morning and come up to Mount Sinai and
wait for me on the top of the mountain. 3 No one will go up
with you and no one is to be seen anywhere on the mountain.
Even the sheep and the cattle are not to graze near the mountain.
4 So Moses cut two slabs of stone like the first. Then he rose
early in the morning and went up Mount Sinai as Yahweh had
commanded, taking in his hands the two slabs of stone. 5 And
Yahweh came down in a cloud and stood there with him, and
Moses called on the name of Yahweh.
6 Then Yahweh passed in front of him and cried out:
—Yahweh, Yahweh is a God full of pity and mercy, slow
to anger and abounding in truth and loving-kindness. 7 He
shows loving-kindness to the thousandth generation and for-
gives wickedness, rebellion and sin; yet he does not leave the
guilty without punishment, even punishing the children and
their children for the sin of the fathers to the third and fourth
generation.
8 Moses hastened to bow down to the ground and worshiped.
9 He then said:
—If you really look kindly on me, my Lord, please come
and walk in our midst and even though we are a stiff-necked
people, pardon our wickedness and our sin and make us
yours.
10 Yahweh said:
—I am making a covenant with you; in the presence of all
the people I will do marvels never yet done in any land or
nation so that all the people among whom you live may see
how awesome is the work of Yahweh that I will do for you.
11 Obey what I command you today.
28 Moses remained there with Yahweh forty days and forty
nights without eating bread or drinking water. He wrote on

the slabs the words of the Covenant—the Ten Commandments.

In Deuteronomy Moses will compile again all Israel's history. The crossing of the Red Sea will be the beginning of its history as chosen people, and the Covenant the final document of its faith.

You can see:
Psalms 105 and 106. These are two meditations: the first one about the fundamental events of salvation; and the second about the capital sins of the chosen people in the desert.

DEUTERONOMY

Introduction

Even if this book was probably written as introduction to the ***Historical Books*** *that follow, it is for us the end of the* ***Pentateuch****, the fifth of the Five Books.*

Its name means "Second Law" because it is a recompilation of the most important laws of Israel. All these laws are placed on the lips of Moses because of his prestige and to show that they follow in the same spirit, even though its writings take place several centuries later.

DECALOGUE AND EXHORTATION

4 44 This is the Law which Moses gave to the children of
Israel. 45 These are the precepts, decrees, and laws which
Moses made known to the children of Israel after their depar-
ture from Egypt.

5 1 Moses gathered the whole of Israel and said to them:
—Listen, Israel, to the laws and norms which I teach you
this day. Learn them and be careful to put them into practice.
2 Yahweh, our God, made a covenant with us in Horeb,
and his covenant 3 was not only with our fathers, but with us
as well who are all alive here today. 4 Yahweh spoke with us
face to face from the midst of the fire in the mountain. 5 And
I stood between Yahweh and you to transmit his word to you,

since you could not go up the mountain for fear of the great
fire.

These were his words:

6 'I am Yahweh, your God, who brought you out of the land
of Egypt, the house of slavery.

7 —'Do not have other gods before me.

8 'Do not have idols, do not make any figure of things in the
heaven or here below on the earth, or in the waters under the
earth. 9 Do not kneel before them or worship them, because I,
Yahweh, am your God, a jealous God who punishes the children until the third and fourth generation for the wickedness
of their parents who hate me. 10 But I am merciful to the thousandth generation to those who love me and obey my commandments.

11 'Do not take the name of Yahweh, your God, in vain
because Yahweh will not leave unpunished him who takes his
name in vain.

12 'Take care to keep holy the sabbath day, as Yahweh, your
God, commands you. 13 You have six days to work and do
your tasks. 14 But the seventh day is the Day of Rest in honor
of Yahweh, your God. Do not do any work, you or your child,
or your servant, or your ox, or your donkey, or any of your
animals. Neither will the foreigner who lives in your land
work. Your servant will rest just like you. 15 Remember that
you were once enslaved in the land of Egypt from where
Yahweh, your God, brought you out with his powerful hand
and outstretched arm. For that reason, Yahweh, your God,
commands you to observe the sabbath.

16 'Honor your father and your mother as Yahweh, your
God, has commanded, and you will live long and it will be
well with you in the land which Yahweh, your God, gives you.

17 'Do not kill.

18 'Do not commit adultery.

19 'Do not steal.

20 'Do not give false testimony against your neighbor.

21 'Do not desire the wife of your neighbor. Do not covet the
house of your neighbor, or his field, or his servant, or his ox,
or his donkey, or anything that is his.'

[22] These are the words of Yahweh said to the whole assembly on the mountain when he spoke from the midst of the fire
and the thick cloud. He said only this and he wrote these
words on the two slabs of stone which he gave to me.

6 [1] —'These are the commandments, the norms and the
laws that Yahweh, your God, has commanded me to teach you
so that you may observe them in the land which is going to be
yours. [2] Fear Yahweh, observe his commandments all the days
of your life and his norms that I teach you today. So also for
your children and your children's children that they may live
long.

[3] 'Listen, then, Israel, observe these commandments and
put them into practice. If you do this, you will be well and you
will multiply in this land flowing with milk and honey, as
Yahweh, the God of your fathers, promised you.

[4] 'Listen, Israel: Yahweh, our God, is One Yahweh. [5] And
you shall love Yahweh, your God, with all your heart, with all
your soul and with all your strength. [6] Engrave on your heart
the commandments that I pass on to you today. [7] Repeat them
over and over to your children, speak of them when you are
at home and when you travel, when you lie down and when
you rise. [8] Brand them on your hand as a sign, and keep them
always before your eyes. [9] Engrave them on your doorposts
and on your city gates.

[13] —'Fear Yahweh, your God, serve him and call on his
Name when you have to swear an oath.

[16] 'You shall not put Yahweh, your God, to the test, as you
did in Massah.

[17] 'Observe the precepts, the commandments and the
norms that Yahweh has commanded you.

[18] 'You shall do what is right and good in the eyes of
Yahweh that you may be happy and may come to possess the
splendid land which he swore to your fathers [19] he would give
you after having destroyed all your enemies before you.

[20] 'And when your child asks you one day: What are these
precepts, these commandments and these norms which
Yahweh has commanded us? [21] You shall answer your child:
We were Pharaoh's slaves in Egypt, but Yahweh led us out of

Egypt with prodigious deeds. 22 And we have seen the great
and wonderful things, the awesome marvels he has done
against Pharaoh and all his people. 23 And he took us out from
there to lead us into the land which he promised to our
fathers. 24 Yahweh has commanded us to put into practice all
these precepts and to fear him, our God. Because of this, we
are happy and alive today, 25 and we shall be perfect in his
eyes if we observe and practice these commandments as he
has told us to do.

Moses, forty years later, just before dying, before entering the promised land, asks the people to renew the covenant, so that they will not forget what God has done with its people, and so that they will transmit that to their descendants.

29 1 Moses summoned all the people of Israel and said to
them:

—You have seen all that Yahweh did before your eyes in the land of Egypt, to Pharaoh, to his servants and to all his land:

9 —'You are all here today in the presence of Yahweh, your
God: your leaders, your elders, your secretaries, all the people
of Israel, 10 with your sons and daughters, and with your
wives, together with the foreigner who lives in your field, who
cuts the firewood or fetches water for you. 11 You are here in
this place to celebrate a Covenant with Yahweh, your God. 12
Through this oath he makes you his people and he becomes
your God, as he said to you and promised to your ancestors,
to Abraham, Isaac and Jacob.

13 'And not only with you do I make this covenant and this
oath today, 14 but I make it both with those who are here with
you today in the presence of Yahweh and with those who are
not here.'

30 11 'These commandments that I give you today are
neither too high nor too far for you.

12 They are not in heaven that you should say:

'Who will go up to heaven to get these commandments that
we may hear them and put them into practice.' 13 Neither are

they at the other side of the sea for you to say: 'Who will cross to the other side and bring them to us, that we may hear them and put them into practice.'

[14] On the contrary, my word is very near you;

it is already in your mouth and in your heart, so that you can put it into practice.

[15] 'See, I set before you on this day life and good, evil and
death. [16] I command you to love Yahweh, your God and follow
his ways. Observe his commandments, his norms and his laws, and you will live and increase, and Yahweh will give you his blessing in the land you are going to possess.

[19] "Let the heavens and the earth listen, that they may be witnesses against you. I have set before you life and death, blessing and curse. Therefore, choose life that you and your
descendants may live, [20] loving Yahweh, listening to his voice,
and being one with him. In this is life for you and length of days in the land which Yahweh swore to give to your ancestors, to Abraham, Isaac and Jacob.'

34 [1] From the barren plain of Moab, Moses went up to Mount Nebo, to the summit of Pisgah, opposite Jericho. And
Yahweh showed him all the Land: from Gilead to Dan, [4] And
Yahweh said to him:

—This is the land about which I swore to Abraham, Isaac and Jacob, promising it to their descendants. I have let you see it with your own eyes, but you shall not enter it.

[5] Moses, the servant of God, died there in the land of Moab, according to the will of Yahweh.

[10] No prophet like Moses has appeared again. Yahweh conversed with him face to face.

Centuries later Israel will come back to these events to repent and renew the covenant.

You can read:
Psalm 106:1–15, 19–22, 43–47. Historical meditation about the seven capital sins of the people of Israel in the desert.

Historical Books

Introduction

We now present the most interesting fragments from several books dealing on the history of Israel, from the occupation of Canaan until the return from the Babylonian Captivity.

In these books we find events, wars, reigns… but, once again, the intention of the authors is religious. The basic argument running through all these books is that Israel is safe as long as it follows the law of God, because God protects them. But when they go to other gods or trespass the laws of God, then ruin reigns and their enemies triumph over them. These are, therefore, historical books with a religious intention.

JOSHUA

Introduction

The book of Joshua tells us about the conquest of Canaan. It is a very theologized history: the events that really happened are presented wrapped in an interpretation full of miracles, showing the astonishing protection of Yahweh.

To enter the Land they have to go through the Jordan River (they are coming from the Western steppes). This passing through the River is presented as a second passing through the Sea, as fantastic as the famous epic.

The conquest of Jericho is also a ritual narration: a sacred procession along the city murals, as a symbolism of the power of God that gives them the Land.

Finally, at the great Assembly of Sichem, Joshua obtains the unity of all tribes. They all renew the Covenant; they all become protagonists of the great adventure of Exodus: the People of God in its entirety is finally rooted in The Promised Land, the Promise has been fulfilled.

3 14 When the people set out from their camp to cross the
Jordan, the priests who carried the Ark of the Covenant went
before them. 15 There was much water in the Jordan, for it was
overflowing its banks at this time of the barley harvest.
Nevertheless, when those who carried the Ark went down to
the river and their feet touched the edge of the water, the
water from upstream stopped flowing. 16 The water stood still,
forming something like a dam very far from that place, near
Adam, the neighboring city of Zarethan. The water flowing

down to the Dead Sea was completely cut off, and so the people could cross opposite Jericho.

17 The priests who carried the Ark of the Covenant remained in the middle of the river which dried up, until all the Israelites had crossed the Jordan.

The conquest of Jericho

6 1 The inhabitants of Jericho had closed the city and had fastened their bolts so that the Israelites could not enter. No one came in and no one went out.

2 But Yahweh said to Joshua:

—I will give you the city, its king and all its men of war.
3 For this, you shall have to go around the city once every day
for six days. 4 Seven priests shall go before the Ark bearing the seven trumpets used in the time of the Jubilee. On the seventh
day, they shall march around the city seven times, 5 and when
they blow the horn, all the people shall come up to attack, shouting their battle cry. At that moment, the walls of the city will fall and everyone shall enter straight ahead of him.

6 Joshua, son of Nun, called the priests and said to them:

—You shall carry the Ark of the Covenant; seven priests shall go ahead with the trumpets they use for the Jubilee.

7 Then Joshua said to the people:

—You shall march around the city and the vanguard of the army shall go before the Ark of Yahweh.

10 Joshua had given this order:

—Do not shout or utter anything, nor let even a single word be heard, until the day comes when I say: Shout and cry out!

11 That day he had the Ark of Yahweh carried around the city once, then all returned to the camp where they spent the night. 12 On the following day, Joshua rose early in the morning, 13 and the priests took the Ark. 15 On the seventh day, the Israelites rose early at dawn and marched around Jericho in the same way as on the previous days. But on that day, they did it seven times. 16 At the seventh time, as the priests blew the trumpets, Joshua ordered the people:

—Shout your battle cry for Yahweh has given you the city.

17 The city and all that is in it shall be given in anathema to Yahweh.

20 The people shouted and the trumpets blew. At this precise moment, the walls of the city fell. Then everyone went straight into the city to the place before him.

27 So Yahweh was with Joshua and made him famous in all the land.

11 23 Joshua seized the whole land as Yahweh had directed Moses and gave it as an inheritance to the Israelites to be
distributed among their tribes. With this, the land rested from
war.

Renewal of the covenant

24 1 Joshua summoned all the tribes of Israel in
Shechem, and assembled the elders, leaders, judges and secretaries. And together they presented themselves before God.

2 Addressing the people, Joshua said to them:

—Yahweh, the God of Israel, commands me to say to you:
"Your ancestors lived beyond the Euphrates River—Terah the
father of Abraham and Nahor—serving other gods. 3 But I
brought Abraham your father from beyond the Euphrates and
led him through the whole land of Canaan. Then I gave him a
son Isaac, that he might have numerous descendants. 4 And to
Isaac, I gave two sons: Esau and Jacob. Esau received the
mountains of Seir as his inheritance, while Jacob and his sons
went down to Egypt.

5 "Then I sent Moses and Aaron to punish Egypt in the way
that you know, that you might leave. 13 I gave you lands which
you have not tilled, cities which you did not build but in
which you now live. I gave you vineyards and olive groves
which you did not plant but from which you now eat.

14 "So fear Yahweh, and be sincere and faithful in serving
him. Set aside those gods your ancestors worshiped in
Mesopotamia and Egypt. Serve only Yahweh. 15 But if you do
not want to serve Yahweh, make known this very day whom
you shall serve—whether they be the gods your ancestors
served in Mesopotamia or the gods of the Amorites who formerly occupied the land in which you now live. As for me, I
and my household will serve Yahweh."

16 The people answered:

—May God not permit that we ever abandon Yahweh to
serve other gods! 17 For it was he who brought us and our
ancestors out of Egypt, the house of slavery. It was he who did
those great wonders that we have seen; he protected us on the
way and through all the land where we passed.

24 The people answered:

—We will serve Yahweh, our God, and obey his commands.

25 On that day at Shechem, Joshua made a covenant with the people and fixed laws and ordinances. 26 He also wrote down everything expressed in the book of the Law of God; he chose a great stone and put it under the oak tree in the sacred place of Yahweh. 27 Then Joshua said to the people:

—This stone shall be a witness to all that Yahweh said to us, for it heard all these words. It shall be a witness against you, lest you deal falsely with Yahweh.

28 Joshua immediately sent the people away and everyone returned to his land.

Judges

Introduction

Israel is established in Canaan, but they have powerful enemies as neighbors, especially the Philistines that are in what today is "the Gaza strip." Israel is not a united people, they do not have a permanent ruler. When difficulties with their neighbors arrive, "Yahweh raises a saving ruler." These ruler are "the Judges."

Once again, what the writers are interested in is the history of the fidelity / infidelity of the people of Yahweh, and the protection / punishment of Yahweh to his people.

Penitential liturgy

2 6 When Joshua dismissed the Israelites, each one of
them went to his inheritance to occupy the land.

7 The people served Yahweh during the lifetime of Joshua
and of the leaders who outlived him, and who had witnessed
all the great works of Yahweh for Israel. 8 Joshua, son of Nun,
the servant of Moses, died at the age of one hundred and ten
years. 9 They buried him at the boundary of his inheritance in
Timnath-heres, in the mountains of Ephraim, north of the
mountain of Gaash. 10 That whole generation died and another one came, but they did not know Yahweh or what he had
done for Israel.

Grand introduction

11 The Israelites treated Yahweh badly for they served the
Baals instead. 12 They abandoned Yahweh, the God of their
ancestors who had brought them out of Egypt, and served
other gods, the gods of the neighboring peoples. They bowed
before those gods and offended Yahweh.

13 When Yahweh saw that they had abandoned him to serve
Baal and Ashtaroth, 14 he became angry with his people and
gave them into the hands of plunderers who left them in misery. He himself sold them to their enemies who completely
surrounded the Israelites, so that these Israelites could no
longer withstand them.

16 Yahweh raised up "judges" (or liberators) who saved the
Israelites from their exploiters. 17 But neither did they obey
those "judges" for they still prostituted themselves to other
gods and worshiped them. They soon left the way of their
fathers who obeyed the commandments of Yahweh; they did
not follow the way of their fathers.

Gideon

6 1 The Israelites treated Yahweh badly, and Yahweh gave
them into the hands of the Midianites for seven years.

11 The Angel of Yahweh came and sat under the sacred tree
at Ophrah, which belonged to Joash, of the family of Abiezer.
Gideon, the son of Joash, was threshing the wheat in the wine-
press to hide it from the Midianites.

12 The Angel of Yahweh said to him:

—Yahweh be with you, valiant warrior.

13 Gideon answered:

—Please, my lord, if Yahweh is with us, why is all this happening to us? Where are the wonders which our fathers
recounted to us? Did they not say that Yahweh led them up
from Egypt? Why has he abandoned us now and given us into
the hands of the Midianites?

14 Yahweh then turned to him and said:

—Go, and with your courage, save Israel from the Midianites. It is I who send you.

15 Gideon answered:

—Pardon me, Lord, but how can I save Israel? My family is the lowliest in my tribe and I am the least in the family of my father.

16 Yahweh said to him:

—I will be with you and you shall defeat the people of Midian with one single stroke.

33 All Midian, Amalek and the people of the East joined forces, crossed the Jordan and invaded the plains of Jezreel.

34 Then the spirit of Yahweh clothed Gideon with strength;
he blew the trumpet and summoned the men of Abiezer. 35 He
sent messengers throughout the whole territory of Manasseh and they joined him. The people of Asher, Zebulun and Naphtali also went out to meet them.

36 Gideon said to God, "If indeed you will save Israel by my
hand, as you have said, grant me this favor. 37 I am going to
spread this woolen fleece on the threshing ground. If the dew falls only on the fleece while all the ground remains dry, then I shall know that you are to save Israel by my hand, as you have promised."

38 So it was: Gideon rose at day-break, squeezed the fleece
and wrung out the dew, filling a cup with water. 39 Gideon
again spoke to God and said to him:

—Don't be angry with me if I dare to speak to you again. Allow me to make another test with the fleece: let it be dry only on the fleece and let dew come on all the ground.

40 That night, Yahweh did so. The fleece remained dry and dew covered all the ground.

7 1 Jerubaal, that is Gideon, rose early with all the people who were with him and they encamped beside the spring of Harod. The Midianite camp was farther north and extended from the hill of Moreb to the plains.

2 Then Yahweh said to Gideon:

—There are too many people with you. If I give the

Midianites into their hands, the Israelites might think that they won over the Midianites by their own strength. [3] So summon your men and say to them that whoever is afraid may go home.

So twenty-two thousand men returned and only ten thousand remained.

[4] Yahweh said to Gideon:

—There are still too many people. Take them down to the water and I myself will test them for you. If I say: This one shall go with you, he will go. And if I say: Not this one, he shall not go.

[5] So Gideon brought them down to the water and Yahweh told him:

—Those who lap the water like a dog, you shall place on one side. And those who kneel down to drink, you shall place on the other side.

[6] Three hundred men lapped the water, and the rest knelt down to drink.

[7] Then Yahweh said to Gideon:

—I will help these three hundred men who lapped the water and give the Midianites into your hands. Let the rest return to their homes.

[8] The three hundred men took the pitchers and the horns of whom Gideon dismissed. Finally, Gideon and his three hundred men faced the Midianites who were encamped below the valley.

[9] That night Yahweh said to him:

—Rise and go down to the camp, because I have given it into your hands.

[15] When Gideon heard the dream and its interpretation, he bowed, returned to the camp of Israel and said:

—Arise, for Yahweh has given the camp of Midian into your hands!

[16] Gideon divided the three hundred men into three groups. Then he handed the trumpets to all and the empty pitchers with lighted torches inside. [17] He said to them:

—Look at me, and do what I do. When I come to the outskirts of the camp, do as I do. [18] When I and those who are with me blow the trumpets then blow yours all around the camp and shout: For Yahweh and for Gideon!

19 With the hundred men with him, Gideon came to the Midianite camp just as the guards were changing shift at the beginning of the midnight watch.

20 Then the Israelites smashed the jars, took the torches in one hand, and blew the trumpets they were holding in the other hand. After blowing the trumpets, the three groups shouted:

—For Yahweh and for Gideon!

21 Everyone stood in his place around the camp while the
Midianites ran, shouting as they fled. 22 As the three hundred
Israelites went on blowing the trumpets, Yahweh made the
Midianites in the camp kill one another. Those who managed
to escape went as far as Beth-shittah toward Zererah, and as
far as the border of Abel-meholah opposite Tabbath.

8 13 After the battle, Gideon, the son of Joash, returned through the slope of Heres.

22 The Israelites said to Gideon:

—Since you have saved us from the Midianites, you shall be our king, and after you, your son and the descendants of your son.

23 But Gideon answered:

—I will not rule over Israel, nor my son, for Yahweh is our king!

32 Gideon the son of Joash died at a happy old age, and he was buried in the tomb of Joash his father, in Ophrah of Abiezer.

33 After the death of Gideon, the Israelites again prostituted
themselves to the Baals and took Baal-Berith as god. 34 The
Israelites no longer remembered Yahweh, their God, who had
freed them from the hands of all the enemies who surrounded
them. 35 Neither were they grateful to the family of Jerubaal-
Gideon for all the good things he had done to Israel.

Samson

13 1 The Israelites again treated Yahweh badly so he
gave them into the hands of the Philistines for forty years.

2 There was a man of Zorah of the tribe of Dan, called
Manoah. His wife could not bear children.

3 The Angel of Yahweh appeared to this woman and said to
her:

—You have not borne children and have not given birth,
but see, you are to conceive and give birth to a son. 4 Because
of this, take care not to take wine or any alcoholic drink, nor
to eat unclean foods from now on, 5 for you shall bear a son
who shall be a Nazirite of Yahweh from the womb of his
mother. Never shall his hair be cut for he is consecrated to
Yahweh. He shall begin the liberation of the Israelites from the
Philistine oppression.

24 The woman gave birth to a son and named him Samson.
The boy grew and Yahweh blessed him. 25 Then the Spirit of
Yahweh began to move him when he was in Mahane Dan
between Zorah and Eshtaol.

14 5 Samson then went down to Timnah, and when he
reached the vineyards at Timnah, a young lion came up roaring toward him. 6 The Spirit of Yahweh then seized Samson.
With bare hands he tore the lion to pieces as he would have
done with a young goat.

15 1 After some time, during wheat harvest, Samson went
to visit his wife, bringing a young goat with him, and he said:

—I want to be with my wife in our room.

But her father would not let him in, 2 saying:

—I thought that you did not like her anymore, so I gave her
to your companion. Is not her younger sister still better? Why
don't you take her instead?

3 Samson replied:

—This time I owe nothing to the Philistines even if I do
them harm.

[4] Samson went out and caught three hundred foxes, took some torches and tied the animals tail to tail. He then placed a torch in between every two tails, [5] set fire to the torches and turned the foxes loose in the grain fields of the Philistines. In this way, he burned the sheaves and the standing grain, together with the vineyards and olive groves.

[6] The Philistines asked:

—Who did this?

And they answered:

—Samson, the son-in-law of the man from Timnah, because this man took his wife and gave her to his companion.

So they went up and burned her and her family. [7] Samson said to them:

—Since you did this, I will not rest until I have had my revenge on you.

[8] So he caused a great havoc upon them.

Samson and Delilah

16 [4] After this, Samson fell in love with a woman in the valley of Sorek; she was called Delilah. [5] The Philistine chiefs said to this woman:

—Charm him and find out where he gets such strength and how we can defeat and tie him up. Each of us shall give you eleven hundred pieces of silver.

[6] So Delilah asked Samson:

—Tell me, please, where do you get such strength and how can others tie you up to subdue you?

[7] Samson answered her:

—If they bind me with seven new and moist bowstrings, then I shall lose my strength and be as any other man.

[8] The Philistine chiefs sent seven new bowstrings that had not been dried to Delilah, and she tied Samson with them. [9] With men hidden in her dwelling, she shouted:

—Samson, here come the Philistines!

Samson broke the bowstrings as if they were burned flax. So they did not find out where his great strength came from.

10 Then Delilah said to Samson:

—You made a fool of me, and you lied to me. Tell me, how can they subdue you?

11 Samson answered her:

—If they bind me this time with seven newly-braided ropes which have never been used, then I shall lose my strength and be like any other man.

12 So Delilah bound him with seven newly-braided ropes. But when she shouted:

—Here come the Philistines!

He again snapped the ropes round his arms like thread.
13 So Delilah said to him:

—How long will you deceive me and lie to me? Tell me how they can subdue you.

He answered her:

—If you braid the seven locks of my hair in the warp of the loom and tighten it with a pin, then I shall lose my strength.

14 She lulled him to sleep, and then braided the seven locks of his hair in the warp of the loom and tightened it with a pin. Then she cried:

—Here come the Philistines!

Samson woke up and pulled the warp with the locks of his hair. And so, Delilah did not find out where his great strength came from.

15 Then Delilah said to him:

—You say that you love me, but your heart is not with me. Three times, you have deceived me and have not told me from whence your great strength comes.

16 And as Delilah insisted and bothered him day after day with her questions, the time came when Samson felt he would die in disgust. 17 So he told her the truth:

—Never has my hair been cut for I am a Nazirite, consecrated to God from the womb of my mother. If my hair is cut, then I shall lose my strength and be like any other man.

18 Delilah understood that he had told her the truth this time, so she called the Philistine chiefs and said:

—Come, because Samson has revealed his secret to me.

They took the money and came to her. [19]Delilah lulled
Samson to sleep upon her knees and called a man to cut the
seven locks of his hair. And she could immediately subdue
him for his strength had left him.

[20]When Delilah shouted:

—Samson, the Philistines!

He awoke and thought that he could still save himself as on other occasions. But he did not know that Yahweh was no longer with him.

[21]So the Philistines seized him, gouged out his eyes, and
brought him to Gaza. There they bound him with two bronze
chains and made him turn the mill in the prison. [22]The hair on
Samson's head, however, began to grow as soon as it was cut.

[23]The Philistine chiefs assembled to offer a great sacrifice to their god Dagon and had a great feast, saying:

—Our god has given Samson, our enemy, into our hands!

[25]As they were very happy, they said:

—Bring out Samson that he may amuse us.

They brought him out of prison and he amused them. Then
they had him placed between the columns [24]and on seeing
him the people praised their god saying:

—Our god has put our enemy into our hands,

Samson who has destroyed our country and killed our men.

[26]Samson then said to the boy who held him by the hand:
—Lead me where I can touch the pillars on which this house rests, so that I may lean on them.

[27]The house was full of men and women, all the Philistine chiefs were also there, and on the roof were about three thousand men and women watching Samson for amusement.

[28]Samson called on Yahweh and exclaimed:

—Lord, Yahweh, please remember me and restore my strength only this once, so that I may avenge myself against the Philistines for my eyes.

[29]Samson grasped the two middle pillars on which the
house rested, leaned on them with his right arm on one pillar
and his left on the other, [30]and cried out, "Let me die with the
Philistines!" He pushed with all his strength and the house fell

upon the chiefs and the people gathered there. Those who joined him in his own death were more than those he had killed during his lifetime.

31 His brothers and the whole family of his father went down to get him. They buried him between Zorah and Eshtaol, in the tomb of his father Manoah.

He had judged Israel for twenty years.

1 Samuel

Introduction

The book of Samuel is artificially divided into two parts: 1 Samuel and 2 Samuel. It is called that way because its main protagonist is Samuel, a mixture of judge and prophet, a "man of God" that rules the destiny of Israel by his prestige and his contact with God. His main function will be to give Israel a king, Saul, and when this king becomes incompetent, substitute him by the one who will be Israel's "king of kings," David who is so important and definitive that he will become the image of the future Messiah, the Savior of the people.

Vocation of Samuel

3 1 The boy Samuel ministered to Yahweh under Eli's care
in a time in which the word of Yahweh was rarely heard;
visions were not seen.

2 One night Eli was lying down in his room, half blind as he
was. 3 The lamp of God was still lighted and Samuel also lay
in the house of Yahweh near the ark of God. 4 Then Yahweh
called:

—Samuel! Samuel!

Samuel answered:

—I am here!

5 and ran to Eli saying:

—I am here, did you not call me?

But Eli said:

—I did not call, go back to sleep.

So he went and lay down.

6 Then Yahweh called again:

—Samuel!

And Samuel stood up and went to Eli saying:

—You called me; I am here.

But Eli answered:

—I did not call you, my son. Go back to sleep.

7 Samuel did not yet know Yahweh and the word of Yahweh had not yet been revealed to him.

8 But Yahweh called Samuel for the third time and, as he went again to Eli saying:

—I am here for you have called me.

Eli realized that it was Yahweh calling the boy.
9 So he said to Samuel:

—Go, lie down, and if he calls you again, answer: "Speak, Yahweh, your servant listens."

10 Then Yahweh came and stood there calling as he did before:

—Samuel! Samuel!

And Samuel answered:

—Speak, for your servant listens.

11 Then Yahweh spoke to Samuel:

—Look, I am about to do something in Israel which will scare everyone who hears about it.
12 On that day I will carry out what I told Eli regarding his family. All will be fulfilled from beginning to end.
13 For I told him that I was about to sentence his family forever. He himself knew that his sons were blaspheming God, but he did not stop them.
14 This is why I have cursed the family of Eli. Their sin shall never be atoned for by sacrifice or by any offering.

15 Samuel lay down until morning and rose up early. Then he opened the doors of Yahweh's house. Samuel was afraid to tell the vision to Eli,
16 but Eli called him and said:

—Samuel, my son.

Samuel answered:

—I am here.

17 Eli asked:

—What did Yahweh tell you? Do not hide it from me. Fear
the punishment of God if you hide from me even one thing he
told you.

18 So Samuel told him everything to the end and Eli said:

—He is Yahweh. Let him do what seems good to him.

19 Samuel grew; Yahweh was with him and made all his
words become true. 20 All Israel, from Dan to Beersheba, knew
that Samuel was really Yahweh's prophet. 21 Yahweh would
appear at Shiloh; there he revealed himself to Samuel by giving him his word.

The Israelites ask for a king. The Monarchy

8 1 When Samuel grew old, he made his sons judges over
Israel. 2 His elder son was Joel and the second was Abijah, and
both of them were judges in Beersheba. 3 But they were not
like their father; they had their vested interests, taking bribes
and perverting justice.

4 Because of this, all the chiefs of Israel gathered together
and went to Samuel in Ramah. 5 They said to him:

—You are already old and your sons are not following your
ways. Give us a king to rule over us as in all the other nations.

6 Samuel was very displeased with what they said:

—Give us a king to rule us.

And he prayed to Yahweh. 7 And Yahweh told him:

—Give to this people all that they ask for. 8 They are not
rejecting you but they have rejected me as their king. They are
now doing to you what they did to me from the day I brought
them out of Egypt until now, forsaking me and serving other
gods. 9 Nevertheless, listen to them, and give them a serious
warning. Tell them how they will be treated by their king.

10 So Samuel answered those who were asking him for a
king, 11 and he told them all that Yahweh said to him:

—Look, these will be the demands of your king: he will

take your sons and assign them to his chariot and his horses
and have them run before his chariot. 12 Some he will assign as
commanders over a thousand men and commanders over
fifty. Others will till his ground and reap his harvest, make his
implements of war and the equipment for his chariots. 13 He
will take your daughters as well to prepare perfumes, to cook
and to bake for him. 14 He will take the best of your fields, your
vineyards and your olive orchards and give them to his officials. 15 He will take a tenth portion of your grain and of your
vineyards and give it to his officers and to his servants. 16 He
will take your menservants and maidservants, the best of your
cattle and your asses for his own work. 17 He will take the
tenth of your flocks and you yourselves will become his
slaves. 18 When these things happen, you will cry out because
of the king whom you have chosen for yourselves. But by
then, Yahweh will not answer you.

19 The people paid no attention to all that Samuel said. They
insisted:

—No! We want a king to govern us as in all the other
nations. 20 Our king shall govern us, lead us and go ahead of
us in our battles.

21 Upon hearing all that his people said, Samuel repeated it
to Yahweh. 22 But Yahweh said to him:

—Listen to them and give them a king.

Samuel then said to the Israelites:

—Go back, all of you, to your own cities.

SAMUEL AND SAUL

9 1 There was a man from the tribe of Benjamin whose
name was Kish. He was the son of Abiel, son of Zeror, son of
Becorath, son of Aphiah, a valiant Benjaminite. 2 Kish had a
son named Saul, a handsome young man who had no equal
among the Israelites, for he was a head taller than any of
them.

3 It happened that the asses of Kish were lost. So he said to
his son Saul:

—Take one of the boys with you and go look for the asses.

[4] They went all over the hill country of Ephraim and the land of Shalishah but did not find them. They passed through the land of Shaalim and the land of Benjamin, but the asses were nowhere to be found.

[5] When they reached the land of Zuph, Saul said to his boy:

—Let us go back, lest my father be more worried about us than about the asses.

[6] But his servant said to him:

—Look, there is a man of God in this city. He is a highly respected man. All that he says comes true. Let us see him for he may be able to help us find what we are looking for.

[10] And Saul said to his boy:

—Well said! Come, let us go.

[14] So they went up to the city and entered it, and saw Samuel coming out towards them on his way up to the high place.

[15] The day before Saul came, Yahweh had already disclosed this to Samuel:

[16] —Tomorrow, about this time, I will send you a man from the land of Benjamin and you shall anoint him to rule over my people Israel. He shall save my people from the hand of the Philistines for I have seen the affliction of my people and their cry has come to me.

[17] So, when Samuel saw Saul, Yahweh told him:

—Here is the man I spoke to you about! He shall rule over my people.

[18] Saul approached Samuel in the gateway and said:

—Tell me, where is the house of the seer?

[19] Samuel answered Saul:

—I am the seer. Go up ahead of me to the high place, for
today you shall eat with me. In the morning, before you leave,
I will tell you all that is in your heart. [20] As for your asses
that were lost three days ago, do not worry about them for
they have been found.

Samuel added:

—For whom is the first place in Israel? Isn't it for you and for all your father's kin?

[21] Saul answered:

—I am a Benjaminite, from the least of the tribes of Israel, and my family is the lowliest of all the families of the tribe of Benjamin. Why do you speak to me in this way?

[22] Samuel took Saul and his boy, brought them into the hall and gave them a place at the head of the table, before some thirty guests. [23] Then Samuel told the cook:

—Bring in the portion which I asked you to put aside.
[24] The cook brought in the leg with the tail portion and set it before Saul, saying to him:

—This has been set aside for you. Please eat.

So Saul ate with Samuel that day.

[25] Then they went down from the high place and entered the city. On the terrace they prepared a bed for Saul where he lay down to sleep.

Saul's anointing

[26] Early the next morning, Samuel called to Saul:

—Get up, for I must send you on your way.

Saul got up and began to walk down the street with Samuel.

[27] As they were going down to the outskirts of the city, Samuel said to Saul:

—Tell your servant to walk ahead. You stay here for a while and I shall give you a message from God.

10 [1] Then Samuel took a vial of oil and poured it on Saul's head. And kissing Saul, Samuel said:

—Yahweh has anointed you to rule over and to lead his people Israel!

Election of the king by lots

[17] After that, Samuel called the people together before Yahweh at Mizpah. [18] He then spoke to the Israelites:

—Thus says Yahweh, the God of Israel: I brought Israel out
of Egypt and I delivered you from the hands of the Egyptians
and from all the kingdoms oppressing you. 19 But you have
this day rejected your God who saves you from all your
calamities and your distress. You have said, 'No! Give us a
king to rule over us.' So now present yourselves before
Yahweh, grouping yourselves into tribes and clans.

25 Samuel then told the people the rights and duties of the
king. He wrote all these in a book and presented it before
Yahweh. Then Samuel sent all the people home. 26 Saul himself
went home to Gibeah with these valiant men whose hearts
God had touched.

11 15 So all the people went to Gilgal and there they proclaimed Saul king before Yahweh. They sacrificed peace offerings and Saul and all Israel celebrated.

13 1 Saul became king and he ruled over Israel for twenty-two years.

14 47 When Saul felt secure as king of Israel, he began to fight against all his surrounding enemies: Moab, the Ammonites, Edom, the kings of Zobah and the Philistines, routing his enemies wherever he went.

Saul is rejected

15 10 Then Yahweh spoke to Samuel:

11 —I feel sorry that I made Saul king because he has turned his back on me and has not kept my command.

Samuel was troubled and cried to Yahweh all night.

12 Early next morning, he went looking for Saul, but was told that Saul had set off for Carmel to erect a monument to himself and then had gone on his way to Gilgal.

13 When finally they met, Saul greeted Samuel:

—May Yahweh bless you,

22 Samuel then said:
—Does Yahweh take as much delight in burnt offerings
and sacrifices, as in obedience to his command? Obedience is
better than sacrifice, and submission better than the fat of
rams. 23 Rebellion is like the sin of divination, and stub-
bornness like holding onto idols. Since you have rejected the
word of Yahweh, he too has rejected you as king.

35 From that day Samuel did not see Saul again until he
died, but he was grieving over Saul because Yahweh regretted
having made him king over Israel.

SAUL AND DAVID

Introduction to David

David is one of the great figures in the history of Israel: a military, political and religious figure. It is the beginning of a new election, of a stable saving institution. To remember him will be an occasion for discovering and maturing the messianic hope.

For this reason David is an exalted and idealized figure, formed by history and legend, by memory and fantasy, making it impossible for us today to separate its components. Most probably right from the beginning diverse traditions about his life and deeds were formed, making it difficult for the author of this book to put them aside or harmonize them.

New variations were added to these loose or braided narrative threads.

A hazardous life can be depicted under a lyric or epic presentation leading towards the throne and to a stable dynasty.

David anointed king

16 1 Yahweh asked Samuel:
—How long will you be grieving over Saul whom I have
rejected as king of Israel? Fill your horn with oil and be on

your way to Jesse the Bethlehemite for I have chosen my king from among his sons.

4 Samuel did what Yahweh commanded and left for Bethlehem. When he appeared, the elders of the city came to him asking, fearfully:

—Do you bring us peace?

5 Samuel replied:

—I come in peace; I am here to sacrifice to Yahweh. Cleanse yourselves and join me in the sacrifice.

He also had Jesse and his sons cleansed and invited them to the sacrifice.

6 As they came, Samuel looked at Eliab the older and thought:

—This must be Yahweh's anointed.

7 But Yahweh told Samuel:

—Do not judge by his looks or his stature for I have rejected him. Yahweh does not judge as man judges; humans see with the eyes; Yahweh sees the heart.

8 Jesse called his son Abinadab and presented him to Samuel who said:

—Yahweh has not chosen this one either.

9 Jesse presented Shammah and Samuel said:

—Nor has Yahweh chosen this one.

10 Jesse presented seven of his sons to Samuel who said:

—Yahweh has chosen none of them.
11 But are all your sons here?

Jesse replied:

—There is still the youngest, tending the flock just now.

Samuel said to him:

—Send for him and bring him to me; we shall not sit down to eat until he arrives.

12 So Jesse sent for his youngest son and brought him to Samuel. He was a handsome lad with ruddy complexion and beautiful eyes. And Yahweh spoke:

—Go, anoint him for he is the one.

13 Samuel then took the horn of oil and anointed him in his brothers' presence. From that day onwards, Yahweh's Spirit took hold of David. Then Samuel left for Ramah.

David, in the court of Saul

14 The spirit of Yahweh had left Saul and an evil spirit sent
by Yahweh tormented him. 15 Saul's servants said to him:

—We know that an evil spirit sent by God is tormenting
you. 16 If you so wish, your servants who stand before you will
look for someone who can play the lyre so when the evil spirit from God comes over you, he will play and you will feel better.

17 So Saul answered them:

—Get someone who can play the lyre well.

18 One of them said:

—A son of Jesse, the Bethlehemite, plays very well. He is,
moreover, a courageous man, intelligent and pleasant to talk
with and Yahweh is with him.

19 So Saul sent messengers to Jesse and asked for his son
David who tended the sheep.

20 Jesse loaded an ass with bread, a wineskin and a kid and
had David take all these to Saul. 21 David then left and entered
Saul's service. Saul grew very fond of David and made him
his armor-bearer. 22 Then he sent word to Jesse, saying:

—Let David remain in my service for I am very pleased
with him.

23 So, whenever the evil spirit from God overpowered Saul,
David would play on the lyre and Saul would feel better for
the evil spirit would leave him.

David and Goliath

17 1 The Philistines prepared their forces for battle and
gathered together at Socoh, a territory of Judah. They
encamped between Socoh and Azekah in Ephesdammim.
2 Saul and the Israelites, meantime, assembled and pitched
camp in the valley of Elah, ready for their encounter with the
Philistines. 3 The Philistines took their position on one hill
while the Israelites took theirs on another hill, with a valley
separating the two forces.

4 Then a champion named Goliath came out from the Philistine camp. He was from Gath and was about three meters tall. 5 He wore a helmet of bronze, and a coat covered with bronze scales. His armor weighed sixty kilos. 6 He had bronze greaves strapped on his legs and a bronze spear slung between his shoulders. 7 The shaft of his spear was the size of a weaver's rod; its head weighed seven kilos. His shield-bearer went before him.

8 He stood in front of the Israelite ranks and shouted:

—Why have you come out in battle array? I am a Philistine and you are Saul's men! Choose a man from among yourselves who can challenge me. 9 If he fights better and kills me, we shall be subject to you; but if I overpower him and kill him, you shall be subject to us.

10 The Philistine added:

—This is my challenge to the Israelite troops this day. Give me a man who can fight with me alone!

11 When they heard this challenge of the Philistine, Saul and his men were afraid and greatly terrified.

32 David said to Saul:

—Let no one be discouraged on account of this Philistine, for your servant will engage him in battle. 33 Saul told David:

—You cannot fight with this Philistine for you are still young, whereas this man has been a warrior from his youth.

34 But David said:

—When I was tending my father's sheep, whenever a lion or bear came to snatch a lamb from the flock, 35 I would run after it, kill it and rescue the victim from its mouth. If it attacked me, I would hold it by its beard and slay it. 36 I have killed lions and bears and will do the same with this uncircumcised Philistine, for he has defied the armies of the living God.

37 David continued:

—Yahweh, who delivered me from the paws of lions and bears, will deliver me from the hands of the Philistine.

Saul then told David:

—Go and may Yahweh be with you!

38 Saul fitted his armor on David, put a bronze helmet on

his head, and clothed him with a coat of mail. [39] David secured his sword over the armor but could not walk because it was his first time. So he said to Saul:

—I cannot move with all these trappings on me because I am not accustomed to wearing them.

David got rid of all this armor, [40] took his staff, picked up five smooth stones from the brook and dropped them inside his shepherd's bag. And with his sling in hand, he drew near to the Philistine.

[41] The Philistine moved forward, closing in on David, his shield-bearer in front of him. [42] When he saw that David was only a lad, (he was of fresh complexion and handsome) he despised him [43] and said:

—Am I a dog that you should approach me with a stick? Cursing David by his gods, [44] he continued:

—Come and I will give your flesh to the birds of the sky and the beasts of the field!

45 David answered the Philistine:

—You have come against me with sword, spear and javelin,
but I come against you with Yahweh, the God of the armies of
Israel whom you have defied. 46 Yahweh will deliver you this
day into my hands and I will strike you down and cut off your
head. I will give the corpses of the Philistine army today to the
birds of the sky and the wild beasts of the earth, and all the
earth shall know that there is a God of Israel. 47 All the people
gathered here shall know that Yahweh saves not by sword or
spear; the battle belongs to Yahweh, and he will deliver you
into our hands.

48 No sooner had the Philistine moved to attack him, than
David rushed to the battleground. 49 Putting his hand into his
bag, he took out a stone, slung it and struck the Philistine on
the forehead; it penetrated his forehead and he fell on his face
to the ground. 50 David triumphed over the Philistine with a
sling and a stone, felling him without using a sword. 51 He
rushed forward, stood over him, took the Philistine's sword
and slew him by cutting off his head.

25 [1]The day Samuel died, all Israel gathered together to mourn him; after which they buried him at his home in Ramah.

Then David went down to the desert of Maon.

Death of Saul

31 [1]Now the Philistines fought against the Israelites who, in their flight, fell mortally wounded on Mount Gilboa.
[2]The Philistines surrounded Saul and his sons and killed Jonathan, Abinadab and Malchishua, Saul's sons. [3]The battle raged around Saul, and he was afraid when he saw that the archers had found him.

[4]Then Saul commanded his armor-bearer:

—Draw your sword and run me through lest these uncircumcised men come and stab me themselves, making fun of me.

But his armor-bearer did not move because he was greatly terrified. So Saul drew his own sword and fell upon it. [5]Seeing that Saul was dead, the armor-bearer also fell upon his sword and died with him. [6]Thus, Saul, his three sons, his armor-bearer and all his men died together on the same day.

2 Samuel

Introduction

The division of the one book of Samuel in two parts is completely artificial; it seems that its purpose was to dedicate to David an entire book.

For the Israelites, David is the greatest king, a figure that places behind Moses and Elijah. Historically, David is a very important king: he receives a nation in disarray and in a few years he makes it the main kingdom on the strip shore; he receives a divided kingdom, and he established a unified monarchy. He gives his kingdom an administrative and religious capital of great influence and attraction; he begins a stable dynasty.

Theologically, he is the beneficiary of a new election and a promise. His election becomes a new article in the Israelite faith; together with his election is Jerusalem, as dwelling place of God; another foundational religious article. As beneficiary of the promise is almost a new patriarch, father of a dynasty, as Abraham was of a numerous people.

Through this promise David pierces the future. On this axle the messianic hope develops and grows. David was an apex, and what followed, even the salomonic splendor, resembles decadence.

David cries over the death of Saul and Jonathan

1 17 David sang a song of lamentation for Saul and his son Jonathan.

David, anointed king at Hebron

2 [1] After this, David consulted Yahweh:

—Shall I go up to one of the cities of Judah?

Yahweh answered him:

—Go!

Then David asked:

—Where shall I go?

He answered:

—To Hebron.

[2] So David went up to Hebron with his two wives,
Ahinoam of Jezreel and Abigail the widow of Nabal of Carmel. [3] David also brought up his men with their families and
they settled in the towns of Hebron.

[4] Then the men of Judah came and there they anointed David king over the nation of Judah.

David learned that the men of Jabesh-Gilead had buried
Saul, [5] so he sent messengers to them with these words:

—May Yahweh bless you for you have dealt kindly with
Saul, your master, and have buried him. [6] May Yahweh show
his love and fidelity to you! I, in turn, will be kind to you for
having done this. [7] Now be brave and strong for although
your master Saul is dead, the people of Judah have anointed
me their king.

Abner and Joab

[11] David was their king in Hebron and he ruled over them for seven years and six months.

[12] Abner, son of Ner, and the menservants of Ishbaal, Saul's son, left Mahanaim for Gibeon.

3 [1] There was a long war between Saul's party and that of David, but David grew stronger while Saul's party grew weaker.

David, king of Israel

5 [1] All the tribes of Israel came to David at Hebron and said:

—We are your bone and flesh. [2] In the past, when Saul was king over us, it was you who led Israel. And Yahweh said to you, 'You shall be the shepherd of my people Israel and you shall be commander over Israel.'

Conquest of Jerusalem

[6] The king and his men set out for Jerusalem to fight the Jebusites who lived there. They said to David:

—If you try to break in here, the blind and the lame will drive you away.

(Which meant that David could not get in).

[7] Yet David captured the fortress of Zion that became the "city of David."

[9] David lived in the fortress, calling it the City of David, and proceeded to build the city around it, from the Millo and inside as well.

[10] And David grew more powerful, for Yahweh, the God of hosts, was with him. [11] Hiram, king of Tyre, sent messengers to David with cedar trees, carpenters and masons to build a house for David. [12] David then understood that Yahweh had made him king over Israel and had exalted his reign for the sake of his people Israel.

The arc, carried to Jerusalem

6 [1] David gathered together once more all the picked men of Israel, numbering thirty thousand in all. [2] Then he and all the people with him in Baala-Judah set forth to bring up from there the ark of God on which Yahweh of hosts pronounced and put his Name, he who rests on the cherubim.

[14] David whirled round dancing with all his heart before Yahweh, [15] shouting joyfully and sounding the horn.

16 As the ark of Yahweh entered the city of David, Michal,
Saul's daughter, looked out of the window; and when she saw
King David leaping and whirling round before Yahweh, she
despised him in her heart. 17 They brought in the ark of
Yahweh and laid it in its place in the tent which David had
pitched for it. Then David offered burnt and peace offerings
before Yahweh. 18 Once the offerings had been made, David
blessed the people in the name of Yahweh of hosts.

20 When David returned to bless his household, Michal,
Saul's daughter, met him and said:

—How the king of Israel honored himself today, exposing
himself before his servants' maids as uncouth men do! 21 But
David said to Michal:

—I did that before Yahweh who chose me instead of your
father and his family, making me commander over Israel,
Yahweh's people. By Yahweh's life I swear that I will dance
and whirl again before him. 22 I will humble myself still more
and you may look at me, but I will not be rejected by the
maids you spoke about.

PROMISE AND SIN

Dynastic promise and prayer of David

7 1 When the king had settled in his palace and Yahweh
had rid him of all his surrounding enemies, 2 he said to
Nathan the prophet:

—Look, I live in a house of cedar but the ark of God is
housed in a tent.

3 Nathan replied:

—Do as it seems fit to you for Yahweh is with you.

4 But that very night, Yahweh's word came to Nathan:

8 Now you will tell my servant David, this is what Yahweh
of hosts says:

—I took you from the pasture, from tending the sheep, to
make you commander of my people Israel. 9 I have been with
you wherever you went, cutting down all your enemies before

you. Now I will make your name great as the name of the
great ones on earth. [10] I will provide a place for my people
Israel and plant them that they may live there in peace. They
shall no longer be harassed, nor shall wicked men oppress
them as before. [11] From the time when I appointed judges over
my people Israel it is only to you that I have given rest from
all your enemies. Yahweh also tells you that he will build you
a house.

[12] When the time comes for you to rest with your ancestors,
I will raise up your son after you, the one born of you and I
will make his reign secure. [13] He shall build a house for my
name and I will firmly establish his kingship forever. [14] I will
be a father to him and he shall be my son. If he does wrong, I
will punish him with the rod, as men do. [15] But I will not withdraw my kindness from him as I did from Saul when I
removed him out of your way. [16] Your house and your reign
shall last forever before me, and your throne shall be forever
firm.

Mepibaal, received by David

9 [1] David asked:

—Is there anyone left of the house of Saul to whom I can show kindness for the sake of Jonathan?

[2] So they called a servant of Saul, named Ziba, and brought him to David who asked:

—So you are Ziba?

He replied:

—I am your servant.

[3] Then the king asked him:

—Is there still someone of the house of Saul to whom I can give God's favor?

Ziba answered the king:

—A son of Jonathan whose feet are crippled still lives. [4] The
king asked him:

—Where is he?

And Ziba replied:

—He is in the house of Machir, son of Ammiel, at Lodebar. [5]So King David sent for him and had him brought from the house of Machir, son of Ammiel, at Lodebar.

[6]When Mepibaal, son of Jonathan, son of Saul arrived, he fell on the ground and paid homage to David who said:

—Mepibaal!

He replied:

—Your servant listens.

[7]David then told him:

—Do not be afraid. I will do you a favor for the sake of your father Jonathan and give you back all the land of Saul your father. Besides, you shall always eat at my table. [8]He bowed down and said:

—What is your servant that you should show concern for a dead dog like myself?

[9]The king called Ziba, Saul's servant, and said to him:

—I have turned over to your master's son everything that Saul and his family possessed. [10]You yourself, your sons and servants shall till the land for him and carry in the harvest so that your master's family may have food, although your master's son Mepibaal shall always eat at my table.

Ziba, who had fifteen sons and twenty servants [11]said to the king:

—Your servant will do whatever my lord the king commands. Yet Mepibaal ate at my table like a king's son.

[12]Mepibaal had a young son named Mica; and all who lived in Ziba's house became Mepibaal's servants. [13]But Mepibaal lived in Jerusalem for he always ate at the king's table. He was lame in both feet.

David and Bathsheba

11 [1]In the spring of that year, when kings usually set out to fight, David sent out Joab, his officers and all the Israelite troops. They slaughtered the Ammonites and attacked Rabbah, while David remained in Jerusalem.

[2]One afternoon, David got up from his siesta and took a

walk on the roof of the royal house. From the rooftop, he saw a woman bathing, and the woman was very beautiful. [3] David sent to inquire about the woman, and was told:

—She is Bathsheba, daughter of Eliam and wife of Uriah, the Hittite.

[4] So David sent messengers to have her brought to him; and he had intercourse with her after she had cleansed herself after her monthly period. Then she returned to her house.

[5] As the woman saw she was with child, she sent word to David:

—I am with child.

[6] David then sent a message to Joab:

—Send me Uriah the Hittite.

So Joab sent Uriah to David. [7] When Uriah came, David asked him about Joab, how the people were and how the war was proceeding; [8] then he told Uriah:

—Go down to your house and wash your feet.

Uriah left the palace and the king had a portion from his table sent to him. [9] Uriah, however, did not go down to his house but slept by the door of the king's palace with all the servants of his lord. [10] David was told that Uriah did not go down to his house, and he said to him:

—Have you not come from a journey? Why did you not go down to your house?

[11] Uriah replied:

—The ark, the men of Israel and Judah are housed in tents while my lord Joab and his servants are encamped in the open country. Shall I go to my house to eat and drink there and sleep with my wife? As you live, I will not do this!

[12] So David said to Uriah:

—Remain here today also and I will dismiss you tomorrow.

Uriah therefore stayed in Jerusalem that day and the day after. [13] David invited him to table and he ate and drank until he was drunk. When evening fell, however, he went to lie down on his couch with the guards of his lord instead of going down to his house.

[14] The next morning, David wrote Joab a letter to be taken by hand by Uriah, [15] in which he said, "Place Uriah in the front

row where the fighting is very fierce and then withdraw from him so that he may be struck down and die." [16] When Joab was attacking the city, he assigned Uriah to a place which he knew was being defended by strong warriors. [17] And the defenders attacked the men of Joab. Some of David's soldiers and officers were killed; Uriah the Hittite also died.

[18] Then Joab sent a messenger to tell David everything that had happened during the battle. [19] And he said to him:

—When you have finished recounting the outcome of the battle to the king, [20] perhaps he will get angry and ask you, 'Why did you go so near the city to fight? Did you not know they would shoot from the wall? [21] Who killed Abimelech, son of Jerubbesheth? Was it not a woman who dropped a millstone on him from the wall so that he died at Thebez? Why did you go so close to the wall?'; then you shall say: Your servant Uriah the Hittite is also dead.

[22] So the messenger went to tell David all that Joab instructed him. [23] So he answered the king and explained:

—These men had overcome us and pushed us in the field; then we drove them back to the entrance gate. [24] But the archers aimed at your guard from the top of the wall, killing some of them. Your servant Uriah the Hittite has also been killed.

[25] David said to the messenger:

—Try to encourage Joab with this message: Do not let this thing disturb you, for the sword devours one this time and another at another time. Intensify your attacks against the city and overthrow it.

[26] When Uriah's wife heard of the death of her husband, she mourned for him. [27] After her mourning was over, David had her brought to his house. She became his wife and bore him a son. But Yahweh was displeased with what David had done.

David's penance

12 [1] So Yahweh sent the prophet Nathan to David. Nathan went to the king and said to him:

—There were two men in a city: one was rich; the other,

poor. 2 The rich man had many sheep and cattle, 3 but the poor
man had only one little ewe lamb he had bought. He himself
fed it and it grew up with him and his children. It shared his
food, drank from his cup and slept on his lap. It was like a
daughter to him. 4 Now a traveler came to the rich man, but he
would not take from his own flock or herd to prepare food for
the traveler. Instead, he took the poor man's lamb and prepared that for his visitor.

5 David was furious because of this man and told Nathan:

—As Yahweh lives, the man who has done this deserves
death! 6 He must return the lamb fourfold for acting like this
and showing no compassion.

7 Nathan said to David:

—You are this man! It is Yahweh, God of Israel, who
speaks: 'I anointed you king over Israel and saved you from
Saul's hands; 8 I gave you your master's house and your master's wives; I also gave you the nation of Israel and Judah. But
if this were not enough, I would have given you even more.
9 Why did you despise Yahweh by doing what displeases him?
You struck down Uriah the Hittite with the sword and took
his wife for yourself. Yes, you killed him with the sword of the
Ammonites. 10 Now the sword will never be far from your
family because you have despised me and taken the wife of
Uriah the Hittite for yourself.

13 David said to Nathan:

—I have sinned against Yahweh.

Nathan answered him:

—Yahweh has forgiven your sin; you shall not die.

You can read:

The repentance of King David will be portrayed in Psalm 51, attributed to David himself.

In Israel there were other Psalms composed in the style of Psalm 51, to express repentance, for example Psalm 32.

KINGS

Introduction

The two books of Kings narrate the history of the People from David's death till the destruction of Jerusalem and the exile to Babylon. It is a sad history, a history of infidelity and decadence.

David is followed by one of his sons, Solomon. Splendid and full of wisdom he builds the fabulous Temple of Jerusalem. But his alliances with other countries and his marriages with foreign princesses introduce in his court corruption and the cult to foreign gods. From here on, the books narrate the infidelities of Israel along with the misfortunes that follow. The kingdom is divided into two: Israel on the North and Judah on the South. Both kingdom carry out an agitated and vulgar existence, until finally they are destroyed by the great powers of Mesopotamia: Assyria and Babylon.

This history is reflected in the books of the Prophets, who are constantly advising Israel about the danger of their infidelity to Yahweh and the terrible consequences that awaits them unless they convert and fulfill the Covenant

1 KINGS

David's testament

2 1 When David was about to die, he gave his son Solomon
this instruction:
2 —I am about to go the way of all creatures. Be strong and

show yourself a man! 3 Keep the commandments of Yahweh
your God and walk in his ways. Keep his statutes, his commands, his ordinances and declarations written in the law of
Moses, that you may succeed in whatever you do and wherever you go. 4 If you do so, Yahweh will fulfill the promise he
made to me: 'If your sons take care to walk before me faithfully with their whole heart and their whole soul, you shall
always have one of your descendants on the throne of Israel.'

10 Then David rested with his ancestors and was buried in
the city of David. 11 David reigned over Israel for forty years:
seven years in Hebron and thirty-three years in Jerusalem.
12 So Solomon sat on the throne of David his father and his
reign was firmly established.

After Moses, David will be the most famous personage in the history of Israel. He will be the symbol of God's fidelity as it is expressed in the book of Psalms. You can read from Psalms 16 to 50, 67 to 72, 78 and 89.

Vision of Solomon

3 1 Solomon entered into a marriage alliance with
Pharaoh, king of Egypt. He took Pharaoh's daughter and
brought her to the city of David until he had finished building
his own palace, Yahweh's House and the wall around
Jerusalem.

4 The king used to sacrifice at Gibeon, the great high place;
on the altar there he had offered a thousand burnt offerings.
5 It was in Gibeon, during the night, that Yahweh appeared to
Solomon in a dream and said:

—Ask what you want me to give you.

6 Solomon answered:

—You have shown your servant David my father a great
and steadfast love because he served you faithfully and was
righteous and sincere towards you. You have given him proof
of your steadfast love in making a son of his sit on his throne
this day. 7 And now, O Yahweh my God, you have made your
servant king in place of David my father, although I am but a
young boy who does not know how to undertake anything.
8 Meantime, your servant is in the midst of your people whom

you have chosen—a people so great that they can neither be
numbered nor counted.

9 Give me, therefore, an understanding mind in governing
your people that I may discern between good and evil. For
who is able to govern this multitude of people of yours?

10 Yahweh was pleased that Solomon had made this
request. 11 And he told him:

12 —I shall grant you your request. I now give you a wise
and discerning mind such as no one has had before you nor
anyone after you shall ever have.

13 I will also give you what you have not asked for, both
wealth and fame; and no king shall be your equal during your
lifetime. 14 Moreover, if you will walk in my ways, keeping my
statutes and commands, as your father David did, I shall give
you long life.

15 Solomon awoke and knew that this was a dream. So he
went to Jerusalem and, standing before the ark of the covenant
of Yahweh, he offered up burnt offerings and peace offerings,
and gave a feast for all his servants.

The judgment of Solomon

16 Then two harlots came to the king and stood before him.
17 One of the two women said:

—Oh, my lord, this woman and I live in the same house,
and I gave birth to a child while she was there with me.
18 Three days after my child was born, this woman also gave
birth. We were alone, and there was no one in the house but
the two of us. 19 Then this woman's son died during the night
because she lay on him. 20 So during the night, she got up, took
my son from my side while I slept, laid it beside her and her
dead son beside me. 21 When I got up in the morning to nurse
my child, I saw it was dead. But when I looked at it closely in
the morning, I saw that it was not my child.

22 The other woman said:

—No, the living child is mine; the dead child is yours. To
this, the first replied:

—Not so, the dead child is yours; the living child is mine.

And they quarreled this way in the king's presence.

23 Then the king said:

—One says: 'This is my son who is alive; your son is dead'; the other says: 'That is not so, your son is dead; my son is the live one.'

24 And the king said:

—Bring me a sword.

When they brought the king a sword, 25 he gave this order:

—Divide the child in two and give half to one, half to the other.

26 Then the woman whose son was alive said to the king out of pity for her son:

—Oh, my lord, give her the living child but spare its life.

The other woman, however, said:

—It shall be neither mine nor yours. Divide it!

27 Then the king spoke:

—Give the living child to the first woman and spare its life. She is its mother.

28 When all Israel heard of the judgment which the king had given, they revered him, seeing that God's wisdom was in him to render justice.

Riches and wisdom

4 21 Solomon ruled over all the kingdoms from the Euphrates to the land of the Philistines and on to the frontiers of Egypt.

29 God gave Solomon great wisdom and understanding, and knowledge as vast as the sand on the shore, 30 so that his wisdom surpassed that of all the people of the east and of the Egyptians. 31 He was wiser than any man; wiser than Ethan, the Ezrahite, and Heman, Calcot and Darda, sons of Mahol; and his fame spread among all the surrounding nations.

Covenant with Hiram of Tyre

5 1 Now, Hiram King of Tyre sent his servants to Solomon
when he heard that he had been anointed king in place of his
father. For David had always been Hiram's friend. 2 Solomon
then sent this message to Hiram:

3 —You know that David my father could not build a temple for Yahweh his God because his enemies were at war with
him until the time when Yahweh gave him victory over them.
4 But now Yahweh my God has given me peace on all sides
and there is no enemy or calamity that afflicts us. 5 And so I
intend to build a temple for Yahweh my God as Yahweh told
David my father, 'Your son, whom I will set upon your throne,
shall build the House for my Name.' 6 Now, therefore, give
orders to have cedars of Lebanon cut for me. My servants will
join yours and I will pay your servants the wages you set, for
you know that none of us can cut timber like the Sidonians.

Construction of the temple

6 1 In the four hundred and eightieth year after the
Israelites left the land of Egypt, in the fourth year of Solomon's reign over Israel, in the month of Ziv, which is the second month, Solomon began to build the temple of Yahweh.
2 The House which King Solomon built for Yahweh was sixty
cubits long, twenty wide, and thirty high. 3 The vestibule
fronting the Sanctuary was twenty cubits long from side to
side, the width of the temple, and ten cubits deep in front of
the House.

37 In the month of Ziv of the fourth year, the foundation of
Yahweh's House was laid. 38 In the month of Bul, the eighth
month of the eleventh year, the House was finished, complete
and according to all specifications. It took Solomon seven
years to build it.

Dedication of the temple

8 1 Then Solomon assembled before him in Jerusalem the

elders of Israel and all the heads of the tribes, as well as the leaders of the ancestral houses of the Israelites, to bring up the ark of the covenant of Yahweh from the city of David, which is Zion.

2 All the Israelites assembled near King Solomon in the month of Ethanim, the seventh month. 3 When all the elders of Israel arrived, the priests carried the ark of Yahweh 4 and brought it up together with the Tent of Meeting and all the holy vessels that were in the tent.

After the priests and Levites had brought them up, 5 King Solomon with the entire congregation of Israel that had assembled before him and were with him before the Ark, sacrificed so many sheep and oxen that they could neither be counted nor numbered.

6 Then the priests laid the ark of the covenant of Yahweh in its place in the inner sanctuary of the House—the Most Holy Place—underneath the wings of the cherubim. 7 The cherubim had their wings spread out over the place of the ark, providing a covering above the ark and its poles. 8 The poles were so long that their ends were seen from the Holy Place in front of the inner sanctuary but not from the outside. 9 There was nothing in the ark except the two tables of stone which Moses placed there at Horeb, where Yahweh made a covenant with the Israelites when they came out of the land of Egypt.

10 And when the priests came out of the Holy Place, such a cloud filled Yahweh's House 11 that the priests could not continue to minister. Indeed, the glory of Yahweh filled his House.

New apparition and oracle

9 1 After Solomon had finished building Yahweh's House, the royal palace, and everything he wanted to build, 2 Yahweh appeared to him a second time, as he had appeared to him at Gibeon. 3 Yahweh said to him:

—I have heard the prayer and supplication you made before me. I have consecrated this House you have built, that my Name may be there forever. My eyes and my heart will be there forever. 4 As for you, if you will live in my presence, the

way your father David did, with sincerity and uprightness,
doing all that I have commanded you and keeping my decrees
and laws, [5] I will affirm your kingship in Israel forever, as I
promised your father David when I said, 'You shall always
have someone from your family on the throne of Israel.'

[6] But if you or your children refuse to follow me, and dis-
obey my commands and laws which I have set before you; if
they serve and worship other gods, [7] then I will cut off Israel
from the land which I have given them and I will remove from
my sight this House I have consecrated for my Name. Israel
will become a proverb and a byword among all peoples. [8] This
House will be reduced to a heap of stones and everyone passing by will be astonished and jeer: 'Why has Yahweh done
such a thing to this land and to this House?' [9] Then people will
answer: 'Because they abandoned Yahweh their God who
brought their ancestors out of the land of Egypt, and they followed other gods, worshiping and serving them. That is why
Yahweh has brought all this evil on them.'

Visit of the queen of Sheba

10 [1] The queen of Sheba heard about Solomon's fame,
and came to test him with difficult questions. [2] She arrived in
Jerusalem with a vast retinue and with camels loaded with
spices, an abundance of gold and precious stones. When she
came to Solomon, she told him all that she had on her mind
[3] and Solomon answered all her questions. There was nothing
that the king could not explain to her.

[4] And when the queen of Sheba had seen all the wisdom of
Solomon, the palace he had built, [6] she said to the king:

—All that I heard in my own land concerning you and your
wisdom was true. [7] But I did not believe the reports until I
came and saw with my own eyes. And what did I see! I was
told only half the story; for your wisdom and wealth surpass
the report I heard.

[8] Fortunate are your wives! Fortunate are your servants
who are ever in your presence and hear your wisdom!
[9] Blessed be Yahweh your God, who has looked kindly on you
and has put you on the throne of Israel! Because of Yahweh's

eternal love for Israel, he has made you king so that you may dispense justice and righteousness.

10 Then she gave the king a hundred and twenty talents of gold, spices in abundance, and precious stones. Such an abundance of spices as those which the queen of Sheba gave to
King Solomon was never again seen. 13 King Solomon, in turn,
gave the queen of Sheba all that she desired and all that he in his generosity wanted to give her. Then she went back to her own land together with her servants.

Idolatry of Solomon

11 1 King Solomon loved many foreign women besides the daughter of Pharaoh. There were Moabite, Ammonite,
Edomite, Sidonian and Hittite women 2 from nations about
which Yahweh had commanded the Israelites, "You shall not marry them; nor shall they marry you, lest they win over your heart to their gods." Solomon, however, imitated these peoples because of his love. 4 In Solomon's old age, his wives led
him astray to serve other gods and, unlike his father David, his heart was no longer wholly given to Yahweh his God.

5 For he served Astarte the goddess of the Sidonians, and
Milcom, the idol of the Ammonites. 6 He did what displeased
Yahweh and, unlike his father David, was unfaithful to him.
7 Solomon even built a high place for Chemosh, the idol of
Moab, on the mountain east of Jerusalem and also for Molech,
the idol of the Ammonites. 8 He did the same for all his foreign
wives who burned incense and sacrificed to their gods.

9 Yahweh became angry with Solomon because his heart
had turned away from Yahweh, the God of Israel. 10 Yahweh
appeared to him twice and commanded him not to follow other gods. But he did not obey Yahweh's command.
11 Therefore, Yahweh said to Solomon:

—Since this has been your choice and you have kept neither my Covenant nor the statutes I commanded you, I will take the kingdom from you and give it to your servant.
12 Nevertheless, I will not do this during your lifetime for the
sake of your father David; I will take it from your son. 13 But I
will not take it all; I will reserve one tribe for your son for the

sake of David my servant, and for the sake of Jerusalem, the city which I have chosen.

42 Solomon reigned over all Israel in Jerusalem for forty
years. 43 Then he rested with his fathers and was buried in the
city of David; Rehoboam his son reigned in his place.

THE SCHISM: THE TWO KINGDOMS

The schism

12 1 Rehoboam went to Shechem because all Israel had gathered there to make him king.

16 All Israel realized that the king refused to listen to them, and they answered the same way:

—What have we to do with David?

Is the son of Jesse from our tribes?

Let the son of David deal with his own and you, people of Israel, go back to your homes!

And so the Israelites left for their homes. 17 Only the Israelites
who dwelt in the cities of Judah let Rehoboam reign over them.

20 As Jeroboam had returned and was with them at the assembly, having been called by them, they made him king of Israel. And so, with the exception of the tribe of Judah, no one followed the house of David.

21 When Rehoboam came to Jerusalem, he called together
all the people of Judah and the tribe of Benjamin, numbering
a hundred and eighty thousand select warriors, to fight
against the people of Israel in a bid to restore the kingship of
Rehoboam, son of Solomon. 22 But the word of God was directed to Shemaiah, the man of God:

23 —Give Rehoboam, son of Solomon, king of Judah, and all
the people of Judah and Benjamin, and the rest of the people,
this message from Yahweh: 24 'You shall not go up to fight
against your kinsmen, the Israelites. Let everyone return to his
home for I am the author of this.'

When they heard this word they went back home according to what Yahweh had ordered.

The schismatic cult

25 Jeroboam fortified Shechem in the hill country of
Ephraim and lived there. Then, he set out to fortify Penuel.

26 Jeroboam thought, "The kingdom could return to the
house of David. 27 Should this people go up to offer sacrifices
in Yahweh's House in Jerusalem, their heart would turn again
to their master, Rehoboam king of Judah. They would kill me
and go back to him."

28 And so the king sought advice and made two golden
calves. Then he said to the people:

—You have been going up to Jerusalem long enough. Here
are your gods, O Israel, who brought you up out of the land of
Egypt.

29 He put one of these in Bethel, the other in Dan.

Ahab of Israel (874–852)

16 29 Ahab, son of Omri became king in the thirty-eighth
year of Asa, king of Judah, and he reigned over Israel in
Samaria for twenty-two years.

30 Ahab did what displeased Yahweh, even more than all
those who preceded him. 31 Apparently the example and the
sins of Jeroboam son of Nebat were not enough for him; he
even married Jezebel, daughter of Ethbaal, king of the
Sidonians. So he served Baal and worshiped him. 32 He set up
an altar for Baal in the temple of Baal which he built in
Samaria 33 and proceeded to make an Asherah. So Ahab did
everything that could make Yahweh angry, even more than
any of the kings of Israel who ruled before him.

34 During his reign, Hiel of Bethel rebuilt Jericho. On laying
its foundation he sacrificed Abirma, his firstborn. And when
he set up the gates of the city, he sacrificed his youngest son,
Segub, in accordance with the word of Yahweh spoken
through Joshua, son of Nun.

ELIJAH'S CYCLE

Elijah exiled. First miracles

Here begins the cycle of the Prophets. Even though the kings and their reign provide the frame of the events, it is the figure of the prophets the one that guide the selection of the narrative material.

Elijah's cycle. After the introduction about the reign of Ahab, it is Elijah the protagonist. He leaves the stage to other prophets and reappears; he leaves his post to the prophet Micah but reappears again to confront the new king; he disappears completely after naming a successor.

Elijah: the drought

17 1 Now Elijah, the prophet from Tishbe in Gilead, said to Ahab:

—As Yahweh, the God of Israel whom I serve lives, neither dew shall drop nor rain fall except at my command.

2 Then the word of Yahweh came to Elijah:

3 —Leave this place and go eastward. Hide yourself by the brook Cherith, east of the Jordan. 4 You shall drink from the brook and, for your food, I have commanded the ravens to feed you there.

5 So Elijah obeyed the word of Yahweh and went to live by
the brook Cherith, east of the Jordan. 6 There the ravens
brought him bread in the morning and meat in the evening;
and he drank from the brook. 7 After a while, the brook dried
up because no rain had fallen in the land. 8 Then Yahweh
spoke to Elijah:

9 —Go to Zarephath of the Sidonites and stay there. I have
given word to a widow there to give you food.

10 So Elijah went to Zarephath. On reaching the gate of the
town, he saw a widow gathering sticks. He called to her and
said:

—Bring me a little water in a vessel that I may drink.

11 As she was going to bring it, he called after her and said:

—Bring me also a piece of bread.

12 But she answered:

—As Yahweh your God lives, I have no bread left but only
a handful of flour in a jar and a little oil in a jug. I am just now
gathering some sticks so that I may go in and prepare something for myself and my son to eat – and die.

13 Elijah then said to her:

—Do not be afraid. Go and do as you have said, but first
make me a little cake of it and bring it to me; then make some
for yourself and your son. 14 For this is the word of Yahweh,
the God of Israel, 'The jar of meal shall not be emptied nor
shall the jug of oil fail, until the day when Yahweh sends rain
to the earth.'

15 So she went and did as Elijah told her; and she had food
for herself, Elijah and her son from that day on. 16 The jar of
flour was not emptied nor did the jug of oil fail, in accordance
with what Yahweh had said through Elijah.

17 After this, the son of this housewife became ill. And such
was his illness that he stopped breathing. 18 She then said to
Elijah:

—What did you do, O man of God? Have you come to
uncover past sins and cause my son's death?

19 He answered:

—Give me your son.

Taking him from her lap, he carried him up to the upper

room where he was staying and laid him on his own bed.
[20] Then he called on Yahweh:

—O Yahweh, my God, will you afflict even the widow with whom I am residing by letting her son die?

[21] Then he stretched himself on the child three times and called on Yahweh:

—O Yahweh, my God, let this child's breath return to him.

[22] Yahweh listened to the pleading of Elijah and the child's
breath returned to him, and he lived. [23] Elijah then took the
child and brought him down from the upper room. He gave
him to his mother and said:

—See, your son is alive.

[24] Then the woman said to Elijah:

—Now I am certain that you are a man of God, and that your words really came from Yahweh!

Judgment of God at Carmel

18 [1] After several days (in the third year) Yahweh spoke to Elijah and said:

—Go, show yourself to Ahab that I may let it rain on the earth.

[2] So Elijah went to show himself to Ahab.

[17] On seeing Elijah, Ahab said to him:

—Is it you, the plague of Israel?

[18] Elijah replied:

—Who is troubling Israel? Isn't it you and your family who
have disobeyed the commands of Yahweh and followed
instead the Baals? [19] Now, therefore, give an order for the
Israelites to gather before me at Mount Carmel, together with
the four hundred and fifty prophets of Baal who are sustained
by Jezebel.

[20] So Ahab sent for all the people of Israel and gathered the
prophets at Mount Carmel. [21] Then Elijah addressed the people and asked:

—How long will you follow two ways at the same time? If

Yahweh is God, follow him; but if Baal is God then follow him.

The people remained silent. 22 So Elijah continued:

—I am the only prophet of Yahweh left here to face Baal's four hundred and fifty prophets. 23 Get us two bulls. Let them choose one bull for themselves, cut it into pieces and lay it on the wood and I will do the same with the other bull. But we will not set it on fire. 24 Then you shall call on the name of your gods while I shall call on the name of Yahweh. The God who answers with fire is the true one.

Then the people answered:

—That is right.

25 Then Elijah told the prophets of Baal:

—Choose for yourselves one bull and prepare it first, for you are many. Then call on the name of your god lest you are left without fire!

26 So they took the bull and prepared it, and they called on the name of Baal:

—Baal, answer us!

But there was no voice and no one answered them while they went on dancing on one foot around the altar they had built.

27 By noontime, Elijah began to mock them:

—Shout out louder. Baal is a busy god; or he may have gone out or perhaps he has gone on a trip, or he is sleeping and must be wakened!

28 So they shouted louder gashing their skin with knives, as they are used to doing, until they bled. 29 It was already past noon and they were still raving on until the time of the evening offering. But still there was no voice; no one answered or gave a sign of life.

30 Then Elijah said to the people:

—Draw closer to me.

And the people drew closer to him. He then repaired the altar of Yahweh which had been thrown down. 31 He took twelve stones corresponding to the number of tribes of the sons of Jacob whom Yahweh had addressed saying, "Israel shall be your name." 32 With these stones, he built an altar to the Name of Yahweh and dug a trench around it that would

contain about thirty liters. 33 He then arranged the firewood,
cut the bull in pieces and laid them on the wood. Then, he
said:

—Fill four jars with water and pour it on the burnt offering
and on the firewood.

34 He said:

—Do it again.

And they did it again.

—One more time.

And they did it a third time. 35 The water ran around the
altar and filled the trench.

36 When the time of the evening offering came, Elijah the
prophet came near and said:

—O Yahweh, God of Abraham, Isaac and Israel, let it be
known today that you are God in Israel and that I am your servant, doing all these things at your command. 37 Answer me,
O Yahweh, answer me so that this people may know that you,
O Yahweh, are God and that you are turning back their hearts
to you.

38 Then the fire of Yahweh fell and consumed the burnt
offering, together with the wood, the stones also, and the dust;
the water also dried up in the trench.

39 All the people witnessed this. Then they fell on their faces
and said:

—Yahweh is God! Yahweh is God!

40 Then Elijah commanded them:

—Seize the prophets of Baal and let none of them escape.

And so they seized them. Then Elijah brought them down
to the brook Kidron and had them slaughtered there.

41 Elijah then said to Ahab:

—Go up, eat and drink, for the sound of rain is rushing in.

42 So Ahab went up to eat and drink. Elijah, in the meantime, went to the top of Carmel, bowed to the ground and put
his face between his knees. 43 Then he said to his servant:

—Go up and look in the direction of the sea.

The man went up, looked, and said:

—There is nothing.

Then Elijah said:

—Go again!

And seven times he went.

44 At the seventh time, he perceived a little cloud, the size of
a man's hand, rising out of the sea. Elijah told him:

—Go, tell Ahab: Prepare your chariot and go down before
the rain stops you.

45 A little later the sky grew dark with clouds and wind and
a strong rain fell. Ahab was riding on his way to Jezreel; 46 as
for Elijah, the hand of Yahweh was on him, and tucking his
cloak in his belt, he ran before Ahab to the entrance of Jezreel.

Elijah at Horeb mountain

19 1 Ahab told Jezebel everything Elijah had done and
how he had slain all the prophets with the sword. 2 Jezebel
then sent word to Elijah:

—May I be cursed if by this time tomorrow I have not
dealt with you as you dealt with them.

3 Elijah was scared and fled for his life. He reached Beersheba of Judah and left his servant there. 4 He himself disappeared into the desert going on a day's journey. Then he sat
down under a broom tree and prayed to die:

—That is enough, Yahweh, take away my life for I am
dying!

5 He lay down and went to sleep under the broom tree.
Then an angel touched him and said:

—Get up and eat.

6 Elijah looked and saw, at his head, a cake baked on hot
stones and a jar of water. He ate and drank and went back to
sleep. 7 The angel of Yahweh came a second time to him, saying:

—Get up and eat, for the journey is too long for you. 8 He
got up, ate and drank, and on the strength of that food, he
traveled for forty days and forty nights to Horeb, the mount
of God. 9 On reaching the place, he came to the cave and
stayed in it. Then the word of Yahweh came to him:

—What are you doing here, Elijah?

10 He answered:

—I am burning with jealous love for Yahweh, the God of Hosts, because the Israelites have forsaken your covenant, thrown down your altars, and slain your prophets with the sword. No one is left but myself and they are still trying to kill me as well.

11 Then Yahweh said:

—Go up and stand on the mount, waiting for Yahweh.

And Yahweh passed by.

There was first a windstorm, wild wind which rent the
mountains and broke the rocks into pieces before Yahweh, but
Yahweh was not in the wind. After the storm, an earthquake,
but Yahweh was not in the earthquake. 12 After the earthquake, a fire, but Yahweh was not in the fire. After the fire,
the murmur of a gentle breeze. 13 When Elijah perceived it, he
covered his face with his cloak, went out and stood at the
entrance of the cave.

Then he heard a voice addressing him again:

—What are you doing here, Elijah?

14 He answered:

—I am burning with jealous love for Yahweh, the God of hosts, because the Israelites have forsaken your covenant, thrown down your altars and slain your prophets with the sword. No one is left but myself, yet they still seek my life to take it away.

15 Yahweh said to him:

—Take the road back through the desert and go to
Damascus. 18 Yet I will spare seven thousand in Israel who
have not knelt before Baal and whose lips have not kissed
him.

19 So Elijah left. He found Elisha, son of Shaphat, who was
plowing a field of twelve acres and was at the end of the
twelfth acre. Elijah passed by him and cast his cloak over him.
20 Elisha left the oxen, ran after Elijah and said:

—Let me say goodbye to my father and mother; then I will follow you.

Elijah said to him:

—Return if you want, don't worry about what I did.
21 However, Elisha turned back, took the yoke of oxen and
slew them. He roasted their meat on the pieces of the yoke and gave it to his people who ate of it. After this, he followed Elijah and began ministering to him.

2 Kings

Miracles of Elisha

4 [1] The widow of one of the fellow prophets called Elisha saying:

—You know that my husband feared God. But now his creditor has come to collect payment. And as we could not pay, he wanted to take my two sons as slaves.

[2] Elisha said:

—What can I do for you? Tell me what you have in your house?

She answered:

—I have but a little oil for cleaning.

[3] Elisha said to her:

—Go and ask your neighbors for empty jars. [4] Get as many as you can; then go into your house with your sons and close the door. Pour oil into the vessels. And when they are filled, set them aside.

[5] The woman went and locked herself in her house with her sons. They handed her the vessels and she filled them all. [6] She said to one of her sons:

—Bring me another vessel.

And he answered:

—There are no more.

Then the oil stopped flowing. [7] As she went back to tell this to the man of God, he said to her:

—Go and sell the oil to pay for your debts; you and your sons can live on the money that is left.

The Shunamite's son

8 One day Elisha went to Shunem, and a rich woman invited him to eat. Afterwards, whenever he went to that town, he would go to her house to eat.

9 The woman said to her husband:

—See, this man who constantly passes by our house is a holy man of God. 10 If you want, we can make a small upper room for him, and place a bed, a table, a chair and a lamp in it. So when he comes, he may stay and rest.

11 One day when Elisha came, he went to the upper room and lay down. 12 Then he said to Gehazi, his manservant:

—Call this woman.

The young man called her and as the woman stood by the door, 16 Elisha said:

—By this time next year, you will hold a son in your arms.

She answered:

—No, my lord, O man of God, you are deceiving your maidservant.

17 But the woman gave birth to a son precisely at the time Elisha had told her.

18 The boy grew. One day, when he had gone out to his father among the harvesters, he had a severe headache. 19 So the father ordered his servant:

—Carry him to his mother.

20 The servant brought him to his mother, and the boy sat on her lap till noon, when he died. 21 Then the mother went up and laid him on Elisha's bed and she left, closing the door.

32 Elisha came into the house, and found the dead boy lying on his bed. 33 He entered, closed the door behind him, and prayed to Yahweh. 34 Then he lay upon the boy, put his mouth upon the boy's mouth, his eyes upon his eyes, his hands upon the boy's hands, and warmth returned to the boy's body. 35 Elisha came down and began walking to and fro. Then he went upstairs to stretch himself upon the boy, and the boy sneezed seven times and opened his eyes.

36 Elisha then called Gehazi and said:

—Call the woman.

And when she came, Elisha told her:

—Take your son.

37 She bowed at his feet, then she took her son and went out.

Naaman from Syria and Elisha

5 1 Naaman was the army commander of the king of Aram. This man was highly regarded and enjoyed the king's favor, for Yahweh had helped him lead the army of the Arameans to victory. But this valiant man was sick with leprosy.

2 One day some Aramean soldiers raided the land of Israel and took a young girl captive who became a servant to the wife of Naaman. She said to her mistress:

3 —If my master would only present himself to the prophet in Samaria, he would surely cure him of his leprosy.

4 Naaman went to tell the king what the young Israelite
maidservant had said. 5 The king of Aram said to him:

—Go to the prophet, and I shall also send a letter to the king of Israel.

So Naaman went and took with him ten gold bars, six thousand pieces of silver and ten festal garments. 6 On his arrival,
he delivered the letter to the king of Israel. It said, 'I present my servant Naaman to you that you may heal him of his leprosy.'

7 When the king had read the letter, he tore his clothes to show his indignation, 'I am not God to give life or death. And the king of Aram sends me this man to be healed! You see he is just looking for an excuse for war.'

8 Elisha, the man of God, came to know that the king of Israel had torn his clothes, so he sent this message to him:

—Why have you torn your clothes? Let the man come to me, that he may know that there is a prophet in Israel.

9 So Naaman came with his horses and chariots, and
stopped before the house of Elisha. 10 Elisha then sent a messenger to tell him:

—Go to the river Jordan and wash seven times, and your flesh shall be as it was before, and you shall be cleansed.

[11] Naaman was angry, so he went away. He thought:

—On my arrival, he should have personally come out, and then paused and called on the name of Yahweh, his God. And he should have touched with his hand the infected part, and I would have been healed.
[12] Are the rivers of Damascus, Abana and Pharpar not better than all the rivers of the land of Israel? Could I not wash there to be healed?

[13] His servants approached him and said to him:

—Father, if the prophet had ordered you to do something difficult, would you not have done it? But how much easier when he said: Take a bath and you will be cleansed.

[14] So Naaman went down to the Jordan where he washed himself seven times as Elisha had ordered. His skin became soft like that of a child and he was cleansed.

[15] Then Naaman returned to the man of God with all his men. He entered and said to him:

—Now I know that there is no other God anywhere in the world but in Israel. I ask you to accept these gifts from your servant.

[16] But Elisha answered:

—I swear by Yahweh whom I serve, I will accept nothing.

And however much Naaman insisted, Elisha would not accept his gifts.

Death of Elisha

13 [20] Elisha died and they buried him.

A little later, a detachment of Moabites conducted a raid as they used to do at the beginning of every year.
[21] It happened that at that time some people were burying a dead man, when they saw the Moabites. So they quickly threw the body into the grave of Elisha, and then fled to safety. But as soon as the man's body touched the bones of Elisha, the man revived and stood on his feet.

[22] Hazael, king of Aram, oppressed the Israelites throughout the reign of Jehoahaz.
[23] But Yahweh had pity and took compassion on them; he turned towards them because of his

covenant with Abraham, Isaac and Jacob, and would not utterly destroy them, or cast them far from his face.

Azariah of Judah (796–767)

15 27 In the fifty-second year of Azariah, king of Judah,
Pekah, son of Remaliah, began to reign over Israel in Samaria,
its capital. He reigned for twenty years, and he acted badly
towards Yahweh, 28 for he did not turn away from the sins
which Jeroboam made Israel commit.

29 In the time of Pekah, king of Israel, Tiglath-pileser, king
of Assyria, came and seized Iyon, Abel-bethmaacah, Janoah,
Kedesh, Hazor, the territory of Gilead and Galilee, and the
whole land of Naphtali, and deported their inhabitants to
Asshur.

Zedekiah of Judah (597–587)

24 18 Zedekiah was twenty-one years old, and he
reigned in Jerusalem for eleven years. His mother was
Hamutal, daughter of Jeremiah. 19 He did what displeased
Yahweh, as Jehoiakim had done; 20 so the punishment of
Yahweh fell on Jerusalem and Judah, until he cast them far
away from his presence. And Zedekiah rebelled against the
king of Babylon.

Fall of Jerusalem

25 1 In the ninth year of Zedekiah's reign, on the tenth
day of the tenth month, Nebuchadnezzar king of Babylon
marched with his entire army and laid siege to Jerusalem.
They camped outside the city and built siege works all around
it. 2 The city was under siege up to the eleventh year of
Zedekiah.

3 On the ninth day of the fourth month famine became a
serious problem in the city, and throughout the land there was
no bread for the people.

8 On the seventh day of the fifth month in the nineteenth
year of Nebuchadnezzar king of Babylon, Nebuzaradan, commander of the bodyguard and servant of the king of Babylon,
entered Jerusalem and 9 set fire to the House of Yahweh and
the royal palace as well as to all the houses in Jerusalem. 10 The
Chaldean army under the commander of the bodyguard completely demolished all the walls around Jerusalem.

11 Nebuzaradan, commander of the bodyguard, carried off
into exile the last of the Jews left in the city, those who had
deserted to the king of Babylon and the remainder of the arti-
sans. 12 But he left those among the very poor who were capable of working in vineyards and cultivating the soil.

EZRA AND NEHEMIAH

Introduction

These two books, that originally were only one, tell about the history of the people after their return from the Babylonian captivity. Cyrus, the Persian king, has conquered Babylon and has granted permission to the Jews to return to their land and rebuild Jerusalem and the Temple. The priest Ezra and the governor Nehemiah guide the people during this time of reconstruction and in the reorganization of the country. They did that of course based on the Covenant, pillar of the new protection of Yahweh.

The books were probably written towards the year 400 B.C.

EZRA

The return from the desert

1 [1] In the first year of Cyrus, king of Persia, Yahweh wil-
led to fulfill the word he had said through the prophet Jeremiah, so he moved the spirit of Cyrus, king of Persia, to issue
the following command and send it out in writing to be read
aloud everywhere in his kingdom, [2] "Thus speaks Cyrus, king
of Persia: Yahweh, the God of heavens, who has given me all
the kingdoms of the earth, has ordered me to build him a
Temple in Jerusalem, in the land of Judah. [3] To everyone
belonging to his people, may his God be with him! Let them
go up to Jerusalem with the help of their God and there build

the House of Yahweh, the God of Israel, the God who is in
Jerusalem. [4] In every place where the rest of the people of
Yahweh live, let the people of those places help them for their
journey with silver, gold and all kinds of goods and livestock.
Let them also give them voluntary offerings for the House of
Yahweh which is in Jerusalem."

[5] Then they rose up—the heads of the families of Judah and
Benjamin, the priests and the Levites, and all those whose
spirit God had stirred up—and they decided to go and build
the House of Yahweh. [6] And all their neighbors gave them all
kinds of help: gold, silver, livestock and precious objects in
great quantity, besides every kind of voluntary offering.

[7] King Cyrus also brought out the vessels of the House of
Yahweh which Nebuchadnezzar had carried away from
Jerusalem and placed in the house of his gods. [8] Cyrus, the
king, gave them into the hands of Mithredath, the treasurer,
who counted them and turned them over to Sheshbazzar, the
prince of Judah.

[9] This is the list: golden cups for the offering, 30; silver cups
for offering, 1000; knives, 29; [10] other cups of gold, 30; of silver,
410; other vessels, 1000.

[11] Total number of golden and silver vessels: 5400. All this
was brought out by Sheshbazzar when the exiles were
allowed to return to Jerusalem from Babylon.

NEHEMIAH

Reading of the Law

8 [1] In the seventh month, all the people gathered as one
man in the square before the Water Gate, and they asked Ezra
to bring the Book of the Law of Moses, which Yahweh had
given to Israel. [2] Ezra brought the Law before the assembly,
both men and women and all the children who could understand what was being read. It was the first day of the seventh
month. [3] Ezra read the book before all of them from early
morning until midday in the square facing the Water Gate;
and all who heard were attentive to the Book of the Law.

4 Ezra, the teacher of the Law, stood on a wooden platform built for that occasion and to his right were Mattithiah, Shema, Anaiah, Uriah, Hilkiah and Maaseiah; and to his left were Pedaiah, Mishael, Malchijah, Hashum, Hasbaddanah, Zechariah and Meshullam.

5 Ezra opened the book in the sight of all the people, for he
was in a higher place; and when he opened it, all the people
stood. 6 Ezra blessed Yahweh, the great God; and all the people lifted up their hands and answered, "Amen! Amen!" And
they bowed their heads to the ground.

7 The Levites Joshua, Bani and the rest of their brothers
explained the Law to the people who were standing. 8 They
read from the Book of the Law of God, clarifying and interpreting the meaning, so that everyone might understand what they were hearing.

9 Then Ezra, the teacher of the Law, said to the people:

—This day is dedicated to Yahweh, your God, so do not be sad or weep.

He said this because all wept when they heard the reading
of the Law. 10 Then he said to them:

—Go and eat rich foods, drink sweet wine and share with him who has nothing prepared. This day is dedicated to the Lord, so do not be sad. The joy of Yahweh is our strength.

11 The Levites also calmed the people down, saying:

—Do not weep. This day is a festival day. Do not be sad.

12 And the people went their way to eat, drink and share, and they had a great feast, because they had understood the words that had been proclaimed to them.

Maccabees

Introduction

These events happen towards the year 200 B.C. The Israelites are a small estate under the kings of Syria, successors of Alexander Magnus' empire. One of them, Antiochus Epiphanes, tries to force the Israelites to accept Greek customs, completely opposed to the prescriptions of the Law. The people of Israel resist passively but, later on, reach martyrdom before disobeying Yahweh. Afterwards the armed rebellion explodes, steered by one family: the Maccabees.

In these books, besides the regular theme of Yahweh's protection for his people, when the people are faithful there is another very interesting theme: faith in eternal life, and the recompense that the just ones will receive after death.

1 Maccabees

Historical introduction

1 1 Everything began with the conquests of Alexander the
first, son of Philip, the Macedonian. Setting out from Greece,
he killed Darius, king of the Persians and the Medes. Being
already King of Greece, he took the throne of Darius. 2 After
fighting many battles, conquering strongholds and putting to
death the kings of those nations, 3 he reached the ends of the

earth and plundered several nations. And when the world became quiet and subject to his power, he became proud.
7 Alexander had reigned for twelve years when he died.

8 His generals assumed power, each one in the region assigned to him.
9 And immediately after Alexander's death, they made themselves kings and their sons after them, filling the earth with evil for many years.

Persecution of Antiochus Epiphanes

10 From their descendants there came a godless offshoot, Antiochus Epiphanes, son of King Antiochus, who had been held as hostage in Rome. He became king in the one hundred and thirty-seventh year of the Greek era (175 B.C.).

11 It was then that some rebels emerged from Israel, who succeeded in winning over many people. They said:

—Let us renew contact with the peoples around us for we had endured many misfortunes since we separated from them!

12 This proposal was well-received
13 and some eagerly went to the king. The king authorized them to adopt the customs of the pagan nations.
14 With his permission, they built a gymnasium in Jerusalem in the pagan style.
15 And as they wanted to be like the pagans in everything, they made artificial foreskins for themselves and abandoned the Holy Covenant, sinning as they pleased.

20 In the year one hundred and forty-three (169 B.C.), when Antiochus returned after defeating Egypt, he passed through Israel and went up to Jerusalem with a strong army.

21 He arrogantly broke into the sanctuary and removed the golden altar, the lampstand for the light with all its accessories,
22 the table for the bread of offering, the libation vessels, the cups, the golden censers, the curtains and the crowns, and stripped away all the decorations, the golden moldings that used to cover the Temple entrance.
23 He also took possession of the silver, gold, valuable objects and all the hidden treasures he could find.
24 He took everything with him and left for his country, after shedding much blood and making arrogant statements.

[29] After two years, the king sent to the cities of Judah the
chief tax collector and he came to Jerusalem with a strong
army. [30] He spoke to the people with words of peace in order
to deceive them. But when he had gained their confidence, he
suddenly fell on the city and dealt it a terrible blow, killing
many Israelites. [31] He plundered the city, burning and destroying the palaces and the surrounding walls.

[32] He took women and children captive and seized the livestock. [33] Then they rebuilt the city of David with a high and
solid wall protected by strong towers, and this became their
fortress. [34] There they set evil men and apostates who defended it. [35] They stored up weapons and provisions, and everything they looted in the city, posing a constant threat. [36] It
became an ambush for the sanctuary, a grave and constant
threat to Israel.

[41] Antiochus issued a decree to his whole kingdom.

Mattathias' rebellion

2 [15] In the meantime, the king's representatives, who were
forcing the Jews to give up their religion came to Modein to
organize a sacred gathering.

[16] While many Israelites went to them, Mattathias and his
sons drew apart.

[17] The representatives of the king addressed Mattathias,
and said to him:

—You are one of the leaders of this city, an important and
well-known man, and your many children and relatives follow you. [18] Come now and be the first to fulfill the king's
order, as the men of Judah have already done, and the sur-
vivors in Jerusalem as well. You and your sons will be named
Friends of the King and the king will send you gold, silver and
many other gifts.

[19] But Mattathias answered in a loud voice:

—Even if all the nations included in the kingdom should
abandon the religion of their ancestors and submit to the order
of King Antiochus, [20] I, my sons and my family will remain
faithful to the Covenant of our ancestors. [21] May God preserve

us from abandoning the Law and its precepts. 22 We will not
obey the orders of the king nor turn aside from our religion
either to the right or to the left.

27 Mattathias then began to proclaim loudly in the city:

—Everyone who is zealous for the Law and supports the
Covenant, come out and follow me!

28 Immediately he and his sons fled to the mountains and
left behind all they had in the city.

Judah makes alliance with Rome

8 1 In the meantime, Judas was informed about the
Romans. He was told that the Romans were valiant in war and
that they showed goodwill towards all who sided with them;
that they offered friendship to all who approached them, 2 and
were a strong ally in war.

He was told of their wars and of their exploits among the
Gauls whom they conquered and forced to pay taxes, 3 and of
all they had done in Spain to gain possession of the silver and
gold mines, 4 and how they had conquered that land by dint of
intelligence and perseverance, despite its great distance from
their own land. He also learned how they had defeated the
kings who came from the ends of the earth to attack them,
how they managed to conquer and crush them. There were
others who paid them an annual tax.

17 So Judas sent Eupolemus the son of John, and Jason the
son of Eleazar to Rome, entrusting them with the mission to
make a covenant of friendship with the Romans. 18 Since the
Greeks treated the Israelites as slaves, Judas hoped to liberate
them from oppression in this way.

19 The envoys from Judas went to Rome, where they arrived
after a long journey. When they entered the Senate they
addressed the assembly:

20 —Judas Maccabeus, his brothers and the people of Israel
have sent us to you to conclude a covenant of peace with you
and to be numbered among your allies and friends.

21 The Romans approved this proposal.

2 Maccabees

Persecutory laws

6 [1] After a while, the king sent an older Athenian to force the Jews to abandon their ancestral laws and no longer live according to the laws of God. [2] And to have them also profane the temple in Jerusalem and dedicate it to the *Olympian god*. In the same way, he wanted them to dedicate the temple in Mount Gerizim to the *hospitable god,* according to the wishes of the inhabitants of the place.

Martyrdom of Eleazar

[18] Eleazar, one of the prominent teachers of the Law, already old and of noble appearance, was forced to open his mouth to eat the flesh of a pig. [19] But he preferred to die honorably than to live in disgrace, and voluntarily came to the place where they beat him to death. He spit out bravely the piece of meat, [20] as should be done by those who do not want to do things prohibited by the Law, even to save their life.

[21] Those in charge of this impious banquet took him aside, since they had known him for a long time, and tried to convince him to pretend to be eating the meat, but in reality, to eat something allowed by the Law and prepared by himself. [22] In this way, he could escape death, and be treated with humanity for the sake of their long-time friendship.

[23] But he preferred to make a noble decision worthy of his age, of his noble years, of his shining white hair, and of the irreproachable life he had led from childhood. Above all, showing respect for the holy laws established by God, he

answered that he would rather be sent to the place of the dead. And he added:

24 —It would be unworthy to pretend at our age, and to lead many young people to suppose that I, at ninety years, have gone over to the pagan customs. 25 If I led them astray for the sake of this short life I would bring disgrace to my old age. 26 Even if I could now be saved from mortals, I cannot—whether living or dead—escape from the hands of the Almighty. 27 I prefer to bravely sacrifice my life now, as befits my old age. 28 So I shall leave an excellent example to the young, dying voluntarily and valiantly for the sacred and holy laws.

Having said this, he gave himself over to death.

29 Those who escorted him considered his words foolishness, so their previous gentleness turned into harshness.

30 When he was almost at the point of death, he said groaning:

—The Holy Lord, who sees all, knows that though I could have saved myself from death, I now endure terrible sufferings in my body. But in my soul, I suffer gladly because of the respect I have for him.

31 In his death, he left a noble example and a memorial of virtue and strength, not only to the young but to the whole nation.

The seven brothers and their mother

7 1 It happened also that seven brothers were arrested with their mother. The king had them scourged and flogged to force them to eat the flesh of a pig which was prohibited by the Law.

2 One of them, speaking in behalf of all, said:

—What do you want to find out from us? We are prepared to die right now rather than break the law of our ancestors.

3 The king became furious and ordered that pans and caldrons be heated over a fire. 4 When these were red-hot, he commanded that the tongue of their spokesman be cut out, his head scalped, and his hands and feet cut off while his brothers and mother looked on.

5 When he had been thoroughly mutilated, the king ordered that while still breathing, he be brought to the fire and roasted alive. While the smoke from the pan spread widely, the other brothers and their mother encouraged one another to die bravely. And they said:

6 —The Lord God sees all, and in reality, has compassion on us, as Moses declared in his song, and clearly said:

—The Lord will have pity on his servants.

7 When the first had left the world in this way, they brought the second for execution. After stripping the skin with the hair from his head, they asked him:

—Which do you prefer: to eat the flesh of a pig or to be tortured limb by limb?

8 He answered them in the language of his ancestors:

—I will not eat.

And so he, too, was tortured.

9 At the moment of his last breath, he said:

—Murderer, you now dismiss us from life, but the King of the world will raise us up. He will give us eternal life since we die for his laws.

10 After this, they punished the third. He stuck his tongue
out when asked to, bravely stretched forth his hands, 11 and
even had the courage to say:

—I have received these limbs from God, but for love of his laws I now consider them as nothing. For I hope to recover them from God.

12 The king and his court were touched by the courage of this young man, so unconcerned about his own sufferings.

13 When this one was dead, they subjected the fourth to the
same torture. 14 At the point of death, he cried out:

—I would rather die at the hands of mortals, and wait for the promises of God who will raise us up; you, however, shall have no part in the resurrection of life.

15 They took the fifth at once and tortured him. But with his
eyes fixed on the king, 16 he said to him:

—Though you are mortal, you have authority over people
and are able to do what you will. But do not think that our
race has been abandoned by God. 17 Wait, and you shall see

his great power when he torments you and your descendants.

18 After this, they took the sixth who, at the point of death, said:

—Don't be mistaken. We suffer all this because of ourselves for we have sinned against our own God; so these astonishing things have come upon us. 19 But do not think that you are going to remain unpunished, after having made war with God.

20 More than all of them, their mother ought to be admired and remembered. She saw her seven sons die in a single day. But she endured it even with joy for she had put her hope in the Lord. 21 Full of a noble sense of honor, she encouraged each one of them in the language of their ancestors. Her woman's heart was moved by manly courage, so she told them:

22 —I wonder how you were born of me; it was not I who gave you breath and life, nor I who ordered the matter of your body. 23 The Creator of the world who formed man in the beginning and ordered the unfolding of all creation shall in his mercy, give you back breath and life, since you now despise them for love of his laws.

24 Antiochus thought that she was making fun of him and suspected that she had insulted him.

As the youngest was still alive, the king tried to win him over not only with his words, but even promised to make him rich and happy, if he would abandon the traditions of his ancestors. He would make him his Friend and appoint him to a high position in the kingdom. 25 But as the young man did not pay him any attention, the king ordered the mother to be brought in. He urged her to advise her son in order to save his life. 26 After being asked twice by the king, she agreed to persuade her son. 27 She bent over him and fooled the cruel tyrant by saying in her ancestral language:

—My son, have pity on me. For nine months I carried you in my womb and suckled you for three years; I raised you up and educated you until this day. 28 I ask you now, my son, that when you see the heavens, the earth and all that is in it, you know that God made all this from nothing, and the human race as well. 29 Do not fear these executioners, but make yourself worthy of your brothers—accept death that you may again meet your brothers in the time of mercy.

30 When she finished speaking, the young man said:

—What are you waiting for? I do not obey the king's order
but the precepts of the Law given by Moses to our ancestors.
31 And you who have devised such tortures against the
Hebrews, shall not escape the hands of God. 32 Know that we
perish because of our sins. 33 Our living Lord punishes and
corrects us for a short time because he is angry with us, but he
shall again be reconciled with his servants.

34 And you, the most wretched and impious man, do not be
proud or be carried away by your vain hopes. Do not raise
your hand against the children of Heaven, 35 for you have not
yet escaped the judgment of the almighty God, who sees
everything. 36 Our brothers suffered a short time for the sake
of eternal life and have already entered into the friendship of
God. But you, for your part, shall suffer the punishment you
deserve for your arrogance.

37 With my brothers, I give up my body and my soul for the
laws of my fathers, calling on God that he may at once have
pity on our race, and that by trials and afflictions, you may
come to confess that he is the only God. 38 Through me and my
brothers, may the wrath of the Almighty which has justly fall-
en on the whole of our race come to an end.

39 The king was even more infuriated at him than at the
others because of his mockery and he dealt more cruelly with
him. 40 So the youngest also died undefiled, putting his whole
trust in God.

41 After all her sons, the mother also died.

42 This is enough to make known what happened regarding
the pagan sacrifices and the tortures beyond all imagination.

New deeds of Judas

12 38 Judas reorganized his army, and then went to the
city of Adullam. Since it was the week's end, they purified
themselves and celebrated the sabbath there. 39 The next day
the companions of Judas went to take away the bodies of
the dead (it was urgent to do it) and buried them with their
relatives in the tombs of their fathers. 40 They found under the

tunic of each of the dead men objects consecrated to the idols of Jamnia, which the Law forbade the Jews to wear. So it became clear to everyone why these men had died.

[41] Everyone blessed the intervention of the Lord, the just Judge who brings to light the most secret deeds; [42] and they prayed to the Lord to completely pardon the sin of their dead companions.

The valiant Judas urged his men to shun such sin in the future, for they had just seen with their own eyes what had happened to those who sinned. [43] He took up a collection among his soldiers which amounted to two thousand pieces of silver and sent it to Jerusalem to be offered there as a sacrifice for sin.

They did all this very well and rightly inspired by their belief in the resurrection of the dead. [44] If they did not believe that their fallen companions would rise again, then it would have been a useless and foolish thing to pray for them. [45] But they firmly believed in a splendid reward for those who died as believers; therefore, their concern was holy and in keeping with faith.

STORIES

RUTH

Introduction

The book of Ruth is a jewel of Hebrew narrative. Ruth, the Moabite foreigner, will be the great-grandmother of King David, through her wedding to Boaz, a rich farmer from Bethlehem. Out of this story, that probably has a historical root, a beautiful model to trust in God is made; God's piety extends even to a foreigner, because of his goodness and fidelity.

The foreigner girl

1 1 There was a famine in the land during the time of the
Judges, and a man from Bethlehem in Judah departed with
his wife and two sons to sojourn in the country of Moab. 2 The
man was Elimelech, his wife Naomi, and his two sons
Mahlon and Chilion. They were Ephrathites from Bethlehem,
Judah. A little later, after they had settled in Moab. 3 Naomi's
husband Elimelech died. She was left with her two sons,
4 who married Moabite women, one named Orpah and the
other Ruth.

After living in Moab for about ten years, 5 Mahlon and
Chilion also died and Naomi was left bereft of husband and
two sons. 6 Having heard that Yahweh had come to help his
people by giving them food, Naomi prepared to return home.
7 With her two daughters-in-law, she took the road back to
Judah.

8 It was then that Naomi said to her daughters-in-law:

—Go back, each of you, to your mother's house. And may
Yahweh be kind to you, as you have been to your dead and to
me. 9 May he also grant each of you rest in the home of another husband.

She kissed them goodbye. But they wept aloud 10 and said
to her:

—No, we will go back with you to your people.

11 Naomi said:

—Return home, my daughters. Why should you come with
me?

14 Again they sobbed and wept. Then Orpah kissed her
mother-in-law goodbye, but Ruth clung to her.

15 Naomi said:

—Look, your sister-in-law returns to her people and her
gods. You too must return. Go after her.

16 Ruth replied:

—Don't ask me to leave you. For I will go where you go
and stay where you stay. Your people will be my people and
your god, my God. 17 Where you die, there will I die and be
buried. May Yahweh deal with me severely if anything except
death separates us.

18 Realizing that Ruth was determined to go with her,
Naomi stopped urging her.

19 So the two went on till they reached Bethlehem. Their
arrival set the town astir. Women asked:

—Can this be Naomi?

The rich man from town

2 1 Naomi had a well-to-do kinsman, Boaz, from the clan
of her husband Elimelech. 2 And Ruth the Moabite said to
Naomi:

—Let me go to pick up the left-over grain in the field whose
owner will allow me that favor.

Naomi said:

—Go ahead, my daughter.

[3] So she went to glean in the fields behind the harvesters. It happened that the field she entered belonged to Boaz of the clan of Elimelech.

[4] When Boaz came from Bethlehem, he greeted the harvesters:

—Yahweh be with you.

They returned the greeting:

—Yahweh bless you.

[5] Noticing Ruth, Boaz asked the foreman of his harvesters:

—To whom does that young woman belong?

[6] The foreman replied:

—She is the Moabite who came back with Naomi from the
country of Moab. [7] She came this morning and asked leave to
glean behind the harvesters. Since then she has been working
without a moment's rest.

[8] Boaz said to Ruth:

—Listen, my daughter. Don't go away from here to glean in
anyone else's field. Stay here with my women servants. [9] See
where the harvesters are and follow behind. I have ordered
the men not to molest you. They have filled some jars with
water. Go there and drink when you are thirsty. [10] Bowing
down with her face to the ground, she exclaimed:

—Why have I, a foreigner, found such favor in your eyes?

[11] Boaz answered:

—I have been told all about you: what you have done for
your mother-in-law since your husband's death, how you
have gone with her, leaving your own father and mother and
homeland, to live with a people you knew nothing about
before you came here. [12] May Yahweh reward you for this!
May you receive full recompense from Yahweh, the God of
Israel, under whose wings you have come for refuge!

[13] Ruth said:

—May I prove worthy of your favor, my lord. You have consoled your servant with your kind words, though I am not the equal of your maidservants.

[14] Boaz called her at mealtime:

—Come over, have some bread and dip it in the wine.

As she sat among the reapers, he handed her some roasted grain. She ate her fill and had some left over.

15 When she rose to glean, Boaz instructed his men:

—Let her glean even among the sheaves and do not scold her. 16 And pull some stalks from the bundles; leave them scattered for her to glean.

17 She worked until evening and when she threshed what she had gleaned it amounted to about an ephah. 18 Ruth carried back to town the threshed barley, which she showed to her mother-in-law. She also gave her what she had left over from lunch.

19 Naomi asked her daughter-in-law:

—Where did you glean today? Where did you work? May the man who took notice of you be blessed.

Ruth told her mother-in-law about the owner of the field where she had worked.

Ruth said:

—His name is Boaz.

20 Naomi exclaimed:

—May Yahweh bless him! God indeed is merciful both to the living and the dead. This man is a close relative, one with a right of redemption over us.

21 Ruth continued:

—He even told me to stay with his servants until they finish harvesting the grain.

22 Naomi said:

—It will be better for you, my daughter, to go out with his maidservants than to go working in some other field where harm might come to you.

23 Ruth, therefore, stayed close to the maidservants of Boaz, gleaning until the end of the wheat and barley harvests. And she continued living with her mother-in-law.

The night on the threshing floor

3 9 Boaz asked:

—Who are you?

The answer came:

—I am Ruth, your servant. Spread the corner of your cloak over me for you are a kinsman who has right of redemption over me.

10 Boaz said:

—May Yahweh bless you, my daughter! This kindness of yours now is even greater than that which you have shown earlier, for you have not gone after young men, rich or poor.
11 Have no fear, my daughter; I will do for you all that you ask, since all my townsmen know that you are a worthy woman.
12 It is true that I am a close relative, but there is another still closer. 13 Stay here for the night. In the morning, if he wants to claim you—good! But if not—as surely as Yahweh lives—I will claim you myself. Lie here till morning.

15 Then turning to Ruth, Boaz said:

—Hold out the mantle you are wearing.

She did so and he poured into it six measures of barley. He helped her lift the bundle, then went back to town.

16 Ruth returned home to her mother-in-law, who asked:

—How did you fare, my daughter?

She told her everything 17 and added:

—He gave me these six measures of barley because, as he said, he did not want me to go back to my mother-in-law empty-handed.

18 Naomi said:

—Wait, my daughter, till you learn what happens, for he will not rest until it is settled today.

The wedding

4 1 Meanwhile Boaz went to the town gate and sat there waiting for the closer relative about whom he had spoken to Ruth. When he saw him coming, he called him by name and said:

—Come here and sit down.

And so he did.

2 Boaz picked out ten from the city elders and asked them
to sit with them, which they did. 3 Then he said to the other
man who also had right of redemption:

—Naomi, who has come back from Moab, is selling the
piece of land that belonged to our brother Elimelech. 4 I
thought of bringing this matter to you before our elders here,
because as the closer kin you have more right to lay claim to
it. But if you have no wish to redeem it, let me know because
I am next to you in line.

The man replied:

—I am willing to put in my claim. I will redeem it. 5 Boaz
continued:

—If you buy the land from Naomi, you will also have to
take the Moabite Ruth, widow of the late heir, and her sons
will inherit the name and the land of the dead.

6 The man said:

—Then I cannot redeem it, because I might endanger my
own estate. Redeem it yourself.

7 It used to be the custom in Israel that for a contract of
redemption or exchange to become binding, one party had to
take off his sandal and give it to the other. This act legalized
transactions.

8 So the man took off his sandal and said to Boaz:

—Buy it yourself.

9 Boaz turned to the elders and all those present.

—This day you are witnesses that I buy from Naomi all the
holdings of Elimelech, Chilion and Mahlon. 10 I also take
Mahlon's widow, Ruth the Moabite, as my wife to raise up a
family for her late husband, so that the name of the dead will
be restored to his inheritance and be present among his brothers when they gather at the gate of his town. Do you witness
this today?

11 The elders and all those at the gate answered:

—We witness. May Yahweh make the woman coming into
your house like Rachel and Leah, who together built up the
house of Israel. May you prosper in Ephrathah and be of good
standing in Bethlehem. 12 And through the offspring Yahweh
will give you by this woman, may your house become like
that of Perez whom Tamar bore to Judah.

13 So Ruth was taken by Boaz and became his wife. Yahweh
made her conceive and give birth to a son.

14 The women said to Naomi:

—Blessed be Yahweh who has provided you today with an
heir. May he become famous in Israel! 15 He will be your comfort and stay in your old age, for he is born of a daughter-in-
law who loves you and is worth more than seven sons.

16 Naomi took the child as her own and became his nurse.
17 And the women of the neighborhood gave him his name,
saying:

—A son has been born for Naomi.

They named him Obed. He was the father of Jesse, who was David's father.

Prophets

Introduction

We have already met three Prophets that appeared in the Historical Books: Samuel, Elijah and Elisha. There were many more prophets in Israel. They were personages inspired by God to preach to the People, to remind them about the Law, to denounce their sins, the abuses of the kings. They are normal people, of any trade or condition that suddenly feel called by God for that ministry: to denounce the sins of the people, tell them about the punishments that their infidelities can bring to them. They are solitary, exceptional people, called to a very hard life, full of persecutions, often times confronting even kings, the priests and the powerful. We find in them the faith of Israel in its purist form and in their writings (gathered almost always by their disciples) some of the most beautiful and sublime texts of the whole Old Testament.

ISAIAH

Introduction

The book of Isaiah

With the name of Isaiah we have a collection of prophetic writings that actually have several authors. Looking at close range we distinguish three parts: Isaiah I, from 1–39; Isaiah II, "The Book of Consolation," from 40–45; Isaiah III, from 56–66.

The prophet Isaiah

Born towards the year 760, he received his prophetic vocation in 739; he lived in an agitated and decisive time, with the destruction of the Northern kingdom and the invasion of Judah by Sennacherib. In his prophesy he announces the arrival of a savior, a new just king that will heal the wounds of Israel and will conduct them in the path of the Lord. This announcement, that made reference to the successor of the impious king Ahaz, gives wings to Isaiah for dreaming about a future time of peace and blessing, expressed in marvelous poetic images, and that was taken later on as announcement about the future Messiah, the definitive Savior of Israel.

ISAIAH I

Vocation of Isaiah

6 1 In the year that King Uzziah died I saw the Lord seated on a throne, high and exalted; the train of his robe filled the

Temple. [2] Above him were seraphs, each with six wings: two to cover the face, two to cover the feet, and two to fly with.

[3] They were calling to one another:
"Holy, holy, holy is Yahweh Sabaoth.
All the earth is filled with his Glory!"

[4] At the sound of their voices the foundations of the thresh-
old shook and the Temple was filled with smoke. [5] I said:

—Poor me! I am doomed!
For I am a man of unclean lips
living among a people of unclean lips,
and yet I have seen the King,
Yahweh Sabaoth.

[6] Then one of the seraphs flew to me; in his hands was a live
coal which he had taken with tongs from the altar. [7] He
touched my mouth with it and said:

—See, this has touched your lips;
your guilt is taken away
and your sin is forgiven.

[8] Then I heard the voice of the Lord:

—Whom shall I send?

And who will go for us?

I answered:

—Here I am. Send me!

BOOK ABOUT IMMANUEL

Second advice: the sign of Immanuel

7 [10] Once again Yahweh addressed Ahaz:

[11] —Ask for a sign from Yahweh your God, let it come either from the deepest depths or from the heights of heaven.

[12] But Ahaz answered:

—I will not ask, I will not put Yahweh to the test.

[13] Then Isaiah said:

—Now listen, descendants of David.

Have you not been satisfied trying the patience of people,
that you also try the patience of my God? 14 Therefore the Lord
himself will give you a sign:

The Virgin is with child
and bears a son,
and calls his name
Immanuel.

Messianic prophesy

9 1 The people who walk in darkness
have seen a great light.
A light has dawned
on those who live in the land
of the shadow of death.
2 You have enlarged the nation;
you have increased their joy.
They rejoice before you,
as people rejoice at harvest time
as they rejoice in dividing the spoil.
3 For the yoke of their burden,
the bar across their shoulders,
the rod of their oppressors,
you have broken it as on the day of Midian.
4 Every warrior's boot that tramped in war,
every cloak rolled in blood,
will be thrown out for burning,
will serve as fuel for the fire.
5 For a child is born to us,
a son is given us;
the royal ornament is laid upon his shoulder,
and his name is proclaimed:
"Wonderful Counselor, Mighty God,
Everlasting Father, Prince of Peace."
6 To the increase of his powerful rule
in peace, there will be no end.
Vast will be his dominion,
he will reign on David's throne
and over all his kingdom,
to establish and uphold it

with justice and righteousness
from this time onward and forever.
The zealous love of Yahweh Sabaoth
will do this.

Messianic peace

11 1 From the stump of Jesse a shoot will come forth;
from his roots a branch will grow and bear fruit.

2 The Spirit of the Lord will rest upon him—
a Spirit of wisdom and understanding,
a Spirit of counsel and power,
a Spirit of knowledge and fear of the Lord.

3 Not by appearances will he judge,
nor by what is said must he decide,
4 but with justice he will judge the poor
and with righteousness
decide for the meek.

Like a rod, his word will strike the oppressor,
and the breath of his lips slay the wicked.
5 Justice will be the girdle of his waist,
truth the girdle of his loins.

6 The wolf will dwell with the lamb,
the leopard will rest beside the kid,
the calf and the lion cub will feed together
and a little child will lead them.

7 Befriending each other, the cow and the bear
will see their young ones lie down together.
Like cattle, the lion will eat hay.
8 By the cobra's den the infant will play.
The child will put his hand
into the viper's lair.

9 No one will harm or destroy
over my holy mountain,
for as water fills the sea
the earth will be filled
with the knowledge of the Lord.

Return to Zion

35 [1] Let the wilderness and the arid land rejoice,
the desert be glad and blossom.
[2] Covered with flowers,
it sings and shouts with joy,
adorned with the splendor of Lebanon,
the magnificence of Carmel and Sharon.

They, my people, see the glory of Yahweh,
the majesty of our God.
[3] Give vigor to weary hands
and strength to enfeebled knees.

[4] Say to those who are afraid:
"Have courage, do not fear.
See, your God comes, demanding justice.
He is the God who rewards,
the God who comes to save you."

[5] Then will the eyes of the blind be opened
and the ears of the deaf unsealed.
[6] Then will the lame leap as a hart
and the tongue of the dumb sing and shout.
For water will break out in the wilderness
and streams gush forth from the desert.

[7] The thirsty ground will become a pool,
the arid land springs of water.
In the haunts where once reptiles lay,
grass will grow with reeds and rushes.

[8] There will be a highway
which will be called The Way of Holiness;
no one unclean will pass over it
nor any wicked fool stray there.
[9] No lion will be found there
nor any beast of prey.
Only the redeemed will walk there.

[10] For the ransomed of Yahweh will return:
with everlasting joy upon their heads,
they will come to Zion singing,
gladness and joy marching with them,
while sorrow and sighing flee away.

Isaiah II

Introduction

In this book appears the mysterious figure of the "Servant of Yahweh," a personage chosen by God for the salvation of the people; this person does not have regal attributes, neither power, but it is the "suffering servant," who takes upon himself the sins of the people and suffers for them. In this mysterious figure the Church has seen the announcement of Jesus that will not be a triumphant King Messiah, but the one who will give his life until death for the salvation of all.

The Good News

40 1 Be comforted, my people,
be strengthened, says your God.
2 Speak to the heart of Jerusalem, proclaim to her
that her time of bondage is at an end,
that her guilt has been paid for,
that from the hand of Yahweh
she has received double punishment
for all her iniquity.
3 A voice cries:
—In the wilderness prepare the way for Yahweh.
Make straight in the desert a highway for our God.
4 Every valley will be raised up;
every mountain and hill will be laid low.
The stumbling blocks shall become level
and the rugged places smooth.
5 The glory of Yahweh will be revealed,
and all mortals together will see it;
for the mouth of Yahweh has spoken."
6 A voice says: 'Cry.'
and I say: 'What shall I cry?'
All flesh is grass,
and all its beauty as the flower of the field.
10 Here comes your God with might;

his strong arm rules for him;
his reward is with him,
and here before him is his booty.
11 Like a shepherd he tends his flock:
he gathers the lambs in his arms,
he carries them in his bosom,
gently leading those that are with young.

First servant song: God presents his servant

42 1 Here is my servant whom I uphold,
my chosen one in whom I delight.
I have put my spirit upon him,
and he will bring justice to the nations.
2 He does not shout or raise his voice
proclamations are not heard in the streets.
3 A broken reed he will not crush,
nor will he snuff out the light
of the wavering wick.
He will make justice appear in truth.
4 He will not waver or be broken
until he has established
justice on earth;
the islands are waiting for his law.

5 Thus says God, Yahweh,
who created the heavens
and stretched them out,
who spread the earth
and all that comes from it,
who gives life and breath
to those who walk on it:
6 I, Yahweh,
have called you for the sake of justice;
I will hold your hand
to make you firm;
I will make you as a covenant to the people,
and as a light to the nations,

7 to open eyes that do not see,
to free captives from prison,
to bring out to light
those who sit in darkness.
8 I am Yahweh, that is my name,
I will not give my glory to another;
or my praise to graven images.
9 See, the former things have come to pass,
and new things do I declare:
before they spring forth I tell you of them.

Second servant song: the mission

49 1 Listen to me, O islands,
pay attention, peoples from distant lands.
Yahweh called me from my mother's womb;
he pronounced my name before I was born.
2 He made my mouth like a sharpened sword.
He hid me in the shadow of his hand.
He made me into a polished arrow
set apart in his quiver.
3 He said to me: You are Israel, my servant,
Through you I will be known.
4 'I have labored in vain,' I thought
and spent my strength for nothing.
Yet what is due me was in the hand of Yahweh,
and my reward was with my God.
I am important in the sight of Yahweh,
and my God is my strength.
5 And now Yahweh has spoken,
he who formed me in the womb to be his servant,
to bring Jacob back to him,
to gather Israel to him.
6 He said: 'It is not enough
that you be my servant,
to restore the tribes of Jacob,
to bring back the remnant of Israel.
I will make you the light of the nations,

that my salvation will reach
to the ends of the earth.

Third servant song: suffering and trust

50 [4]The Lord Yahweh has taught me
so I speak as his disciple
and I know how to sustain the weary.
Morning after morning he wakes me up
to hear, to listen like a disciple.
[5]The Lord Yahweh has opened my ear.
I have not rebelled,
nor have I withdrawn.
[6]I offered my back to those who strike me,
my cheeks to those who pulled my beard;
neither did I shield my face
from blows, spittle and disgrace.
[7]I have not despaired,
for the Lord Yahweh comes to my help.
So, like a flint I set my face,
knowing that I will not be disgraced.
[8]He who avenges me is near.
Who then will accuse me?
Let us confront each other.
Who is now my accuser?
Let him approach.
[9]If the Lord Yahweh is my help.
who will condemn me?
All of them will wear out like cloth;
the moth will devour them.

Fourth servant song: passion and glory

52 [13]It is now when my servant will succeed;
he will be exalted and highly praised.
[14]Just as many have been horrified

at his disfigured appearance:
'Is this a man? He does not look like one,'
15 so will nations be astounded,
kings will stand speechless,
for they will see something never told,
they will witness something never heard of.

53 1 Who could believe what we have heard,
and to whom has Yahweh revealed his feat?
2 Like a root out of dry ground,
like a sapling he grew up before us,
with nothing attractive in his appearance,
no beauty, no majesty.
3 He was despised and rejected,
a man of sorrows familiar with grief,
a man from whom people hide their face,
spurned and considered of no account.
4 Yet ours were the sorrows he bore,
ours were the sufferings he endured,
although we considered him as one
punished by God, stricken and brought low.
5 Destroyed because of our sins,
he was crushed for our wickedness.
Through his punishment we are made whole;
by his wounds we are healed.
6 Like sheep we had all gone astray,
each following his own way;
but Yahweh laid upon him all our guilt.
7 He was harshly treated,
but unresisting and silent, he humbly submitted.
Like a lamb led to the slaughter
or a sheep before the shearer
he did not open his mouth.
8 He was taken away to detention and judgment—
what an unthinkable fate!
He was cut off from the land of the living,
stricken for his people's sin.
9 They made his tomb with the wicked,
they put him in the graveyard of the oppressors,
though he had done no violence nor spoken in deceit.

10 Yet it was the will of Yahweh to crush him with grief.
When he makes himself an offering for sin,
he will have a long life and see his descendants.
Through him the will of Yahweh is done.
11 For the anguish he suffered,
he will see the light and obtain perfect knowledge.
My just servant will justify the multitude;
he will bear and take away their guilt.
12 Therefore I will give him his portion among the great,
and he will divide the spoils with the strong.
For he surrendered himself to death
and was even counted among the wicked,
bearing the sins of the multitude
and interceding for sinners.

ISAIAH III

Introduction

We practically know nothing about this prophet whom we call Isaiah III; it is not even clear that the following chapters belong to the same one author. The core message seems to come from a prophet that acts shortly after the restoration of Judah, amidst the poverty and disillusionment of the returning exiles. It is obvious that he imitates Isaiah II. Characteristic of this collection is its eschatological character that is looking towards a definitive future.

The light of the New Jerusalem

60 1 Arise, shine, for your light has come.
The Glory of Yahweh rises upon you.
2 Night still covers the earth
and gloomy clouds veil the peoples,
but Yahweh now rises
and over you his glory appears.
3 Nations will come to your light
and kings to the brightness of your dawn.

4 Lift up your eyes round about and see:
they are all gathered and come to you,
your sons from afar,
your daughters tenderly carried.
5 This sight will make your face radiant,
your heart throbbing and full;
the riches of the sea will be turned to you,
the wealth of the nations will come to you.
6 A flood of camels will cover you,
caravans from Midian and Ephah.
Those from Sheba will come,
bringing with them gold and incense,
all singing in praise of Yahweh.

Mission of the prophet

61 1 The Spirit of the Lord Yahweh is upon me,
because Yahweh has anointed me
to bring good news to the poor.
He has sent me to bind up broken hearts,
to proclaim liberty to the captives,
freedom to those languishing in prison;
2 to announce the year of Yahweh's favor
and the day of vengeance of our God;
to give comfort to all who grieve;
3 (to comfort those who mourn in Zion)
and give them a garland instead of ashes,
oil of gladness instead of mourning,
and festal clothes instead of despair.

New creation

65 17 I now create new heavens and a new earth, and the former things will not be remembered, nor will they come to mind again.

18 Be glad forever and rejoice in what I create; for I create Jerusalem to be a joy and its people to be a delight.
19 I will rejoice over Jerusalem and take delight in my people.

The sound of distress and the voice of weeping will not be heard in it any more.

[20] You will no longer know of dead children or of adults who do not live out a lifetime. One who reaches a hundred years will have died a mere youth, but one who fails to reach a hundred will be considered accursed.

JEREMIAH

Introduction

The prophet Jeremiah

Few personalities from the Old Testament are better known and close to us than the prophet Jeremiah, born at Anatot, a town of the tribe of Benjamin, in the middle of the VII century B.C.

First of all, because we know quite well that part of history when he lived, thanks to the biblical documents, together with extra biblical writings of that time (see 2K 22–25). And also because a great part of the book of Jeremiah is autobiographical, written perhaps by his disciple and secretary Baruc.

We can follow the tragic and touching itinerary of Jeremiah: his vocation in the year 627, the first prophetic activity addressing the destroyed Northern Kingdom, the youthful dreams. After a time of silence (622–609), the great tragedy of Josiah and the terrible revelation of the "Northern threat". From there the scorn of the people because the threats do not come thru, the retrenchment and isolation of a bitter prophet, the insults and, finally, the open persecution. His vocation becomes unbearable and he needs the consolation of God. Finally all his threatening oracles begin to take place.

The prophet tries to gather a group of Jews so that sacred history would continue in Palestine; he is taken by force to Egypt where he pronounces his last oracles. He ends as an anti-Moses, that is, doing backwards the road of liberation, loosing the institutions and the Promised Land, returning to Egypt, where the name of the Lord is no longer invoked. The prophet runs this path in a passionate way. He feels torn between solidarity with his people and the word of God, between obedience to the divine mission and solidarity with his suffering people. His life and passion seem in many aspects an anticipation of the one like Christ.

The book of Jeremiah

Regarding the materials, usually three groups are distinguishable: the first one formed by the original oracles of the prophet and his confessions. The second comprises the biographical narrations, where there are also oracles of the prophet. The third is formed by Jeremiah's discourses.

It was necessary, often times, to reestablish the order or point out the interruptions in the presentation, to make the text more legible.

Jeremiah stands out for his capacity to create images. He stands also by his lyricism and for his intense emotions.

1 1 These are the words of Jeremiah son of Hilkiah, one of
the priests at Anathoth in the territory of Benjamin. 2 The word
of Yahweh came to him in the thirteenth year of the reign of
Josiah son of Amon, king of Judah. 3 It came again during the
reign of Jehoiakim son of Josiah, king of Judah, until the
eleventh year of Zedekiah son of Josiah, king of Judah. In the
fifth month of that year, the inhabitants of Jerusalem were
taken into exile.

Vocation and first oracle

4 A word of Yahweh came to me:

5 —Even before I formed you in the womb I have known you; even before you were born I had set you apart, and appointed you a prophet to the nations!

6 I said:

—Ah, Lord Yahweh! I do not know how to speak; I am still young!

7 But Yahweh replied:

—Do not say; 'I am still young', for now you will go whatever be the mission I am entrusting to you, and you will speak
of whatever I command you to say. 8 Do not be afraid of them,
for I will be with you to protect you—it is Yahweh who speaks!

[9]Then Yahweh stretched out his hand and touched my mouth and said to me:

—Now I have put my words in your mouth. [10]See! Today I give you authority over nations and over kingdoms
to uproot and to pull down,
to destroy and to overthrow,
to build and to plant.

[11] A word of Yahweh came to me again:

—Jeremiah what do you see?

I said:

—I see the branch of a watching tree.

[12] And Yahweh said to me:

—You are right. I too am watching to fulfill my word. [13]The word of Yahweh came to me a second time:

—What do you see?

I replied:

—I see a boiling caldron coming from the north and it is tilted towards this direction.

Then Yahweh said to me:

[14]—From the north disaster will boil down on all the people of this land. [15]I am calling all the kingdoms of the north—it is Yahweh who speaks.

Each of them will come and encamp
at the entrance of the gates of Jerusalem;
against all its surrounding walls
and against all the cities of Judah.
16 I will pass judgment on my people
because of the evil they do in forsaking me;
they have burned incense to foreign gods
and worshipped gods their hands have made.
17 But you, get ready for action;
stand up and say to them all
that I command you.
Be not scared of them
or I will scare you in their presence!
18 See, I will make you a fortified city,
a pillar of iron with walls of bronze,
against all the nations,
against the kings and princes of Judah,
against the priests and the people of the land.
19 They will fight against you
but shall not overcome you,
for I am with you to rescue you
—it is Yahweh who speaks.

Sermon on the temple

7 1 These words were spoken by Yahweh, to Jeremiah:
—2 Stand at the gate of Yahweh's house and proclaim this
in a loud voice: Listen to what Yahweh says, all you people of
Judah (who enter these gates to worship Yahweh). 3 Yahweh
the God of Israel says this:

Amend your ways
and your deeds
and I will stay with you in this place.
4 Rely not on empty words
such as: 'Look, the Temple of Yahweh!
The Temple of Yahweh!
This is the Temple of Yahweh!'
5 It is far better for you
to amend your ways
and act justly with all.

6 Do not abuse the stranger,
orphan or widow
or shed innocent blood in this place
or follow false gods to your own ruin.
7 Then I will stay with you
in this place,
in the land I gave to your ancestors
in times past and forever.
8 But you trust in deceptive
and useless words.
9 You steal, kill,
take the wife of your neighbor;
you swear falsely,
worship Baal
and follow foreign gods who are not yours.
10 Then, after doing
all these horrible things,
you come and stand before me
in this temple that bears my Name
and say, 'Now we are safe.'
11 Is this house on which rests my Name
a den of thieves? I have seen this myself
—it is Yahweh who speaks.

At the potter's house

18 1 This is the word of Yahweh that came to Jeremiah:

2 —Go down to the potter's house and there you will hear what I have to say.

3 So I went to the potter's house and found him working at the wheel.

4 But the pot he was working on was spoiled in his hands, so he reworked it all over again into another pot that suits his desire.

5 Meanwhile Yahweh sent me his word:

6 —People of Israel, can I not do with you what this potter does? As clay in the potter's hand so are you in my hands.

7 At times I warn a nation or a kingdom that I will uproot
or destroy it. 8 But if they change their ways, I then relent and
refrain from doing the harm I had intended to do.

9 At other times I declare that a nation or kingdom will be
built up and planted 10 but then they do what displeases me
and do not listen to me, so I decide to reverse the good deeds
that I intend to do.

11 And Yahweh added:

—Now tell the people of Judah and to those who live in Jerusalem:

Yahweh says to you,
'Listen, I am planning to destroy you;
I am hatching a devastating plot against you!
Turn from your evil ways;
rectify your conduct and your deeds.'

The broken jar

19 1 This was an order of Yahweh to Jeremiah:

—Go and buy a jar from the potter. Take with you some
elders of the people and a few senior priests, 2 and go out to
the valley of Ben-Hinnom at the entrance to the Potsherd
Gate. Proclaim there what I tell you.

10 Then, you shall break the jar before the people who have
accompanied you 11 and you will tell them that I, Yahweh the
God of hosts, will smash the people of this city like the shattered jar of the potter which is beyond repair.

14 Then Jeremiah left Topheth where Yahweh had sent him
to prophesy, and stood in the porch of the House of Yahweh.
There he told all the people:

15 —Listen to the word of Yahweh, God of Israel: I am about
to bring on this city and the towns surrounding the disaster that I have already foretold, because they are a stiff-necked people and will not listen to me.

Jeremiah's confessions

20 7 Yahweh, you have seduced me
and I let myself be seduced.

You have taken me by force and prevailed.
I have become a laughingstock all day long;
they all make fun of me,
8 for every time I speak
I have to shout, "Violence! Devastation!"
Yahweh's word has brought me
insult and derision all day long.
9 So I decided to forget about him
and speak no more in his name.
But his word in my heart becomes like a fire
burning deep within my bones.
I try so hard to hold it in,
but I cannot do it.
10 I hear many people whispering,
'Terror is all around!
Denounce him! Yes, denounce him!'
All my friends watch me to see if I will slip:
'Perhaps he can be deceived,' they say;
'then we can get the better of him
and have our revenge.'
11 But Yahweh, a mighty warrior, is with me.
My persecutors will stumble and not prevail;
that failure will be their shame
and their disgrace will never be forgotten.
12 Yahweh, God of hosts, you test the just
and probe the heart and mind.
Let me see your revenge on them,
for to you I have entrusted my cause.
13 Sing to Yahweh! Praise Yahweh and say:
he has rescued the poor
from the clutches of the wicked!

JEREMIAH'S BIOGRAPHICAL WRITINGS

Jeremiah, judged and released

26 1 At the beginning of the reign of Judah's king Jehoiakim son of Josiah, the word of Yahweh came to Jeremiah:
2 Yahweh says this:

—Stand in the courtyard of Yahweh's House and say to all who come from the towns of Judah to worship in Yahweh's house—all that I command you to say; do not omit anything!
3 Perhaps they will listen to you. Perhaps each one will turn from his wicked ways. Then I will change my mind and forget the destruction that I have planned to inflict on them because of their wicked deeds.

4 Tell them: This is what Yahweh says:

—You have not obeyed me and you have failed to walk
according to my Law which I have set before you. 5 You have
not heeded my servants, the prophets, whom I have persistently sent to you. If you stubbornly close your ears to them,
6 I will treat this House of mine as I treated the sanctuary of Shiloh and let all the nations see that Jerusalem is a cursed city.

7 The priests, the prophets and all the people heard what
Jeremiah said in Yahweh's House. 8 When Jeremiah finished
saying all that Yahweh had commanded, he was besieged by the priests and prophets saying:

—You are bound to die! 9 How dare you speak in Yahweh's
Name telling us that this House will be treated like Shiloh and this city is to become a deserted ruin.

And all the people gathered around Jeremiah in the House of Yahweh.

10 Upon hearing this, the leaders of Judah came up from the king's palace to the House of Yahweh and took their place at
the entrance of the New Gate. 11 Then the priests and the
prophets said to the leaders of the people:

—This man must die for he has spoken against the city as you have heard with your own ears!

12 Jeremiah replied:

—I have been sent by Yahweh to prophesy against this
House and this city all that you have heard. 13 Hence, reform
your ways and your deeds and obey Yahweh your God that he may change his mind and not bring upon you the destruction he had intended.

14 As for me I am in your hands; do with me whatever you
consider just and right. 15 But know that I am innocent and if
you take my life you commit a crime that is a curse on your-

selves, on the city and the people. In truth it was Yahweh who sent me to say all that I said in your hearing.

16 Then the leaders, backed by the people, said to the priests and the prophets:

—This man does not deserve death; he spoke to us in the Name of Yahweh.

24 As for Jeremiah he was befriended by Ahikam, son of Shaphan, and was not handed over to those who wanted him put to death.

Restoration oracle

30 1 This is another word that came to Jeremiah from Yahweh:

2 Yahweh, God of Israel says:

—Write in a book all that I have communicated to you, 3 for
the days are coming when I shall bring my captive people
Israel and Judah back to the land I gave to their ancestors as
their inheritance.

Ezekiel

Introduction

His life

We do not know the date of his birth. Being from a priestly family, he surely received his formation in the Temple, where he most probably officiated until the time of the Exile. In Exile he receives the prophetic vocation, making him a kind of a younger brother to Jeremiah: both are the interpreters of tragedy, in the Motherland and in Exile.

His activity is divided into two stages by a violent break. The first stage lasts about seven years, until the fall of Jerusalem. His job there is to systematically destroy the false hope. The fall of Jerusalem seals the validity of his prophesies. A time of forced silence follows. The prophet begins the second stage: while undermining all hope in human powers, he asserts the judgment of God in History. Only afterwards begins to appear a new hope, founded only in the grace and fidelity of God.

His work

The same happens here as with the other prophets: the book of Ezekiel is not fully the work of Ezekiel. Firstly, because his literary activity is oral, made for recitation, divulged by the prophet and his disciples. What today we know as the book of Ezekiel is the work of his school.

Reading this book we should discover above all the dynamism of a divine action that, through the deserved cross of the people, a pure gift of resurrection will follow.

Theophany

1 1 On the fifth day of the fourth month of the thirtieth
year when I was with the exiles by the river Kebar, the heavens opened and I had visions from Yahweh.

2 On the fifth of the month (it was the fifth year of the exile
of King Jehoiakin).

Vocation

2 1 He said to me:

—Son of man, stand up for I am about to speak to you.

2 A spirit came upon me as he spoke and kept me standing
and then I heard him speak:

3 —Son of man, I am sending you to the Israelites, to a people who have rebelled against me; they and their fathers have
sinned against me to this day. 4 Now I am sending you to these
defiant and stubborn people to tell them 'this is the Lord Yahweh's word.' 5 So, whether they listen or not this set of rebels
will know there is a prophet among them. 6 But you, son of
man, do not fear them or what they say, for they will be as
thorns for you and you will be sitting on a nest of scorpions.
Don't be afraid of their words when you are facing this set of
rebels. 7 Tell them what I say whether they choose to listen or
not, for they are rebels. 8 Listen then, son of man, to what I say
and don't be a rebel among rebels. Open your mouth and take
in what I'm about to say.

9 I looked and saw a hand stretched out in front of me holding a scroll. 10 He unrolled it before me; on both sides were
written lamentations, groanings and woes.

The prophet as sentinel

3 16 After seven days the word of Yahweh came to me:

17 —Son of man, I have made you a watchman for the
House of Israel. With the word you hear from my mouth you
will warn them in my name. 18 When I say to the wicked, 'You

will surely die,' if you do not speak to warn the wicked man
to give up his evil ways and so live, he shall die for his sin, and
I will hold you responsible for his death. 19 But if you have
warned the wicked man and he has not given up his wickedness and evil ways, he shall die for his sin but you will save
yourself. 20 When the righteous man turns from what is good
to do evil I shall put an obstacle in his path: he shall die. Since
you did not warn him, he will die for his sin. His good deeds
will not be remembered and I shall hold you responsible for
his death. 21 But when you have warned the righteous man to
keep him from sinning and he has not sinned, he will live for
sure for he was warned and you will save your life.

Punishment and reconciliation

36 16 The word of Yahweh came to me in these terms:
17 —Son of man, when Israel occupied her own land she
defiled it by her way of life and her actions. To me her conduct
was like the uncleanness of a woman in her period.

18 I poured out my fury on them because of the blood they
shed in the land and because they defiled it with their filthy
idols. 19 Then I scattered them among the nations and dispersed them in other lands. I judged them according to their
conduct and their actions.

20 But when they were brought to other nations, my holy
Name was profaned because others said of them: 'The people
of Yahweh had to be exiled from his land!' 21 Then I was concerned for my holy Name, profaned by Israel among the
nations where she had been dispersed. Now you shall say to
the people of Israel:

22 —It is not for your sake that I am about to act, but
because of my holy Name that you have profaned in the
places where you have gone. 23 I will make known the holiness
of my great Name, profaned among the nations because of
you, and they will know that I am Yahweh when I show them
my holiness among you.

24 —For I will gather you from all the nations and bring you
back to your own land. 25 Then I shall pour pure water over
you and you shall be made clean—cleansed from the defile-

ment of all your idols. [26] I shall give you a new heart and put a new spirit within you. I shall remove your heart of stone and give you a heart of flesh. [27] I shall put my spirit within you and move you to follow my decrees and keep my laws. [28] You will live in the land I gave your ancestors; you shall be my people and I will be your God.

[29] —I will free you from all your uncleanness. I shall summon the wheat and make it plentiful and so keep famine away from you. [30] I shall see that the fruits of the earth and the produce of the fields are plentiful and that you no longer suffer the disgrace of famine among the nations. [31] Then you will remember your evil ways and wicked actions and loathe yourselves for the sins you committed and for your detestable practices. [32] I want you to know that it is not for your sake I am doing this, word of Yahweh. Be ashamed and humbled because of your conduct, Israel!

The bones and the spirit

37 [1] The hand of Yahweh was upon me. He brought me out and led me in spirit to the middle of the valley which was full of bones. [2] He made me walk to and fro among them and I could see there was a great number of them on the ground all along the valley and that they were very dry.

[3] Yahweh said to me:

—Son of man, can these bones live again?

I said:

—Lord Yahweh, only you know that.

[4] He then said:

—Speak on my behalf concerning these bones; say to them:

Dry bones, hear the word of Yahweh! [5] Yahweh says: I am going to put spirit in you and make you live. [6] I shall put sinews on you and make flesh grow on you; I shall cover you with skin and give you my spirit, that you may live. And you will know that I am Yahweh.

[7] I prophesied as I had been commanded and then there was a noise and commotion; the bones joined together. [8] I looked and saw that they had sinews, that flesh was growing

on them and that he was covering them with skin. But there was no spirit in them.

9 So Yahweh said to me:

—Speak on my behalf and call on the Spirit, son of man! Say to the Spirit: This is the word of Yahweh: Spirit, come from the four winds. Breathe into these dead bones and let them live!

10 I prophesied as he had commanded me and breath entered them; they came alive, standing on their feet—a great, immense army!

11 He then said to me:

—Son of man, these bones are all Israel. They keep saying:
'Our bones are dry, hope has gone, it is the end of us.' 12 So
prophesy! Say to them: This is what Yahweh says: I am going
to open your tombs; I shall bring you out of your tombs, my
people, and lead you back to the land of Israel. 13 You will
know that I am Yahweh, O my people! when I open your
graves and bring you out of your graves, 14 when I put my
spirit in you and you live. I shall settle you in your land and
you will know that I, Yahweh, have done what I said I would
do.

Daniel

Introduction

The book

What we read today in the book of Daniel is a complex work, set aside by itself in the Old Testament.

Beginning with the language in which the book is written: some chapters are written imitating the classic Hebrew; other in Aramaic, and others in Greek.

The distribution of forms and themes does not coincide with the division of languages.

Data

We could date the book between the years 167 and 164 B.C.

It is impossible to decide if all the legendary materials belonged since the beginning to Daniel or if it had been gathered around the hero. In any case, the Babylonian ambiance is fictitious; the author does not show special interest in the historical precision in these writings.

Apocalypses

The book of Daniel is a book all by itself in the Old Testament.

It has not entered as a prophetic book; it is part of the "writings," a more facile and more welcoming concept. But in the Greek and Latin bibles and in Christian tradition, Daniel is one of the four major prophets.

The apocalyptic literature is heir to prophesy.

Apocalypses is presented as a revelation of God, made to a cho-

sen person, about history and its unraveling. It is intended for the community during a time of crisis, to re-enkindle hope.

God is the one who reveals, but through dreams and prophetic visions. The visions are explained by an angel.

The theme is history and its unraveling.

It is a past history that arrives to the present and that through the genre's fiction presents as future events, foretold by the seer.

It is about the definitive and universal establishment of the kingdom by the Lord of History.

The style uses allegory as basic procedure.

Pseudonymia: the author, faithful to the fiction of foretelling history, has to attribute his work to a great figure of the past. It seems that our author has chosen one of the personages quoted by Ezekiel.

DANIEL'S HISTORY

Daniel in the Babylonian court

1 1 In the third year of Jehoiakim's reign as king of Judah,
King Nebuchadnezzar of Babylon besieged Jerusalem. 2 The
Lord delivered into his hands King Jehoiakim of Judah, and
some of the vessels from the temple of God as well. These he
carried off to the land of Shinar and placed in the treasure
house of his god.

3 King Nebuchadnezzar ordered his chief eunuch
Ashpenaz to bring in some of the Israelites from the royal family and the nobility: 4 young men without physical defect,
handsome, intelligent and wise, well-informed, quick to learn
and understand, and suitable for service in the king's palace.
They were to be taught the language and literature of the
Chaldeans. 5 They were allotted a daily portion of food and
wine from the king's table and were to be trained for three
years, after which they were to enter the king's service.

6 Among these were young men of Judah: Daniel,
Hananiah, Mishael, and Azariah.

17 To these four youths God gave wisdom and proficiency

in literature, and to Daniel the gift of interpreting visions and
dreams.

18 At the end of the period set by the king for the youths'
training, the chief eunuch presented them to Nebuchadnezzar.
19 The king talked with them and found none to equal Daniel,
Hananiah, Mishael, and Azariah. These four became members
of the king's court. 20 In any matter of wisdom and discernment about which the king consulted, he found them ten
times better than all the magicians and enchanters in his
whole kingdom.

The dream of Nebuchadnezzar

2 1 In the second year of Nebuchadnezzar's reign, he had
a series of troubling dreams which rendered him sleepless.
2 The king summoned magicians, enchanters, sorcerers and
Chaldean diviners to interpret his dreams. When they arrived
and stood in his presence, 3 the king said:

—I had a terrible dream and I want to know its meaning.

4 The Chaldeans answered in Aramaic:

—Live forever, O King! Tell your servants the dream, and
we will give you its meaning.

5 But the king replied:

—You have to tell me the dream and interpret it, too. That
is my decision. If you won't do it, I will have you cut into
pieces and your houses razed to the ground. 6 But if you can
tell me the dream and its meaning, I will give you presents
and reward you with great honor.

10 The Chaldeans exclaimed:

—No one on earth can do what your majesty asks. Never
has any king, however great and mighty, asked such a thing of
any magician, enchanter or diviner. 11 What the king demands
is too difficult. No one can tell him that except the gods who
do not live among mortals.

12 This made the king so furious that he ordered all the wise
men of Babylon executed. 13 Upon issuance of the decree to
put the wise men to death, a search was also made for Daniel
and his companions to have them killed. 24 After this Daniel

went to Arioch, the commander appointed by the king to execute the wise men of Babylon. Daniel said to him:

—Do not execute the wise men yet. Bring me to the king, and I will interpret his dreams.

25 At once Arioch took Daniel to the king and said:

—Here is a man found among the Judean captives who says he can interpret the king's dream.

26 The king asked Daniel, who had been named Beltheshazzar:

—Can you tell me what my dream was and what it means?

27 Daniel answered:

—No wise man, enchanter, magician or diviner can interpret the king's dream.
28 But there is a God in heaven who reveals mysteries, and he has shown King Nebuchadnezzar what will happen in the future. I will tell you the dream and visions you had.

29 As you lay in bed, O King, your thoughts turned to the future, and he who reveals mysteries showed you what is to happen.
30 This mystery has been revealed to me not because I am wiser than anybody else but so that you may know what it means and what went on in your mind.

31 In your vision you saw a statue—very large, very bright, terrible to look at.
32 Its head was of pure gold, its chest and arms of silver, its belly and thighs of bronze,
33 its legs of iron, its feet partly of iron and partly of baked clay.
34 As you watched, a rock cut from a mountain but not by human hands, struck the statue on its feet of iron and clay, smashing them.
35 All at once the iron, clay, bronze, silver and gold crumbled into pieces as fine as chaff on the threshing floor in summer. The wind swept them off and not a trace was left. But the rock that struck the statue became a great mountain that filled the whole earth.

36 That was the dream. Now the interpretation.
37 You, O king, are king of kings, to whom the God of heaven has given dominion, strength, power and glory,
38 and into whose hand he has placed humankind, the beasts of the field and the birds of the air, making you ruler over them. You are that head of gold.

39 After you, another kingdom inferior to yours will rise.

Then a third kingdom of bronze will rule the whole world.
40 Last shall be a fourth kingdom strong as iron and just as iron
breaks and crushes everything else, so will it break and smash
all the others. 41 The partly-clay and partly-iron feet and toes
mean that it will be a divided kingdom; yet it will have some
of the strength of iron, just as you saw iron mixed with clay.
42 And as the toes were partly iron and partly clay, the kingdom will be partly strong and partly weak. 43 Just as you saw
the iron mixed with baked clay, the people will be a mixture
but will not remain united, any more than iron mixes with
clay.

44 In the time of those kings the God of heaven will set up a
kingdom never to be destroyed or delivered up to another
people. It will crush all those kingdoms and put an end to
them. And it will endure forever. 45 This is the meaning of your
vision of a rock cut from a mountain not by human hands, the
rock which struck the statue and broke into pieces the iron,
bronze, clay, silver and gold. The great God has shown the
king what will happen in the future. The dream is true and its
interpretation reliable.

46 King Nebuchadnezzar fell prostrate before Daniel and
ordered that oblation and incense be offered to him.

47 The king said to Daniel:

—Surely your God is the God of gods, the Lord of kings
and the revealer of mysteries. That is why you were able to
reveal this mystery.

48 The king gave Daniel a high position and showered gifts
on him. He made him governor of the entire province of
Babylon and in charge of all its wise men. 49 At Daniel's
request the king appointed Shadrach, Meshach and Abednego
administrators of the province of Babylon, while Daniel himself remained at the king's court.

The golden statue

3 1 King Nebuchadnezzar had a golden statue, sixty
cubits high and six cubits wide, erected on the plain of Dura
in the province of Babylon.

3 All those summoned came together for the dedication and

stood before the statue set up by King Nebuchadnezzar.
4 There a herald proclaimed aloud:

—Nations and peoples of every language, you are hereby
commanded 5 to fall down and worship the golden statue as
soon as you hear the music played on the horn, flute, zither,
lyre, harp, pipes and all other instruments. 6 Whoever fails to
do this will at once be thrown into a burning furnace.

8 It was then that Chaldean diviners came to the king accus-
ing the Jews. 9 They said to King Nebuchadnezzar:

—Live forever, O king! 10 You issued a decree that upon
hearing the sound of the horn, flute, zither, lyre, harp, pipes
and other musical instruments, everyone must fall down and
worship the golden statue, 11 and whoever failed to do so was
to be thrown into a burning furnace. 12 There are some Jews,
those whom you appointed administrators of Babylon: Shadrach, Meshach and Abednego, who gave no heed to your
order. They would not serve your gods or worship the golden
image you set up.

16 Shadrach, Meshach and Abednego answered:

—King Nebuchadnezzar, we need not defend ourselves
before you on this matter. 17 If you order us to be thrown into
the furnace, the God we serve will rescue us. 18 But even if he
won't, we would like you to know, O king, that we are not
going to serve your gods or worship the golden statue you
have set up.

19 Nebuchadnezzar's face reddened with fury as he
looked at Shadrach, Meshach and Abednego. He ordered the
furnace heated seven times hotter than usual 20 and commanded some of his strongest soldiers to bind Shadrach,
Meshach and Abednego and throw them into the burning
furnace.

21 At once they were bound and thrown into the furnace,
with their hats, shoes and garments on, 22 for the king's order
was very urgent. So fierce was the fire in the furnace that it
devoured even the men who threw Shadrach, Meshach and
Abednego into it. 23 The three, bound fast, fell into the midst of
the blazing furnace.

The text in italics is originally written in Greek. Azariah's "Penitential Prayer" is written following the style and with the theme of Psalm 51, that you can read in the book of Psalms in this Bible. And the "Canticle of the Three Youth" gets its inspiration from Psalms 136 and 148 that can also be read in the book of Psalms.

Azariah's penitential prayer

24 *They walked in the midst of the flames, singing to God and praising the Lord.*

25 *Azariah stood up in the midst of the fire and prayed aloud:*

26 *Blessed and worthy of praise are you,*
O Lord God of our fathers!
your name is glorious forever!

Canticle of the three youth

49 *But the angel of the Lord came down into the furnace beside*
Azariah and his companions; he drove the flames of the fire outside
the furnace, and blew upon them, 50 *in the middle of the furnace, a*
coolness like that of wind and dew, so that the fire did not touch them or cause them pain or trouble them.

51 *Then the three began singing together, glorifying and blessing God within the furnace, and saying:*

52 *—Blessed are you, Lord, God of our fathers,*
be praised and exalted forever.
Blessed is your holy and glorious name,
celebrated and exalted forever.

Confession of Nebuchadnezzar

91 Then King Nebuchadnezzar suddenly rose up in great amazement and asked his counselors:

—Did we not throw three men bound into the fire?

They answered:

—Certainly.

92 The king said:

—But I can see four men walking about freely through the

fire without suffering any harm, and the fourth looks like a son of the gods.

93 Nebuchadnezzar approached the mouth of the blazing furnace and said:

—Shadrach, Meshach and Abednego, servants of the Most High God, come out and come here.

So they came out from the midst of the fire.

94 The officials, prefects, governors and counselors of the king drew near to examine them: the fire had no effect on their bodies, their hair was not singed, their trousers were not burned, and they did not even have the smell of smoke.

95 Nebuchadnezzar exclaimed:

—Blessed be the God of Shadrach, Meshach and Abednego who sent his angel to free his servants who, trusting in him, disobeyed the king's order and preferred to give their bodies to the fire rather than serve and worship any other god but their God.

96 I give this command, therefore: From every race, nation and language, anyone who speaks irreverently of the God of Shadrach, Meshach and Abednego shall be cut into pieces and his house shall be destroyed, for there is no other god who can save like this.

97 And the king promoted Shadrach, Meshach and Abednego in the province of Babylon.

The banquet of Belshazzar

5 1 King Belshazzar gave a great banquet for his nobles, a
thousand of them attended and he drank wine with them.
2 Under the influence of wine, he ordered that the gold and silver vessels his father Nebuchadnezzar had taken from the
temple in Jerusalem be brought in so that he and his nobles,
his wives and concubines might drink from them. 3 The gold
and silver vessels taken from God's temple were brought in,
and the king and his nobles, his wives and concubines drank
from them. 4 While they drank wine, they praised the gods of
gold and silver, of bronze and iron, of wood and stone.

5 Suddenly a man's fingers appeared opposite the lamp-

stand and wrote on the plastered wall of the king's palace.
Watching the hand as it wrote, the king turned pale. [6] So terrified was he that his knees knocked and his legs gave way.

[7] He shouted, calling for his enchanters and Chaldean diviners:

—Whoever reads this writing and tells me its meaning will be clothed in purple, wear a gold chain around his neck, and be made the third highest ruler in my kingdom.

[8] All the king's wise men came, but none could read the
writing or tell its meaning. [9] King Belshazzar became very
frightened and his face grew even more pale. His nobles were likewise terrified and confused.

[10] Hearing the troubled voices of the king and his nobles, the queen entered the banquet hall and said:

—Live forever, O king! Do not be alarmed and become
pale. [11] In your kingdom is a man who has the spirit of the holy gods. He was found to have discernment and god-like wisdom during your father's lifetime. He was in fact appointed chief of the magicians, enchanters and diviners by your father
King Nebuchadnezzar. [12] This man Daniel, whom the king called Beltheshazzar, knew how to interpret dreams, explain riddles and solve difficult problems. Call for Daniel and he will tell you what the writing means.

[13] Daniel was brought in and questioned by the king.

—Are you Daniel, one of the exiles my father brought from
Judah? [14] I have heard that you have the spirit of the gods, that
you have insight and extraordinary wisdom. [15] Wise men and
enchanters were brought here, but none of them could read
this writing and tell its meaning. [16] I have heard that you can
interpret dreams and solve problems. If you can read this writing and tell me what it means, you will be clothed in purple, wear a gold chain around your neck, and be appointed third in rank in my kingdom.

[17] Daniel replied:

—You may keep your gifts or give them to someone else. Just the same I will read and interpret the writing for you.

[24] So he sent the hand that wrote the inscription [25] which
read MENE, MENE, TEKEL, PARSIN. And these words mean:
[26] MENE, God has numbered the days of your reign and put

an end to it; 27 TEKEL, you have been weighed on the scales
and found wanting; 28 PARSIN, your kingdom has been divided and given to the Medes and the Persians.

29 On Belshazzar's order, Daniel was clothed in purple,
given a gold chain to wear around his neck, and proclaimed
the third highest ruler in the kingdom.

30 That very night, however, the Chaldean king Belshazzar
was slain.

6 1 Darius the Mede, at the age of sixty-two, took over the
kingdom.

Daniel In the lion's den

2 Darius appointed one hundred and twenty satraps
throughout the whole kingdom. They were made accountable
to three administrators, one of whom was Daniel. This was to
ensure that no loss or harm should come to the king. 3 Because
of the extraordinary spirit residing in him, Daniel excelled
above all the other administrators and satraps, so that the king
planned to give him authority over the entire kingdom.

4 This provoked envy among the administrators and
satraps, who tried to find grounds for filing charges against
Daniel as regard his performance of official duties. But he was
so trustworthy that neither corruption nor negligence could
be found in him. 5 Finally the men decided: 'We will never find
any grounds for charges against this man Daniel except in
something that has to do with the law of his God.'

11 There the men spying on him found Daniel kneeling in
prayer and asking God for help. 12 So they went to the king
and reminded him about the prohibition:

—O king, did you not publish a decree that anyone who prays or makes petition to any god or man except to you would be thrown into the lions' den?

The king answered:

—Yes, and the decree stands, in accordance with Medo-Persian laws which cannot be altered or annulled.

13 Then they said:

—But the Jewish exile Daniel pays no attention to you and
to your decree. Three times a day he still prays to some god
other than you.

14 Greatly aggrieved at what he heard, the king decided to
help Daniel. He made every effort till sundown to save him.

15 But the men kept coming to him and insisting:

—Remember, O king, that under the Medo-Persian laws
every decree or prohibition issued by the king is irrevocable.

16 The king, therefore, could not help giving the order that
Daniel be brought and thrown into the lions' den. The king
said to Daniel:

—May your God, whom you serve faithfully, save you.

17 A stone was placed at the mouth of the den, and the king
sealed it with his own signet ring and with that of his nobles,
so that Daniel's situation might remain unchanged. 18 Then the
king returned to his palace and spent a sleepless night, refus-
ing food and entertainment. 19 Very early next morning, he
rose and hurried to the lions' den. 20 As he came near he called
in an anguished voice:

—Daniel, servant of the living God, did your God whom
you serve faithfully save you from the lions?

21 Daniel answered:

—Live forever, O king! 22 My God sent his angel who closed
the lions' mouths so that they did not hurt me. God did that
because I am innocent in his sight. Neither have I wronged
you, O king.

23 The king felt very glad and ordered Daniel released from
the lions' den. No wound was found on him for he had trusted in his God. 24 At the king's order, the men who had
accused Daniel were thrown into the lions' den, together with
their wives and children. No sooner had they reached the
floor of the den than the lions lunged at them and tore them
to pieces.

25 King Darius wrote to the nations, to peoples of every language:

—'Peace to you all! 26 I decree that throughout my kingdom
people should reverence and fear the God of Daniel.

For he is the living God,
and forever he endures;
his kingdom will not be crushed,
his dominion will never cease.
27 He rescues and he delivers;
he performs signs and wonders
And he came to Daniel's rescue
saving him from the lions' tooth and claw.'

28 Daniel greatly prospered during the reign of Darius and the reign of Cyrus the Persian.

Psalms

Introduction

The Psalms are the prayer of Israel. They are the expression of human experience addressed towards God. They are the expression of a people's life impelled by God. God's history is the life of the people, because he creates and suffers with the people. All these was transformed into prayers, alive and varied, on the hands of very different authors. Tradition attributes many psalms to king David: it is just a convention, the same as attributing to Solomon the wisdom compositions. An anonymous chain of poets, throughout centuries is a more realistic way to describe the authors of these writings.

The hymns sing praises and they are usually communitarian: their themes are the actions of God in creation and history. Close to them is thanksgiving for personal or communitarian favors. From needs spring up supplications, so varied in themes; the praying person motivates his petition so as to convince or to move God. At times, from supplications springs up an act of trust, based on past experiences or in God's promises.

The sinner confesses his sins and asks for forgiveness in the penitential psalms. Others we could call meditations because they deal about human life or about the history of Israel.

In what follows we will give the Hebraic numbering, adding in parenthesis the Greco Latin number. The psalms are also privileged prayer of the Christian community as well as of an individual. Many psalms were prayed by Jesus, thus giving them the plenitude of meaning hidden in them.

8

[2] O Lord, our Lord,
how great is your name throughout the earth!
And your glory in the heavens above.
[3] Even the mouths of children and infants
exalt your glory in front of your foes
and put to shame enemies and rebels.
[4] When I observe the heavens,
the work of your hands,
the moon and the stars you set in their place—
[5] what is the mortal that you be mindful of him,
the son of man, that you should care for him?
[6] Yet you made him a little lower than the angels;
you have crowned him with glory and honor.
[7] You made him rule over the works of your hands;
you have put all things under his feet
[8] sheep and oxen without number
and even the beasts of the field,
[9] the birds of the air, the fish of the sea,
and all that swim the paths of the ocean.
[10] O Lord, our Lord,
how great is your name all over the earth!

23 (22)

[1] The Lord is my shepherd, I shall not want.
[2] He makes me lie down in green pastures.
He leads me beside the still waters,
[3] he restores my soul.
He guides me through the right paths
for his name's sake.
[4] Although I walk through the valley of the shadow of death,
I fear no evil,
for you are beside me:
your rod and your staff comfort me.
[5] You spread a table before me
in the presence of my foes.

You anoint my head with oil;
my cup is overflowing.
6 Goodness and kindness will follow me
all the days of my life,
I shall dwell in the house of the Lord
as long as I live.

24 (23)

1 The earth and its fullness belong to the Lord,
the world and all that dwell in it.
2 He has founded it upon the ocean
and set it firmly upon the waters.
3 Who will ascend the mountain of the Lord?
Who will stand in his holy place?
4 Those with clean hands and pure heart,
who desire not what is vain,
and never swear to a lie.
5 They will receive blessings from the Lord,
a reward from God, their savior.
6 Such are the people who seek him,
who seek the face of Jacob's God.
7 Lift up, O gateways, your lintels,
open up, you ancient doors,
that the King of glory may enter!
8 Who is the King of glory?
The Lord, the strong, the mighty,
the Lord, valiant in battle.
9 Lift up your lintels, O gateways,
open up, you ancient doors,
that the King of glory may enter!
10 Who is the King of glory?
The Lord of Hosts,
he is the King of glory!

32 (31)

Blessed is the one whose sin is forgiven,
whose iniquity is wiped away.
2 Blessed are those in whom the Lord sees no guilt
and in whose spirit is found no deceit.
3 When I kept my sin secret,
my body wasted away,
I was moaning all day long.
4 Your hand day and night lay heavy upon me;
draining my strength, parching my heart
as in the heat of a summer drought.
5 Then I made known to you my sin
and uncovered before you my fault,
saying to myself,
"To the Lord I will now confess my wrong."
And you, you forgave my sin,
you removed my guilt.
6 So let the faithful ones pray
to you in time of distress;
the overflowing waters will not reach them.
7 You are my refuge;
you protect me from distress
and surround me with songs of deliverance.
8 I will teach you,
I will show you the way to follow.
I will watch over you and give you counsel.

51 (50)

3 Have mercy on me, O God, in your love.
In your great compassion blot out my sin.
4 Wash me thoroughly of my guilt;
cleanse me of evil.
5 For I acknowledge my wrongdoings
and have my sins ever in mind.
6 Against you alone have I sinned;
what is evil in your sight I have done.

You are right when you pass sentence
and blameless in your judgment.
7 For I have been guilt-ridden from birth,
a sinner from my mother's womb.
8 I know you desire truth in the heart,
teach me wisdom in my inmost being.
9 Cleanse me with hyssop and I shall be clean,
wash me, I shall be whiter than snow.
10 Fill me with joy and gladness;
let the bones you have crushed rejoice.
11 Turn your face away from my sins
and blot out all my offenses.
12 Create in me, O God, a pure heart;
give me a new and steadfast spirit.
13 Do not cast me out of your presence
nor take your holy spirit from me.
14 Give me again the joy of your salvation
and sustain me with a willing spirit.
15 Then I will show wrongdoers your ways
and sinners will return to you.
16 Deliver me, O God, from the guilt of blood,
and of your justice I shall sing aloud.
17 O Lord, open my lips,
and I will declare your praise.
18 You take no pleasure in sacrifice;
were I to give a burnt offering,
you would not delight in it.
19 O God, my sacrifice is a broken spirit;
a contrite heart you will not despise.
20 Shower Zion with your favor:
rebuild the walls of Jerusalem.
21 Then you will delight in fitting sacrifices,
in burnt offerings and bulls offered on your altar.

78 (77)

Give heed, O my people, to my teaching;
listen to the words of my mouth!
2 I will speak in parables,
I will talk of old mysteries

3 which we have heard and known,
which our ancestors have told us.
4 We will not keep them hidden from our children;
we will announce them to the coming generation:
the glorious deeds of the Lord,
his might and the wonders he has done.
5 He issued decrees for Jacob
and set up a law in Israel,
which he commanded our ancestors
to teach their children,
6 so the next generation would learn
and teach their own children.
7 They would then put their trust in God,
and not forget his deeds and his commands.
8 And not be like their ancestors,
stubborn and rebellious people,
a people of inconstant heart
whose spirit was fickle.
9 Well-armed with bow,
the Ephraimites took flight
when the time came to do battle.
10 It is because they did not keep
God's covenant
and refused to live by his law.
11 They forgot the marvels he had done,
12 what their ancestors had seen
in the land of Egypt,
in the fields of Zoan.
13 He divided the sea and led them across;
he made the water stand like a wall.
14 By day he led them with a cloud,
and by night with a fiery light.
15 In the desert he split rocks
to give them abundant drink.
16 He made streams come out of a rock
and caused water to flow like a river.
17 Yet they sinned even more against him
and rebelled against the Most High
in the desert.
18 They tested God,
demanding the food they craved.

19 They blasphemed against God, saying:
'Can God spread a table in the desert?
20 He made water flow out of the rock;
can he also give his people bread or meat?'
21 When the Lord heard this he was enraged;
a fire raged against Jacob,
his anger flared against Israel,
22 for they had no faith in God
nor trust in his deliverance.
23 Yet he commanded the skies
above and opened the doors of heaven;
24 he rained down manna upon them
and fed them with the heavenly grain.
25 They ate and had more than their fill
of the bread of angels.
26 Then from heaven he stirred the east wind,
and by his power let loose the south wind,
27 to rain down meat on them like dust.
Birds as thick as the sand on the seashore
28 fell inside their camp,
lying all around their tents.
29 They ate till they were satisfied,
for he had given them what they craved.
36 But they flattered him with their mouths,
they lied to him with their tongues,
37 while their hearts were unfaithful;
they were untrue to his covenant.
38 Even then, in his compassion,
he forgave their offenses
and did not destroy them.
Many a time he restrained his anger
and did not fully stir up his wrath.
39 He remembered that they were but flesh,
a breeze that passes and never returns.
40 How often did they rebel against him
in the wilderness,
how often did they grieve him in the desert!
41 Again and again they tested him,
and provoked the Holy One of Israel.
42 They did not remember his power
in redeeming them from the oppressor.

52 Then he led forth his people like a flock,
and guided them like sheep through the desert.
53 He led them safely, they did not fear,
but the sea engulfed their enemies.
54 He brought them to his holy land,
to the mountain his right hand had won.
55 He drove out peoples before them
and gave them the land as their inheritance;
they pitched their tents in it.
69 He built his sanctuary like heaven,
like the earth he founded forever.
70 He chose David his servant
and took him from the sheepfolds;
71 from tending the sheep and their young,
he brought him to shepherd Jacob,
the people of Israel, his inheritance.
72 And with upright heart David pastured them;
with skillful hands he led them.

104 (103)

1 Bless the Lord, my soul!
Clothed in majesty and splendor;
O Lord, my God, how great you are!
2 You are wrapped in light as with a garment;
you stretch out the heavens like a tent,
3 you build your upperrooms above the waters.
You make the clouds your chariot
and ride on the wings of the wind;
4 you make the winds your messengers,
and fire and flame your ministers.
5 You set the earth on its foundations,
and never will it be shaken.
6 You covered it with the ocean like a garment,
and waters spread over the mountains.
7 But at your rebuke the waters flee,
at the sound of your thunder they take to flight.
8 Brought to the mountains, they flow down again
to settle in the valleys.

9 You set a limit they could not cross,
never again to flood the earth.
10 You make springs gush forth in valleys
winding among mountains and hills,
11 giving drink to the beasts of the field,
quenching the thirst of wild donkeys.
12 Birds build their nests close by
and sing among the branches of trees.
13 You water the mountains from your abode
and fill the earth with the fruit of your work.
14 You make grass grow for cattle
and plants for man to cultivate,
that he may bring forth food from the earth:
15 wine to gladden his heart,
oil to make his face shine,
and bread to make him strong.
16 The Lord waters his trees to their fill,
the cedars of Lebanon which he planted.
17 The birds build their nests,
the stork has its home in the pine trees.
18 High mountains are for wild goats,
the cliffs a refuge for badgers.
19 You made the moon to mark the seasons,
and the sun that knows when to set;
20 when you bring the darkness of the night,
all the beasts of the forest begin to prowl:
21 the young lions roaring for their prey
claiming their food from God.
22 When the sun rises, the beasts steal away,
returning to rest in their dens.
23 Man then goes out to his work,
and toils till evening comes.
24 How varied O Lord, are your works!
In wisdom you have made them all—
the earth full of your creatures.
25 Behold the sea, wide and vast,
teeming with countless creatures,
living things both great and small,
26 a strange world reserved for the ships,
for Leviathan, the dragon you made to play with.
27 They all look to you
for their food in due time.

28 You give it to them,
and they gather it up;
you open your hand,
they are filled with good things.
29 When you hide your face they vanish,
you take away their breath, they expire
and return to dust.
30 When you send forth your spirit,
they are created,
and the face of the earth is renewed.
31 May the glory of the Lord endure forever;
may the Lord rejoice in his works!
32 He looks on the earth, and it quakes;
he touches the mountain, and it smokes.
33 I will sing to the Lord all my life;
I will sing praise to God while I live.
34 May my song give him pleasure,
as the Lord gives me delight.
35 May sinners vanish from the earth,
and may the wicked be no more.
Bless the Lord, my soul!

105 (104)

1 Give thanks to the Lord, call on his name;
make known his works among the nations.
2 Sing to him, sing his praise,
proclaim all his wondrous deeds.
3 Glory in his holy name;
let those who seek the Lord rejoice.
4 Look to the Lord and be strong;
seek his face always.
5 Remember his wonderful works,
his miracles and his judgments,
6 you descendants of his servant Abraham,
you sons of Jacob, his chosen ones!
7 He is the Lord our God;
his judgments reach the whole world.
8 He remembers his covenant forever,

his promise to a thousand generations,
9 the covenant he made with Abraham,
the promise he swore to Isaac.
10 He confirmed his decree to Jacob,
to Israel his eternal covenant:
11 'To you I will give the land of Canaan
as part of your inheritance.'
12 When they were few in number,
strangers in the land,
13 wandering from nation to nation,
from one kingdom to another,
14 he allowed no one to oppress them,
and for their sake he rebuked kings:
15 "Touch not my anointed ones,"
he warned, "do my prophets no harm!"
16 Then he sent a famine
and ruined the crop that sustained the land;
17 he sent a man ahead of them, Joseph,
who was sold as a slave;
18 his feet in shackles, his neck in irons
19 till what he foretold came to pass,
and the Lord's word proved him true.
20 The king sent for him, set him free,
the ruler of the peoples released him.
21 He put him in charge of his household
and made him ruler of all his possessions,
22 that he might train his princes
and teach his elders wisdom.
23 Then Israel came to Egypt,
Jacob settled in the land of Ham.
24 The Lord made his people fruitful
and much stronger than their foes,
25 whose hearts he turned to hate his people,
to deal deceitfully with his servants.
37 He led Israel out of the alien land,
laden with silver and gold,
and none were left behind.
38 Egypt was glad when they departed,
so filled were they with dread.
39 He spread a cloud as covering,
and fire to give them light at night.

40 They asked for food;
he gave them quails and fed them
with bread from heaven.
41 He opened the rock, and water gushed out,
flowing like a river through the desert.
42 For he remembered his promise to Abraham,
his servant.
43 So he led forth his people with joy,
his chosen ones with singing.
44 He gave them the lands of the nations,
and let them take the fruit of others' toil,
45 that they might keep his statutes
and remain obedient to his laws.

106 (105)

Alleluia!
1 Give thanks to the Lord, for he is good,
for his love endures forever.
2 Who can count the Lord's mighty deeds,
or declare all his praises?
3 Blessed are they who always do just and right.
4 Remember me, O Lord,
when you show favor to your people;
rescue me when you deliver them;
5 let me see the triumph of your faithful,
let me share the joy of your nation,
and join your people in praising you.
6 We have sinned like our ancestors;
we have done wrong and acted wickedly.
7 When they were in Egypt,
our ancestors had no regard
for your wondrous deeds;
they forgot the abundance of your love;
they rebelled against the Most High
by the Sea of Reeds.
8 Yet he saved them for his name's sake,
to make his mighty power known.
9 He rebuked the sea, and it dried up;
he led them through the deep as on dry land.

10 He saved them from hostility,
freeing them from the hand of the enemy.
11 Waters covered their pursuers,
and none of them was left alive.
12 Then they believed his promises
and all at once sang his praises.
13 But soon they forgot his works
and did not wait for his counsel.
14 They gave way to wanton craving
and tempted God in the desert.
15 He gave them what they wanted,
then sent them a wasting disease.
16 In the camp they grew envious
of Moses and Aaron,
the holy one of the Lord.
17 So the earth opened, swallowed Dathan,
and buried the company of Abiram;
18 fire broke out against them,
burning up the wicked.
19 They made a calf at Horeb
and worshiped the molten image.
20 They exchanged the glory of God
for the image of a bull that eats grass.
21 They forgot their Savior God,
who had done great things in Egypt,
22 wonderful works in the land of Ham,
and awesome deeds by the Sea of Reeds.
23 So he spoke of destroying them,
but Moses, his chosen one,
stood in the breach before him
to shield them from destruction.
24 Yet they despised the promised land,
for they had no faith in his word.
25 They grumbled in their tents
and would not listen to the voice of the Lord.
26 So he swore to them with his hand raised
that he would let them perish in the desert,
27 scatter their descendants among the nations
and disperse them over the lands.
28 They joined the rites of Baal-peor
and ate sacrifices to lifeless gods.

29 Their deeds provoked the Lord to anger,
and a plague broke out among them.
30 But Phinehas stood up and intervened,
and the plague came to an end.
31 This was credited to his uprightness,
making him remembered for all ages.
32 Angered by them at Meribah's waters,
the Lord took it out on Moses
33 for the rash words he uttered,
when they rebelled against God.
34 They dared not destroy the pagans,
as the Lord commanded;
35 they mingled with these nations
and learned to do as they did.
36 In serving the idols of the pagans,
they were trapped
37 into sacrificing children to demons,
38 shedding the innocent blood
of their sons and daughters
to the idols of Canaan,
polluting the country with blood.
39 They defiled themselves by what they did,
playing the harlot in their worship.
40 The anger of the Lord grew intense
and he abhorred his inheritance.
41 He handed them over to the nations,
and their foes ruled them with arrogance.
42 Brought by the enemy into subjection,
they suffered the agony of oppression.
43 He delivered them many a time,
but they went on defying him
and sinking deeper into their sin.
44 But he heard their cry of affliction
and looked on them with compassion.
45 Remembering his covenant,
he relented for their sake,
because of his great love.
46 He let them be pitied by all those
who held them captive.
47 Save us, O Lord, our God,
gather us from among the nations,

that we may give thanks to you
and praise your holy name.

* * *

48 Blessed be the Lord, God of Israel,
from eternity to eternity.
Let all the people say:
"Amen!" Praise the Lord!

132 (131)

1 Remember David, O Lord,
and all his readiness.
11 The Lord swore to David
a promise, and he will remain true to it:
'I will keep your descendance
on your throne.
12 If your sons keep my covenant
and the decrees I have taught them,
their sons, too,
will sit forever upon your throne.'
13 For the Lord has chosen Zion;
he has desired it for his dwelling:
14 'This is my resting place forever;
this I prefer, here will I dwell.
15 I will bless its fruits,
its bread, and the poor will be satisfied.
16 I will clothe its priests with glory
and its faithful will sing in gladness.
17 From here a savior shall come forth,
a son of David;
here shall shine forever the lamp of my anointed.
18 In shame will I clothe his enemies,
but upon his head a crown shall shine.'

136 (135)

1 *Alleluia!*
Give thanks to the Lord, for he is good,
his kindness endures forever.
2 Give thanks to the God of gods,
his kindness endures forever.
3 Give thanks to the Lord of lords,
his kindness endures forever.
4 He alone does great marvels,
his kindness endures forever.
5 In wisdom he made the heavens,
his kindness endures forever.
6 He set the earth upon the waters,
his kindness endures forever.
7 He made the great lights,
his kindness endures forever,
8 the sun to rule over the day,
his kindness endures forever,
9 the moon and stars to rule the night,
his kindness endures forever.

148

1 *Alleluia!* Praise the Lord from the heavens;
praise him in the heavenly heights.
2 Praise him, all his angels; praise him,
all his heavenly hosts.
3 Praise him, sun and moon;
praise him, all you shining stars.
4 Praise him, you highest heavens
and you waters above the skies.
5 Let them praise the name of the Lord,
at whose command they were made.
6 He established them forever
and gave each a fixed and lasting duty.
7 Praise the Lord from the earth,
you sea creatures and all the depths,

8 clouds and snow, hail and lightning,
storm winds that do his bidding,
9 you mountains and all you hills,
you fruit trees and cedars,
10 you wild beasts and tame animals,
you creeping things and winged fowl.
11 Kings of the earth and nations,
princes and all rulers of the world,
12 young men and maidens, old and young together,
13 let them praise the name of the Lord.
For his name alone is exalted;
his majesty is above earth and heaven.
14 He has given his people glory;
he has given a praise to his faithful,
to Israel, the people close to him.
Alleluia.

SAPIENTIAL BOOKS

PROVERBS

Introduction

The doctrines or teachings of this anthology have two main axes, each with an extreme pole: one is the wise/foolish, the other is honorable/wicked. These two axes intertwine, because being wise has an ethical component, while wickedness is considered foolish.

God is present in this wise and ethical world: He possesses wisdom and grants good sense to human beings.

Proclamation of Wisdom

8 22 Yahweh created me first,
at the beginning of his works.
23 He formed me from of old,
from eternity, even before the earth.
24 The abyss did not exist when I was born,
the springs of the sea had not gushed forth,
25 the mountains were still not set in their place
nor the hills, when I was born
26 before he made the earth or countryside,
or the first grains of the world's dust.
27 I was there when he made the skies
and drew the earth's compass on the abyss,
28 when he formed the clouds above
and when the springs of the ocean emerged;
29 when he made the sea with its limits,
that it might not overflow.

When he laid the foundations of the earth,
30 I was close beside him,
the designer of his works,
and I was his daily delight,
forever playing in his presence,
31 playing throughout the world
and delighting to be with humans.
32 Now then, my sons, listen to me:
happy are those who follow my ways.

Job

Introduction

The book of Job is drama with little action and a lot of passion. It brings forward the passion that a great, unresigned writer has portrayed in the main character of the book. Uneasy with the traditional doctrine about retribution, he opposed a concrete fact to a principle.

Our author brings his case to the extreme: he makes the innocent protagonist suffer so that his cry would come "from the depth."

The action is very simple: Job's friends defend God's justice as an impartial judge that rewards the good ones and punishes the bad ones. Job is not interested in this kind of justice by God because his own experience tells him otherwise. To prove his innocence to God, Job risks his own life. God, as the final judge, gives the final answer to Job and his friends. While being challenged, God answers and questions Job to lead him towards the mystery of God.

Through the dialogues, of a good conventional man, that gives thanks to God because everything goes well for him, comes a deep man, capable of assuming and representing the sorrowful humanity that searches God with audacity.

The book of Job is an especially modern book; it is provocative, not apt for conformists. It is difficult to read it without being challenged and it is difficult to understand it unless one takes sides.

Prologue on earth

1 1 Job, a blameless and upright man who feared God and
shunned evil, once lived in the land of Uz. 2 He had seven sons
and three daughters. 3 Owner of seven thousand sheep, three
thousand camels, five hundred yoke of oxen, five hundred
donkeys and a large number of servants, he was considered
the greatest man among the people of the East.

4 His sons used to take turns holding banquets in their
homes and they would invite their three sisters to dine and
drink with them.

Prologue in heaven

6 One day the heavenly beings came to present themselves
before Yahweh, and Satan came with them. 7 Yahweh asked
Satan:

—Where have you been?

Satan answered:

—Going up and down the earth, roaming about.

8 Yahweh asked again:

—Have you noticed my servant Job? No one on earth is as
blameless and upright as he, a man who fears God and avoids
evil.

9 But Satan returned the question:

—Does Job fear God for nothing? 10 Have you not built a
protective wall around him and his family and all his possessions? You have blessed and prospered him, with his livestock
all over the land. 11 But stretch out your hand and strike where
his riches are, and I bet he will curse you to your face.

12 Yahweh said to Satan:

—Very well, all that he has is in your power. But do not lay
a finger upon the man himself.

So Satan left the presence of Yahweh.

Job's trials

13 One day, while his sons and daughters were feasting in
the house of their eldest brother, 14 a messenger came to Job
and said:

—Your oxen were plowing, and your donkeys were graz-
ing nearby 15 when the Sabaeans came and carried them off.
They killed the herdsmen. I alone escaped to tell you.

16 While he was still speaking, another messenger came:

—God's fire fell from the sky and burned all your sheep
and the shepherds as well. I alone have escaped to tell you.

17 He had hardly finished speaking when another messenger arrived:

—Three raiding teams of Chaldeans have killed your servants and carried off your camels. I alone have escaped to tell
you.

18 He was still speaking when another messenger came and
said to Job:

—Your sons and daughters were eating and drinking in the
house of their eldest brother 19 when suddenly a great wind
blew across the desert and struck the house. It collapsed on
the young people and they all died. I alone have escaped to
tell you.

20 In grief Job tore his clothes and shaved his head. Then he
fell to the ground and worshiped, 21 saying:

—Naked I came from my mother's womb,

naked shall I return.

Yahweh gave, Yahweh has taken away.

Blessed be his name!

22 In spite of this calamity, Job did not sin by blaspheming
God.

2 1 Once more the heavenly beings came to present themselves before Yahweh, and again Satan was with them.
2 Yahweh asked Satan:

—Where have you been?

Satan answered:

—Going up and down the earth, roaming about.

3 Yahweh asked again:

—Have you noticed my servant Job? No one on earth is as blameless and upright as he, a man who fears God and avoids evil. He still holds fast to his integrity even if you provoked me to ruin him without cause.

4 Satan replied:

—Skin for skin! For his own life, anyone will give everything he owns. 5 But lay your hand against his own flesh and bones and he will curse you to your face.

6 Yahweh said to Satan:

—Very well, he is in your power. But spare his life.

7 So Satan left the presence of Yahweh and afflicted Job with festering sores from the soles of his feet to the top of his head. 8 Job took a potsherd to scrape himself and sat among the ashes.

9 His wife said to him:

—Do you still hold on to your integrity? Curse God and die!

10 Job replied:

—You talk foolishly. If we receive good things from God, why can't we accept evil from him?

In spite of this calamity, Job did not utter a sinful word.

Job's friends

11 Three of Job's friends—Eliphaz the Temanite, Bildad the Shuhite, and Zophar the Naamathite—heard of the misfortune that came upon him. They set out from their own homes and journeyed together to offer their sympathy and consolation to Job. 12 Failing to recognize him from the distance, they wept aloud, tore their garments and poured dust upon their heads. 13 For seven days and seven nights, they sat on the ground beside him. They did not say a word to Job, for they saw how terribly he suffered.

3 [1] At length it was Job who spoke, cursing the day of his
birth. [2] This is what he said:

[3] —Cursed be the day I was born,
and the night which whispered:
A boy has been conceived.
[25] For what I fear has come upon me,
what I dread has befallen me.
[26] I find no rest, I find no ease;
only turmoil, nothing of peace!

4 [1] Eliphaz the Temanite spoke next:
[6] —Should you not rely on your piety,
and find assurance in your integrity?
[7] Have you seen a guiltless man perish,
or an upright man done away with?
[8] As I see it, those who plow evil
or those who sow trouble reap the same.
[17] Can a mortal be just in the eyes of God?
Can a man be pure before his Maker?

5 [8] If I were you, I would appeal to God
and lay before him my case,
[9] for wonders are past all reckoning,
his miracles beyond all counting.

10 He pours rain down on the earth
and sends water upon the fields.
11 He sets the lowly on high,
turns grief into joy.
17 Blessed is the one whom God corrects;
reject not, therefore, the lessons of the Almighty,
18 He cures the wounds he has inflicted;
he strikes but he also heals.
19 From six troubles he will rescue you;
at the seventh no harm will touch you.
20 In famine he saves you from death;
in war, from the threat of the sword.
21 You will be protected from the lash of the tongue,
and have no dread of marauding bands.
27 This we have examined and found true.
This we have heard, and you should know.

7 1 Job replied:
—Man's life on earth is a thankless job,
his days are those of a mercenary.
2 Like a slave he longs for the shade of evening,
like a hireling waiting for his wages.
3 Thus I am allotted months of boredom
and nights of grief and misery.
4 In bed I say, "When shall the day break?"
On rising, I think, "When shall evening come?"
and I toss restless till dawn.
5 My body is full of worms and scabs;
my skin festers with its boils and cracks.
6 My days pass swifter than a weaver's shuttle,
heading without hope to their end.
7 My life is like wind, you well know it,
O God; never will I see happiness again.

10 1 Since I loathe my life,
I shall pour forth my complaint;
I shall speak of my soul's torment.
2 I shall say to God: Do not condemn me,
but tell me what is your quarrel with me?

29 [1]Job continued his discourse:
[2]—Oh, that I were in months gone by,
in the days when God watched over me,
[3]when his light shone upon my head
and I walked with it through darkness.
[4]Oh, that I were in my prime,
when God's friendship blessed my home,
[5]when the Almighty was still with me
and my children were around me!

32 [1]The three men made no further reply to Job, because
in their opinion, he was guiltless. [2]But Elihu, son of Barachel
the Buzite, of the family of Ram, became angry with Job for
justifying himself before God. [3]He was also angry with the
three friends for their failure to refute Job, because they had
allowed God to be condemned.

38 [1]Then Yahweh answered Job out of the storm:
[2]—Who is this that obscures divine plans
with ignorant words?
[3]Gird up your loins like a man;
I will question you and you must answer.
[4]Where were you when I founded the earth?
Answer, and show me your knowledge.
[5]Do you know who determined its size,
who stretched out its measuring line?
[6]On what were its bases set?
Who laid its cornerstone,
[7]while the morning stars sang together
and the heavenly beings shouted for joy?
[8]Who shut the sea behind closed doors
when it burst forth from the womb,
[9]when I made the clouds its garment
and thick darkness its swaddling clothes;
[10]when I set its limits
with doors and bars in place,
[11]when I said, "You will not go beyond these bounds;
here is where your proud waves must halt?"
[12]Have you ever commanded the morning,

or shown the dawn its place,
13 that it might grasp the earth by its edges
and shake the wicked out of it,
14 when it takes a clay color
and changes its tint like a garment;
15 when the wicked are denied their own light,
and their proud arm is shattered?
16 Have you journeyed to where the sea begins
or walked in its deepest recesses?
17 Have the gates of death been shown to you?
Have you seen the gates of Shadow?
18 Have you an idea of the breadth of the earth?
Tell me, if you know all this.
19 Where is the way to the home of light,
and where does darkness dwell?
20 Can you take them to their own regions,
and set them on their homeward paths?
21 You know, for you were born before them,
and great is the number of your years!
22 Have you entered the storehouse of the snow
or seen the storehouse of the hail,
23 which I reserve for times of woe,
for days of war and battle?
24 What is the way to the place
where lightning is dispersed,
or the place whence the east wind
begins spreading over the earth?
25 Who has cut a channel for the torrents of rain,
and a path for the thunderstorm,
26 to bring rain to no-man's-land
and to the unpeopled wilderness,
27 to enrich the wasted and desolate ground,
to make the desert bloom with green?
28 Does the rain have a father?
Who fathers the drops of dew?
29 From whose womb comes the ice,
and who gives birth to the frost from the skies,
30 when the waters lie as hard as stone,
when the surface of the deep is frozen?
31 Can you bind the chains of the Pleiades,
or loosen the bonds of Orion?

32 Can you guide the morning star in its season,
or lead the Bear with its train?
33 Do you know the laws of the heavens,
and can you establish their rule on earth?
34 Can you raise your voice to the clouds
and order their waters to pour down?
35 Will lightnings flash at your command
and report to you, "Here we are?"
36 Who has given the ibis foresight
or endowed the cock with foreknowledge?
37 Who has the wisdom to count the clouds?
Who tilts the water jars of heaven
38 so that the dust cakes into a mass
and clods of earth stick together?
39 Can you hunt the woods to appease
the hunger of the lioness and her whelps,
40 as they crouch in their dens
or lie in wait in the thicket?
41 Who provides prey for the raven
when its young cry out to God
and roam about desperate for food?

40 1 Yahweh said to Job:
2 —Must a faultfinder contend with the Almighty?
Let him who would correct God answer.
3 Job said:
4 —How can I reply, unworthy as I am!
All I can do is put my hand over my mouth.
5 I have spoken once, now I will not answer;
Oh, yes, twice, but I will do no further.

42 1 This was the answer Job gave to Yahweh:
2 —I know that you are all powerful;
no plan of yours can be thwarted.
3b I spoke of things I did not understand,
too wonderful for me to know.
5 My ears had heard of you,
but now my eyes have seen you.
6 Therefore I retract all I have said,
and in dust and ashes I repent.

12 Yahweh blessed Job's latter days much more than his earlier ones. He came to own fourteen thousand sheep, six thousand camels, a thousand yoke of oxen, and a thousand she-donkeys. 13 He was also blessed with seven sons and three daughters. 14 The first daughter he named Dove, the second Cinnamon, and the third Bottle of Perfume. 15 Nowhere in the land was there found any woman who could compare in beauty with Job's daughters. Their father granted them an inheritance along with their brothers.

16 Job lived a hundred and forty years; he saw his children and their children to the fourth generation. 17 He died old and full of years.

Sirach

Introduction

The prologue written by the Greek translator gives information about the author and epoch.

The 'Wisdom of Ben Sirach' was a book that was read so often in the early Church that it got the name and designation of "Ecclesiasticus".

The Jews in general, and a portion of the early Church, did not consider this book as canonical, even though it was read in the church.

Some Jewish authors make reference to it in the Middle Ages.

As the book itself tells us, the author spent his time in studying, teaching and explaining what traditionally was understood as wisdom or good sense or prudence or knowledge. It fosters observation, experience and reflection as a source of knowledge; still the author underlines the value of tradition, the need of prayer.

43 1 The pride of the heights above is the clear firmament.
How glorious is the spectacle of the heavens!
2 When the sun rises and appears, it proclaims:
—I am your marvelous work, Most High!
3 At noon, it dries up the land;
who can bear its burning heat?
4 You may stoke a furnace to produce heat,
but three times greater
is the heat of the sun burning the mountains,

and sending out fiery vapors,
blinding the eyes with its rays.
5 How great is the Lord who made it
and whose word directs its rapid course!
6 He also made the moon,
exact in marking the months
and the passage of time.
7 With its full light gradually decreasing,
the moon determines and rules over the feast days.
8 The month also takes its name from the moon.
How marvelously does it increase in its phases,
providing a signal for the heavenly hosts,
brightly shining in the expanse of the sky!
9 The bright radiance of the stars
accounts for the beauty of the sky.
What a brilliant ornament they are
for the heights of the Lord!
10 At the command of the All Holy
they stand as appointed
and never fail to keep watch.
11 Look at the rainbow and praise
the One who made it.
How magnificent it is in splendor!
12 It forms a circle of glory in the sky,
a bow that is bent by the hands of its Maker.
13 At his order the snow falls
and lightning strikes according to his decrees.
14 The storerooms of heaven are opened
and clouds fly away like birds.
15 It is his power that thickens the clouds,
making them freeze and break into hailstones.
16a He has only to look and the mountains are shaken;
17a the voice of his thunder terrifies the earth.
16b At his will the south wind blows,
17b as do cyclones and hurricanes from the north.
18 The snow flutters down like birds
and alights on the ground like locusts.
The eye marvels at the beauty of its whiteness
and the mind is amazed to see it fall.
19 He sprinkles frost on the earth like salt;
it freezes and becomes like thorny spikes.

20 The cold north wind blows
and turns the water into ice.
Ice forms on all stagnant water
giving it a freezing coat of armor.
21 He wears down the mountains
and scorches the desert,
withering the green grass as if by fire.
22 A mist is a timely remedy,
and dew after the heat restores it all to life.
23 According to his plan he stilled
the great deep and planted islands in it.
24 Those who cross the seas tell of its dangers,
and we listen in astonishment to what they relate:
25 It is all about strange and marvelous adventures
with marine animals and monsters of all kinds.
26 Thanks be to God, all turns out well
and everything is held together by his word.
27 We shall not give further examples;
one last word: He is everything.
28 Where shall we find the strength to glorify him?
For he is the Mighty One, greater than all his works.

OTHER BOOKS

JONAH

Introduction

The book of Jonah is so brief, so well known and so misunderstood; and it has given rise to many false interpretations. Some, naively, read it as history, and of course they find it unbelievable and even ridiculous.

Others include it among the Prophets as if dealing with a personage that really existed.

The book of Jonah is a novel about adventures, completely fictitious, with a religious, moralizing intention: its thesis is to show God's goodness, who is worried about each person's life. It is a God that threatens and announces his punishments with the aim of not having to punish anybody. Jonah is his speaker, a person who is not worthy of that mission, neither, in his mediocrity, capable of understanding the forgiving heart of God.

1 1 The word of Yahweh came to Jonah, son of Amittai:

2 —Go to Nineveh, the great city, and preach against it, because I have known its wickedness.

3 But Jonah decided to flee from Yahweh and go to Tarshish. He went down to Joppa, found a ship bound for Tarshish, and paid the fare. Then he boarded it and went into the hold of the ship, journeying with them to Tarshish, far away from Yahweh.

4 Yahweh stirred up a storm wind on the sea, so there was a sea tempest, which threatened to destroy the ship.

5 The sailors took fright, and each cried out to his own god. To lighten the ship, they threw its cargo into the sea.

6 Meanwhile Jonah had gone into the hold of the ship, where he lay fast asleep. The captain came upon him and said:

—How can you sleep? Get up and call on your god. Perhaps he will be mindful of us and will not allow us to die here.

7 The sailors said to each other:

—Let us cast lots to find out who is responsible for this disaster.

So they did, and the lot fell on Jonah.

8 They questioned him:

—So you are responsible for this evil that has come upon us? Tell us where you are from. What is your country, your nationality?

9 And Jonah told them his story:

—I am a Hebrew and I worship Yahweh, God of heaven who made the sea and the land.

10 As they knew that he was fleeing from Yahweh, the sailors were seized with great fear and said to him:

—What a terrible thing have you done!

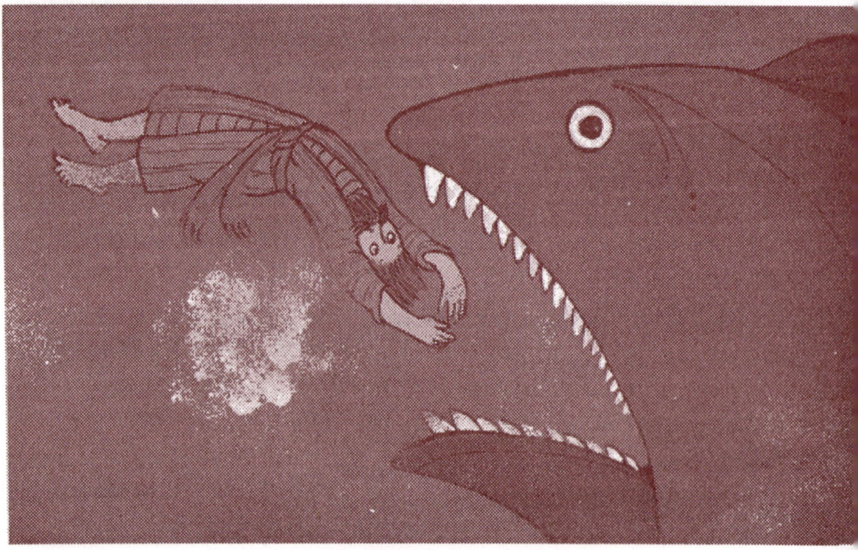

11 —What shall we do with you now to make the sea calm down?

The sea was growing more and more agitated.

12 He said to them:

—Pick me up and throw me into the sea. It will quiet down, for I know it is because of me that this storm has come.

13 The sailors, however, still did their best to row back to land. But they could not, for the sea had grown much rougher
than before. 14 Then they called on Yahweh:

—O Yahweh, do not let us perish for taking this man's life. Do not hold us guilty of shedding innocent blood. For you, Yahweh, have done this as you have thought right.

15 They took Jonah and threw him overboard, and the raging sea grew calm again. 16 At this the men were seized with
great fear of Yahweh. They offered a sacrifice to Yahweh and made vows to him.

2 1 Yahweh provided a large fish which swallowed Jonah. He remained in the belly of the fish for three days and three nights.

2 From the belly of the fish Jonah prayed to Yahweh, his God:

[3]—In my distress I cried to Yahweh,
and he answered me;
from the belly of the netherworld
you heard my voice when I called.
[4] You cast me into the abyss,
into the very heart of the sea,
and the currents swirled about me;
all your breakers and your billows
passed over engulfing me.
[5] Then I thought:
I have been cast out from your presence,
but I keep on looking to your holy Temple.
[6] The waters engulfed me up to my throat;
all around me was the abyss;
wrapped about my head were seaweeds.
[7] I went down to the roots of the mountains,
the bars of the netherworld closed upon me,
but you brought my life up from the pit,
Yahweh, my God.
[8] When my soul was fainting within me,
I remembered Yahweh,
and before you rose my prayer
up to your holy Temple.
[9] Those who worship worthless idols
lose your grace
[10] but I, with songs of praise,
will offer to you sacrifices.
What I have vowed, I will make good—
deliverance comes from Yahweh, my God.

[11] Then Yahweh gave his command to the fish, and it belched out Jonah onto dry land.

3 [1] The word of Yahweh came to Jonah a second time:

[2]—Go to Nineveh, the great city, and announce to them the message I give you.

[3] In obedience to the word of Yahweh, Jonah went to
Nineveh. It was a very large city, and it took three days just to
cross it. [4] So Jonah walked a single day's journey and began
proclaiming:

—Forty days more and Nineveh will be destroyed.

5 The people of the city believed God. They declared a fast,
and all of them, from the greatest to the least, put on sackcloth.

6 Upon hearing the news, the king of Nineveh got up from
his throne, took off his royal robe, put on sackcloth and sat
down in ashes. 7 He issued a proclamation throughout
Nineveh:

—By the decree of the king and his nobles, no people or
beasts, herd or flock, will taste anything; neither will they eat
nor drink. 8 But let people and beasts be covered with sackcloth. Let everyone call aloud to God, turn from his evil ways
and violence. 9 Who knows? God may yet relent, turn from his
fierce anger and spare us.

10 When God saw what they did and how they turned from
their evil ways, he had compassion and did not carry out the
destruction he had threatened upon them.

4 1 But Jonah was greatly displeased at this, and he was
indignant. 2 He prayed to Yahweh and said:

—O Yahweh, is this not what I said when I was yet in my
own country? This is why I fled to Tarshish. I knew that you
are a gracious and merciful God, slow to anger and full of
love, and you relent from imposing terrible punishment. 3 I
beseech you now, Yahweh, to take my life, for now it is better
for me to die than to live.

4 But Yahweh replied:

—What right have you to be angry?

5 Jonah then left the city. He went to a place east of it, built
himself a shelter and sat under its shade to wait and see what
would happen to Nineveh. 6 Then Yahweh God provided a
castor—oil plant and made it grow up over Jonah to give
shade over his head and to ease his discomfort. Jonah was
very happy about the plant.

7 But the next day, at dawn, God sent a worm which
attacked the plant and made it wither. 8 When the sun rose,
God sent a scorching east wind; the sun blazed down upon Jonah's head, and he grew faint. His death wish returned and he
said:

—It is better for me to die than to live.

9 Then God asked Jonah:

—Do you have a right to be angry about the castor oil plant?

Jonah answered:

—I am right to be angry enough to wish to die.

10 Yahweh said:

—You are concerned about a plant which cost you no labor to make it grow. Overnight it sprang up, and overnight it per-
ished. 11 But Nineveh has more than a hundred and twenty thousand people who cannot distinguish right from left and they have many cattle as well. Should I not be concerned for such a great city?

SUMMARY OF ISRAEL'S HISTORY

Dates		*Narrated in*
1800	Period of the Patriarchs	Book of Genesis
1250	Exit from Egypt. Moses	Exodus
1200	Conquest of Canaan Joshua	Joshua
1200-1030	Period of the Judges	Judges
1030-931	Saul – David – Solomon	Samuel and 1 Kings
931	Division of the Monarchy: Israel (North) and Judah (South)	1 Kings
722	Assyrians invade the Northern kingdom	2 Kings
587	Babylonians invade the Southern kingdom Babylonian exile	2 Kings
538	Return from exile. The kingdom is under Persians First and later under Syrians	Nehemiah and Ezra
167	Persecution against Jews for their religious practices. Maccabean revolt.	Maccabees
63	Pompey conquers Judeah and it becomes a Roman Province.	
37	Herod the Great, king under Roman rule.	
+/- 7	Jesus' birth	Gospels
+/- 30	Jesus' death	Gospels

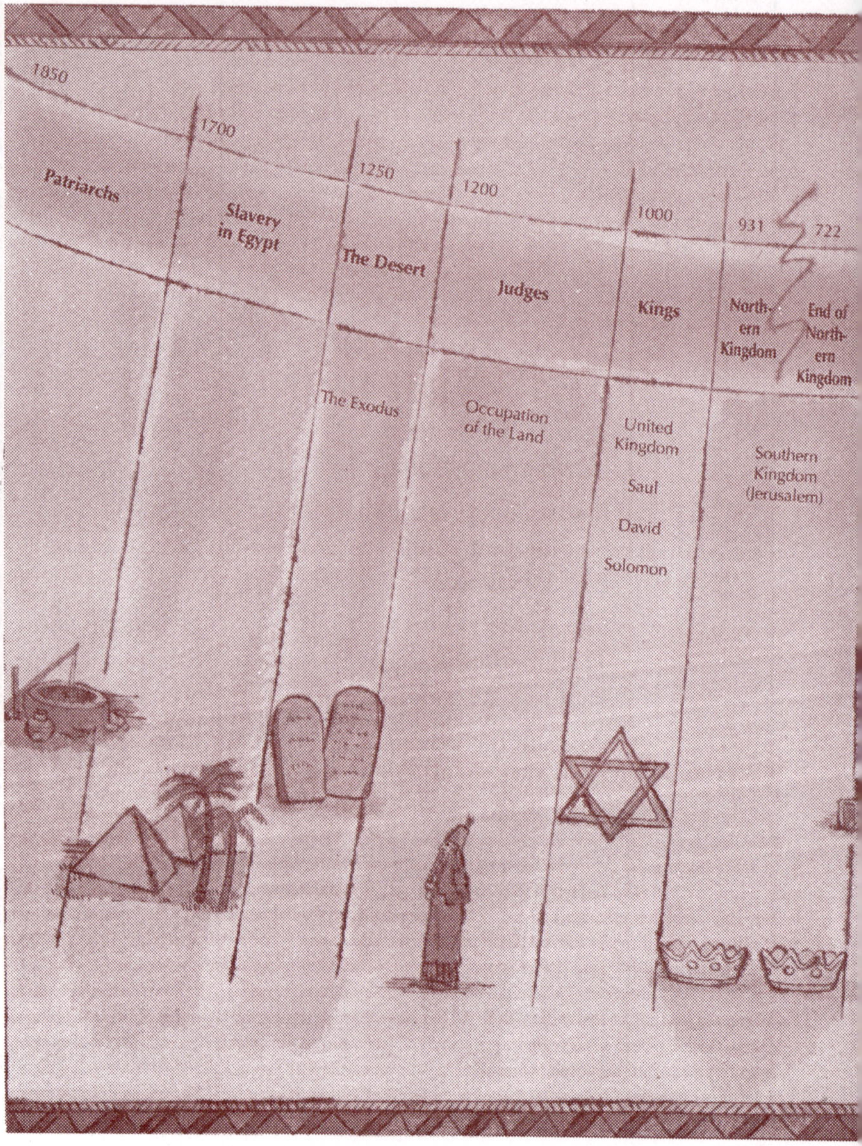
1850
1700
1250
1200
1000
931
722
Patriarchs
Slavery in Egypt
The Desert
Judges
Kings
North-ern Kingdom
End of North-ern Kingdom
The Exodus
Occupation of the Land
United Kingdom
Saul
David
Solomon
Southern Kingdom (Jerusalem)

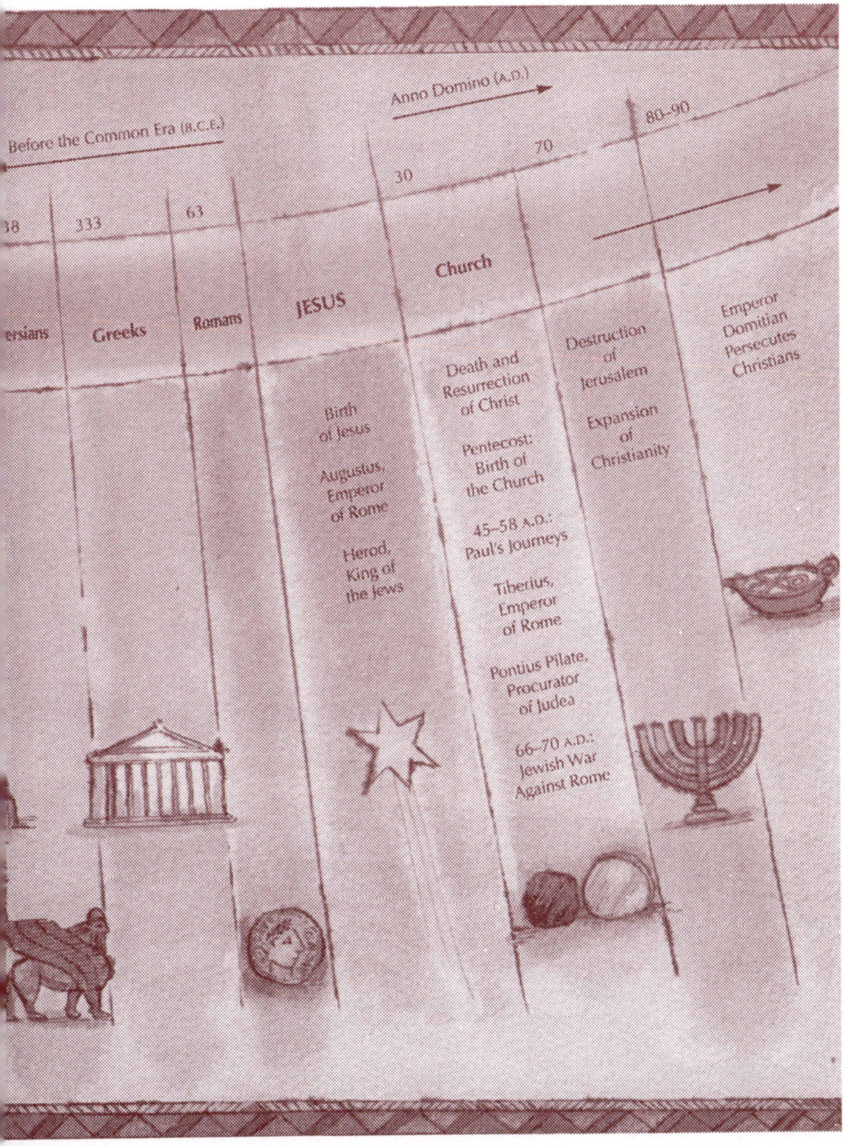

Anno Domino (A.D.)
Before the Common Era (B.C.E.)
38
333
63
30
70
80–90
ersians
Greeks
Romans
JESUS
Church
Birth of Jesus
Augustus, Emperor of Rome
Herod, King of the Jews
Death and Resurrection of Christ
Pentecost: Birth of the Church
45–58 A.D.: Paul's Journeys
Tiberius, Emperor of Rome
Pontius Pilate, Procurator of Judea
66–70 A.D.: Jewish War Against Rome
Destruction of Jerusalem
Expansion of Christianity
Emperor Domitian Persecutes Christians

NEW TESTAMENT

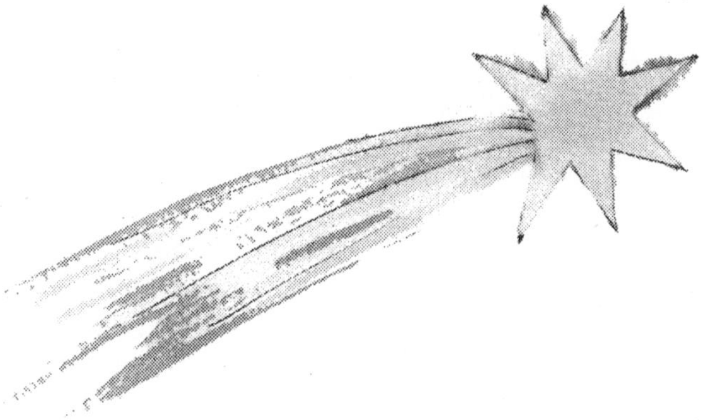

GOSPELS

Introduction

"Gospel" could mean many things: the Good News that Jesus announced; the preaching of the Good News; and the writings that gather that Good News.

In the Gospels we find a lot of history, the deeds and sayings of Jesus, and a lot of geography, the places where these things happened. But the intention of an evangelist is not to narrate facts and sayings as a reporter: they want to transmit their faith, their Faith in Jesus the Son of God. That is why their narrations are colored by their faith in Jesus; Jesus is alive from the faith in The Risen One.

These books were written with materials gathered from previous writings. The deeds and sayings of Jesus had witnesses, especially his closer and more constant disciples. When Jesus left this world, the communities of believers repeated in the Eucharist these deeds and sayings of Jesus. And when people wanted to be part of the community of believers they were taught the deeds and words of Jesus.

These writings were oral traditions first. There was no need to put them into writing because the witnesses were still alive and would not allow deviations. Little by little, with the passage of time and the disappearance of witnesses, the need to put it in writing arrived. At the beginning there were only fragments: stories of the Passion, collections of miracles, collections of sayings, of parables... These collections were used in the Eucharist and in catechesis.

Starting around the years 60 or 70, there were people who gathered these catechesis and made out of them a continuous writing about the activity of Jesus. These are our Gospels. These were not the only ones written. In the latest part of the First Century many "gospels" were written, but the Christian communities paid more attention to some of them over others to the point that some were rejected as not worthy of faith. Finally the four that we know today were accepted as "canonical", that is, completely trustworthy and these are: Matthew, Mark, Luke and John.

The first three ones are called "Synoptic" because they complement each other to the point that we could almost construct a detailed life of Jesus. The fourth gospel, called the gospel of John, is quite different in its presentation and style.

It seems that the first to be written was the one of Mark, and that Matthew and Luke knew it and copied it almost entirely adding materials from other sources that Mark did not know.

The Gospel According to Matthew

Introduction

As time went by, the followers of Jesus as Messiah are just one more group; they were looked upon with suspicion or tolerance. It seems that it is in this context that the gospel of Matthew finds its roots: perfectly familiar with the Jewish customs and traditions.

It presents continuity and newness. Continuity, because in Jesus, the awaited Messiah, the promises of the Scriptures are fulfilled. But it takes distance from Jewish customs and interpretations.

Matthew's community feels in continuity with Israel: they are the authentic Israel that has already entered into the final stage. Jesus has proclaimed the imminence of the "reign of God" and through his death and resurrection has performed the final act. The community gathers now in fidelity to Jesus, the Messiah and Teacher, new Moses and son of David.

Old traditions have attributed this gospel to Matthew. The infancy narratives resemble an overture announcing what will follow: identification-persecution-liberation-acknowledgement from Jews and pagans.

Announcement to Joseph

1 18 This is how Jesus Christ was born. Mary his mother
had been given to Joseph in marriage but before they lived
together, she was found to be pregnant through the Holy
Spirit. 19 Then Joseph, her husband, made plans to divorce her

in all secrecy. He was an upright man, and in no way did he want to discredit her. [20] While he was pondering over this, an angel of the Lord appeared to him in a dream and said:

—Joseph, descendant of David, do not be afraid to take Mary as your wife. She has conceived by the Holy Spirit, [21] and now she will bear a son. You shall call him 'Jesus' for he will save his people from their sins.

[22] All this happened in order to fulfill what the Lord had said through the prophet: [23] *The virgin will conceive and bear a son, and he will be called Emmanuel* which means: God-with-us. [24] When Joseph woke up, he did what the angel of the Lord had told him to do and he took his wife to his home. [25] So she gave birth to a son and he had not had marital relations with her. Joseph gave him the name of Jesus.

Homage from the Magi

2 [1] When Jesus was born in Bethlehem, in Judea, during the days of King Herod, wise men from the east arrived in Jerusalem. [2] They asked:

—Where is the newborn king of the Jews? We saw the rising of his star in the east and have come to honor him.

[3] When Herod heard this he was greatly disturbed and with him all Jerusalem. [4] He immediately called a meeting of all high-ranking priests and the scribes, and asked them where the Messiah was to be born.

[5] They told him:

—In the town of Bethlehem in Judea; for this is what the prophet wrote: [6] *And you, Bethlehem, in the land of Judah, you are by no means the least among the clans of Judah, for from you will come a leader, the one who is to shepherd my people Israel.*

[7] Then Herod secretly called the wise men and asked them the precise time the star appeared. [8] Then he sent them to Bethlehem with the instruction:

—Go and get precise information about the child. As soon as you have found him, report to me, so that I too may go and honor him.

[9] After the meeting with the king, they set out. The star that

they had seen in the East went ahead of them and stopped over the place where the child was. [10] The wise men were overjoyed on seeing the star again. [11] They went into the house and when they saw the child with Mary his mother, they knelt and worshiped him. They opened their bags and offered him their gifts of gold, incense and myrrh. [12] In a dream they were warned not to go back to Herod, so they returned to their home country by another way.

John the Baptist

3 [1] In the course of time John the Baptist appeared in the desert of Judea and began to proclaim his message:

[2] —Change your ways, the Kingdom of heaven is now at hand!

[3] It was about him that the prophet Isaiah had spoken when he said, *A voice is shouting in the desert: prepare a way for the Lord; make his paths straight.*

Baptism of Jesus

[13] At that time Jesus arrived from Galilee and came to John at the Jordan to be baptized by him. [14] But John tried to prevent him, and said:

—How is it you come to me: I should be baptized by you!

[15] But Jesus answered him:

—Let it be like that for now that we may fulfill the right order.

John agreed.

[16] As soon as he was baptized, Jesus came up from the
water. At once, the heavens opened and he saw the Spirit of
God come down like a dove and rest upon him. [17] At the same
time a voice from heaven was heard: "This is my Son, the
Beloved; he is my Chosen One."

Jesus being tested

4 [1] Then the Spirit led Jesus into the desert that he be put
to the test by the devil. [2] After spending forty days and nights
without food, Jesus was hungry. [3] Then the devil came to him
and said:

—If you are the Son of God, order these stones to turn into bread.

[4] But Jesus answered:

—Scripture says: *one does not live on bread alone, but on every word that comes from the mouth of God.*

[5] Then the devil took Jesus to the holy city, set him on the highest wall of the temple, and said to him:

[6] —If you are the Son of God, throw yourself down, for scripture says, *God has given orders to his angels about you. Their hands will hold you up lest you hurt your foot against a stone.*

[7] Jesus answered:

—But scripture also says: *You shall not put to the test the Lord your God.*

[8] Then the devil took Jesus to a very high mountain and showed him all the nations of the world in all their greatness and splendor. And he said:

[9] —All this I will give you, if you kneel and worship me.
[10] Then Jesus answered:

—Be off, Satan! Scripture says: *worship the Lord your God and serve him alone.*

[11] Then the devil left him, and angels came to serve him.

In Galilee

12 When Jesus heard that John had been arrested, he withdrew into Galilee. 13 He left Nazareth and went to settle down
in Capernaum, a town by the lake of Galilee, at the border of
Zebulun and Naphtali. 17 From that time on Jesus began to
proclaim his message:

—Change your ways: the kingdom of heaven is near.

Calling of the first disciples

18 As Jesus walked by the lake of Galilee, he saw two brothers, Simon called Peter, and Andrew his brother, casting a net
into the lake, for they were fishermen. 19 He said to them:

—Come, follow me, and I will make you fish for people.

20 At once they left their nets and followed him. 21 He went
on from there and saw two other brothers, James, the son of
Zebedee, and his brother John in a boat with their father
Zebedee, mending their nets. Jesus called them. 22 At once they
left the boat and their father and followed him.

23 Jesus went around all Galilee, teaching in their synagogues, proclaiming the good news of the Kingdom, and cur-
ing all kinds of sickness and disease among the people.

Sermon on the mount: the Beatitudes

5 1 When Jesus saw the crowds, he went up the mountain.
He sat down and his disciples gathered around him. 2 Then he
spoke and began to teach them:

3 —Fortunate are those who are poor in spirit, for theirs is
the kingdom of heaven.

4 Fortunate are those who mourn, they shall be comforted.
5 Fortunate are the gentle, they shall possess the land.
6 Fortunate are those who hunger and thirst for justice,
for they shall be satisfied.
7 Fortunate are the merciful, for they shall find mercy.
8 Fortunate are those with a pure heart,
for they shall see God.

9 Fortunate are those who work for peace,
they shall be called children of God.
10 Fortunate are those who are persecuted
for the cause of justice,
for theirs is the kingdom of heaven.

11 —Fortunate are you, when people insult you and persecute you and speak all kinds of evil against you because you
are my followers. 12 Be glad and joyful, for a great reward is
kept for you in God. This is how this people persecuted the
prophets who lived before you.

38 —You have heard that it was said: *An eye for an eye and
a tooth for a tooth.* 39 But I tell you this: do not oppose evil
with evil; if someone slaps you on your right cheek, turn
and offer the other. 40 If someone sues you in court for your
shirt, give your coat as well. 41 If someone forces you to go
one mile, go also the second mile. 42 Give when asked and
do not turn your back on anyone who wants to borrow from
you.

43 —You have heard that it was said: *Love your neighbor and
do not do good to your enemy.* 44 But this I tell you: Love your
enemies, and pray for those who persecute you, 45 so that you
may be children of your Father in Heaven. For he makes his
sun rise on both the wicked and the good, and he gives rain to
both the just and the unjust.

46 If you love those who love you, what is special about

that? Do not even tax collectors do as much? 47 And if you are friendly only to your friends, what is so exceptional about that? Do not even the pagans do as much? 48 For your part you shall be righteous and perfect in the way your heavenly Father is righteous and perfect.

Prayer

6 5 —When you pray, do not be like those who want to be seen. They love to stand and pray in the synagogues or on street corners to be seen by everyone. I assure you, they have already been paid in full. 6 When you pray, go into your room, close the door and pray to your Father who is with you in secret; and your Father who sees what is kept secret will reward you.

7 When you pray, do not use a lot of words, as the pagans do, for they hold that the more they say, the more chance they

have of being heard. 8 Do not be like them. Your Father knows
what you need, even before you ask him.

9 This, then, is how you should pray:

Our Father in heaven,
holy be your name,
10 your kingdom come
and your will be done,
on earth as in heaven.
11 Give us today our daily bread.
12 Forgive us our debts
just as we have forgiven those who are in debt to us.
13 Do not bring us to the test
but deliver us from the evil one.'

14 —If you forgive others their wrongs, your Father in heav-
en will also forgive yours. 15 If you do not forgive others, then
your Father will not forgive you either.

Several warnings

7 1 —Do not judge and you will not be judged. 2 In the
same way you judge others, you will be judged, and the meas-
ure you use for others will be used for you. 3 Why do you look
at the speck in your brother's eye and not see the plank in
your own eye? 4 How can you say to your brother: 'Come, let
me take the speck from your eye,' as long as that plank is in
your own? 5 Hypocrite, take first the plank out of your own
eye, then you will see clear enough to take the speck out of
your brother's eye.

6 —Do not give what is holy to the dogs, or throw your
pearls to the pigs: they might trample on them and even turn
on you and tear you to pieces.

7 —Ask and you will receive; seek and you will find;
knock and the door will be opened. 8 For everyone who asks,
receives; whoever seeks, finds; and the door will be opened
to him who knocks. 9 Would any of you give a stone to your
son when he asks for bread? 10 Or give him a snake, when he
asks for a fish? 11 As bad as you are, you know how to give
good things to your children. How much more, then, will

your Father in heaven give good things to those who ask him!

12 —So, do to others whatever you would that others do to you: there you have the Law and the Prophets.

Healings

8 2 A leper came forward. He knelt before him and said:

—Sir, if you want to, you can make me clean.

3 Jesus stretched out his hand, touched him, and said:

—I want to, be clean again.

At that very moment the man was cleansed from his leprosy.
4 Then Jesus said to him:

—See that you do not tell anyone, but go to the priest, have yourself declared clean, and offer the gift that Moses ordered as proof of it.

5 When Jesus entered Capernaum, an army captain approached him to ask his help:

6 —Sir, my servant lies sick at home. He is paralyzed and suffers terribly.

7 Jesus said to him:

—I will come and heal him.

8 The captain answered:

—I am not worthy to have you under my roof. Just give an order and my boy will be healed.
9 For I myself, a junior officer, give orders to my soldiers. And if I say to one: 'Go,' he goes, and if I say to another: 'Come,' he comes, and to my servant: 'Do this,' he does it.

10 When Jesus heard this he was astonished and said to those who were following him:

—I tell you, I have not found such faith in Israel.
11 I say to you, many will come from east and west and sit down with Abraham, Isaac and Jacob at the feast in the kingdom of heaven;
12 but the heirs of the kingdom will be thrown out into the darkness; there they will wail and grind their teeth.

13 Then Jesus said to the captain:

—Go home now. As you believed, so let it be.

And at that moment his servant was healed.

Discipleship

19 A teacher of the Law approached him and said:

—Master, I will follow you wherever you go.

20 Jesus said to him:

—Foxes have holes and birds have nests, but the Son of Man has nowhere to lay his head.

21 Another disciple said to him:

—Lord, let me go and bury my father first.

22 But Jesus answered him:

—Follow me, and let the dead bury their own dead.

Calming the tempest

23 Jesus got into the boat and his disciples followed him.
24 Without warning a fierce storm hit the lake, with waves
sweeping the boat. But Jesus was asleep.

25 They woke him and cried:

—Lord save us! We are lost!

26 But Jesus answered:

—Why are you so afraid, you of little faith?

Then he stood up and ordered the wind and sea; and it
became completely calm. 27 The people were astonished. They
said:

—What kind of man is he? Even the winds and the sea obey him.

Calling of Matthew

9 9 As Jesus moved on from there, he saw a man named Matthew at his seat in the custom-house, and he said to him:

—Follow me.

And Matthew got up and followed him. 10 Now it happened, while Jesus was at table in Matthew's house, many tax collectors and other sinners joined Jesus and his disciples. 11 When the Pharisees saw this they said to his disciples:

—Why is it that your master eats with those sinners and tax collectors?

12 When Jesus heard this he said:

—Healthy people do not need a doctor, but sick people do. 13 Go and find out what this means: *What I want is mercy, not sacrifice.* I did not come to call the righteous but sinners.

Two healings

18 While Jesus was speaking to them, an official of the synagogue came up to him, bowed before him and said:

—My daughter has just died, but come and place your hands on her, and she will live.

19 Jesus stood up and followed him with his disciples.

20 Then a woman who had suffered from a severe bleeding for twelve years came up from behind and touched the edge of his cloak. 21 For she thought:

—If I only touch his cloak, I will be healed.

22 Jesus turned, saw her and said:

—Courage, my daughter, your faith has saved you.

And from that moment the woman was cured.

23 When Jesus arrived at the official's house and saw the flute players and the excited crowd, he said:

24 —Get out of here! The girl is not dead. She is only sleeping!

And they laughed at him. 25 But once the crowd had been turned out, Jesus went in and took the girl by the hand, and she stood up. 26 The news of this spread through the whole area.

The Father and the Son

11 [25] On that occasion Jesus said:

—Father, Lord of heaven and earth, I praise you, because you have hidden these things from the wise and learned and revealed them to simple people. [26] Yes, Father, this is what pleased you.

[27] —Everything has been entrusted to me by my Father. No one knows the Son except the Father, and no one knows the Father except the Son and those to whom the Son chooses to reveal him.

[28] —Come to me, all you who work hard and who carry heavy burdens and I will refresh you. [29] Take my yoke upon you and learn from me for I am gentle and humble of heart; and you will find rest. [30] For my yoke is good and my burden is light.

12 [15] As Jesus was aware of the plot, he went away from that place. Many people followed him and he cured all who were sick. [16] Then he gave them strict orders not to make him known. [17] In this way Isaiah's prophecy was fulfilled:

[18] *Here is my servant whom I have chosen, the one I love, and with whom I am pleased. I will put my Spirit upon him and he will announce my judgment to the nations.*

[19] *He will not argue or shout, nor will his voice be heard in the streets.* [20] *The bruised reed he will not crush, nor snuff out the smoldering wick. He will persist until justice is made victorious.*

The mother and brothers of Jesus

[46] While Jesus was still talking to the people, his mother and his brothers wanted to speak to him and they waited outside. [47] So someone said to him:

—Your mother and your brothers are just outside; they want to speak with you.

[48] Jesus answered:

—Who is my mother? Who are my brothers?

49 Then he pointed to his disciples and said:

—Look! Here are my mother and my brothers. 50 Whoever
does the will of my Father in heaven is for me brother, sister,
or mother.

Parables

13 1 That same day Jesus left the house and sat down by
the lakeside. 2 As many people gathered around him, he got in
a boat. There he sat while the whole crowd stood on the shore,
3 and he spoke to them in parables about many things.

4 Jesus said:

—The sower went out to sow and, as he sowed, some seeds
fell along the path and the birds came and ate them up. 5 Other
seeds fell on rocky ground where there was little soil, and the
seeds sprouted quickly because the soil was not deep. 6 But as
soon the sun rose the plants were scorched and withered
because they had no roots. 7 Again other seeds fell among thistles; and the thistles grew and choked the plants. 8 Still other
seeds fell on good soil and produced a crop; some produced a
hundredfold, others sixty and others thirty. 9 If you have ears,
then hear!

18 —Now listen to the parable of the sower.

19 When a person hears the message of the Kingdom but
without taking it to himself, the devil comes and snatches
away what was sown in his heart. This is the seed that fell
along the footpath.

20 —The seed that fell on rocky ground stands for the one
who hears the word and accepts it at once with joy. 21 But such
a person has no roots. No sooner is he harassed or persecuted
because of the word, than he gives up.

22 —The seed that fell among the thistles is the one who
hears the word, but then the worries of this life and the love of
money choke the word, and it does not bear fruit.

23 —As for the seed that fell on good soil it is the one who
hears the word and understands it; this bears fruit and pro-
duces a hundred, or sixty, or thirty times more.

31 Jesus put another parable before them:
—The kingdom of heaven is like a mustard seed that a man
took and sowed in his field. 32 It is smaller than all other seeds,
but once it has fully grown, it is bigger than any garden plant;
like a tree, the birds come and rest in its branches.

33 He told them another parable:
—The kingdom of heaven is like the yeast that a woman
took and buried in three measures of flour until the whole
mass of dough began to rise.

34 Jesus taught all this to the crowds by means of parables;
he did not say anything to them without using a parable.
35 So what the Prophet had said was fulfilled: *I will speak in
parables. I will proclaim things kept secret since the beginning of
the world.*

44 —The kingdom of heaven is like a treasure hidden in a
field. The one who finds it buries it again; and so happy is he,
that he goes and sells everything he has, in order to buy that
field.

45 —Again the kingdom of heaven is like a trader who is
looking for fine pearls. 46 Once he has found a pearl of exceptional quality, he goes away, sells everything he has and buys
it.

Miracle of the loaves

14 14 When Jesus went ashore, he saw the crowd gathered there and he had compassion on them. And he healed
their sick. 15 Late in the afternoon, his disciples came to him
and said:

—We are in a lonely place and it is now late. You should
send these people away, so they can go to the villages and buy
something for themselves to eat.

16 But Jesus replied:
—They do not need to go away; you give them something
to eat.

17 They answered:
—We have nothing here but five loaves and two fishes.

18 Jesus said to them:

—Bring them here to me.

19 Then he made everyone sit down on the grass. He took
the five loaves and the two fishes, raised his eyes to heaven,
pronounced the blessing, broke the loaves and handed them
to the disciples to distribute to the people. 20 And they all ate,
and everyone had enough; then the disciples gathered up the
leftovers, filling twelve baskets. 21 About five thousand men
had eaten there besides women and children.

22 Immediately Jesus obliged his disciples to get into the boat and go ahead of him to the other side, while he sent the crowd away.

Walking on the water

23 And having sent the people away, he went up the mountain by himself to pray. At nightfall, he was there alone.
24 Meanwhile, the boat was very far from land, dangerously
rocked by the waves for the wind was against it.

25 At daybreak, Jesus came to them walking on the lake.
26 When they saw him walking on the sea, they were terrified,
thinking that it was a ghost. And they cried out in fear. 27 But
at once Jesus said to them:

—Courage! Don't be afraid. It's me!

28 Peter answered:

—Lord, if it is you, command me to come to you walking on the water.

29 Jesus said to him:

—Come.

And Peter got out of the boat, walking on the water to go
to Jesus. 30 But, in face of the strong wind, he was afraid and
began to sink. So he cried out:

—Lord, save me!

31 Jesus immediately stretched out his hand and took hold of him, saying:

—Man of little faith, why did you doubt?

32 As they got into the boat, the wind dropped.

Peter's confession

16 13 After that Jesus came to Caesarea Philippi. He asked his disciples:

—Who do people say the Son of man is?

14 They said:

—For some of them you are John the Baptist, for others Elijah or Jeremiah or one of the prophets.

15 Jesus asked them:

—But you, who do you say I am?

16 Peter answered:

—You are the Messiah, the Son of the living God.

17 Jesus replied:

—It is well for you, Simon Barjona, for it is not flesh or blood that has revealed this to you but my Father in heaven.
18 And now I say to you: You are Peter (or *Rock*) and on this rock I will build my Church; and never will the powers of death overcome it. 19 I will give you the keys of the kingdom of heaven: whatever you bind on earth shall be bound in heaven, and what you unbind on earth shall be unbound in heaven.

20 Then he ordered his disciples not to tell anyone that he was the Christ.

First announcement about the passion and resurrection

21 From that day Jesus began to make it clear to his disciples that he must go to Jerusalem; he would suffer many things from the Jewish authorities, the chief priests and the teachers of the Law. He would be killed and be raised on the third day.

22 Then Peter took him aside and began to reproach him:

—Never, Lord! No, this must never happen to you.

23 But Jesus turned to him and said:

—Get behind me, Satan! You are an obstacle in my path. You are thinking not as God does, but as people do.

[24] Then Jesus said to his disciples:

—If you want to follow me, deny yourself, take up your
cross and follow me. [25] For whoever chooses to save his life
will lose it, but the one who loses his life for my sake will find
it. [26] What will one gain by winning the whole world if he
destroys himself? There is nothing you can give to recover
your own self.

Communitarian instruction

18 [1] At that time the disciples came to Jesus and asked him:

—Who is the greatest in the kingdom of heaven?

[2] Then Jesus called a little child, set the child in the midst of
the disciples, [3] and said:

—I assure you that unless you change and become like little children, you cannot enter the kingdom of heaven. [4] Whoever becomes lowly like this child is the greatest in the kingdom of heaven, [5] and whoever receives such a child in my
name receives me.

19 [1] When Jesus had finished this teaching, he left Galilee
and arrived at the border of Judea, on the other side of the
Jordan River. [2] A great crowd was with him and there, too, he
healed their sick.

The rich youth

[16] It was then that a young man approached him and asked:

—Master, what good work must I do to receive eternal life?

[17] Jesus answered:

—Why do you ask me about what is good? Only one is Good. If you want to enter eternal life, keep the commandments.

[18] The young man said:

—Which commandments?

Jesus replied:

—*Do not kill, do not commit adultery, do not steal, do not bear false witness,* [19] *honor your father and mother, and love your neighbor as yourself.*

[20] The young man said to him:

—I have kept all these commandments, what is still lacking?

[21] Jesus answered:

—If you wish to be perfect, go and sell all that you possess and give the money to the poor and you will become the owner of a treasure in heaven. Then come back and follow me.

[22] On hearing this answer, the young man went away sad for he was a man of great wealth.

[23] Then Jesus said to his disciples:

—Truly I say to you: it will be hard for one who is rich to
enter the kingdom of heaven. [24] Yes, believe me: it is easier for
a camel to go through the eye of a needle than for the one who is rich to enter the kingdom of heaven.

[25] On hearing this the disciples were astonished and said:

—Who, then, can be saved?

[26] Jesus looked steadily at them and answered:

—For humans it is impossible, but for God all things are possible.

[27] Then Peter spoke up and said:

—You see we have given up everything to follow you: what will be our lot?

[28] Jesus answered:

—You who have followed me, listen to my words: on the Day of Renewal, when the Son of Man sits on his throne in glory, you, too, will sit on twelve thrones to rule the twelve
tribes of Israel. [29] As for those who have left houses, brothers,
sisters, father, mother, children or property for my Name's sake, they will receive a hundredfold and be given eternal life.
[30] Many who are now first will be last, and many who are now
last will be first.

The workers in the vineyard

20 1—This story throws light on the kingdom of heaven.
A landowner went out early in the morning to hire workers
for his vineyard. 2 He agreed to pay the workers a salary of a
silver coin for the day, and sent them to his vineyard.

3—He went out again at about nine in the morning, and
seeing others idle in the square, 4 he said to them: 'You, too,
go to my vineyard and I will pay you what is just.' So they
went.

—The owner went out at midday and again at three in
the afternoon, 5 and he did the same. 6 Finally he went out
at the last working hour—it was the eleventh—and he saw
others standing there. So he said to them: 'Why do you
stay idle the whole day?' 7 They answered: 'Because no one
has hired us.' The master said: 'Go and work in my vineyard.'

8—When evening came, the owner of the vineyard said to
his manager: 'Call the workers and pay them their wage,
beginning with the last and ending with the first.' 9 Those who
had come to work at the eleventh hour turned up and were
given a denarius each (a silver coin). 10 When it was the turn of
the first, they thought they would receive more. 11 But they,
too, received a denarius each. So, on receiving it, they began
to grumble against the landowner.

12—They said: 'These last hardly worked an hour, yet you
have treated them the same as us who have endured the day's
burden and heat.' 13 The owner said to one of them: 'Friend, I
have not been unjust to you. Did we not agree on a denarius a
day? 14 So take what is yours and go. I want to give to the last
the same as I give to you. 15 Don't I have the right to do as I
please with my money? Why are you envious when I am
kind?'

16—So will it be: the last will be first, the first will be last.

Triumphant entry in Jerusalem

21 1 When they drew near Jerusalem and arrived at Beth-

phage, on the mount of Olives, Jesus sent two of his disciples,
2 saying:

—Go to the village in front of you, and there you will find
a donkey tied up with its colt by her. Untie them and bring
them to me. 3 If anyone says something to you, say: The Lord
needs them but he will send them back immediately.

4 This happened in fulfillment of what the prophet said:
5 *Say to the daughter of Zion: See, your king comes to you in all simplicity, riding on a donkey, a beast of burden, with its colt.*

6 The disciples went as Jesus had instructed them, 7 and
they brought the donkey with its colt. Then they threw their
cloaks on its back, and Jesus sat on them.

8 Many people also spread their cloaks on the road, while
others cut leafy branches from the trees and spread them on
the road. 9 The people who walked ahead of Jesus and those
who followed him began to shout:

—*Hosanna to the Son of David! Blessed is he who comes in the name of the Lord! Hosanna, glory in the highest!*

10 When Jesus entered Jerusalem, the whole city was disturbed. The people asked:

—Who is this man?

11 And the crowd answered:

—This is the Prophet Jesus from Nazareth of Galilee.

The main commandment

22 34 When the Pharisees heard how Jesus had silenced
the Sadducees, they came together. 35 One of them, a teacher of
the Law, tried to test him with this question:

36 —Teacher, which is the most important commandment in
the Law?

37 Jesus answered:

*—You shall love the Lord, your God, with all your heart, with all
your soul and with all your mind.* 38 This is the first and the most
important of the commandments. 39 But after this there is
another one very similar to it: *You shall love your neighbor as
yourself.* 40 The whole Law and the Prophets are founded on
these two commandments.

25 14 —Imagine someone who, before going abroad,
summoned his servants to entrust his property to them. 15 He
gave five talents of silver to one, then two to another, and one
to a third, each one according to his ability; and he went away.

16 —He who received five talents went at once to do busi-
ness with the money and gained another five. 17 The one who
received two did the same and gained another two. 18 But the
one with one talent dug a hole and hid his master's money.

19 —After a long time, the master of those servants returned
and asked for a reckoning. 20 The one who received five talents
came with another five talents, saying: 'Lord, you entrusted me
with five talents, but see I have gained five more with them.' 21
The master answered: 'Very well, good and faithful servant,
since you have been faithful in a few things, I will entrust you
with much more. Come and share the joy of your master.'

22 —Then the one who had two talents came and said:
'Lord, you entrusted me with two talents; I have two more
which I gained with them.' 23 The master said: 'Well, good and
faithful servant, since you have been faithful in little things, I
will entrust you with much more. Come and share the joy of
your master.'

24 —Finally, the one who had received one talent came and
said: 'Master, I know that you are an exacting man. You reap

what you have not sown and gather what you have not
invested. 25 I was afraid, so I hid your money in the ground.
Here, take what is yours.' 26 But his master replied: 'Wicked
and worthless servant, you know that I reap where I have not
sown and gather where I have not invested. 27 Then you
should have deposited my money in the bank, and you would
have given it back to me with interest on my return.'

28 —Therefore, take the talent from him, and give it to the
one who has ten. 29 For to all those who have, more will be
given, and they will have an abundance; but from those who
are unproductive, even what they have will be taken from
them. 30 As for that useless servant, throw him out into the
dark where there will be weeping and gnashing of teeth.

The judgment of nations

31 —When the Son of Man comes in his glory with all his
angels, he will sit on the throne of his Glory. 32 All the nations
will be brought before him, and as a shepherd separates the
sheep from the goats, 33 so will he do with them, placing the
sheep on his right and the goats on his left.

34 —The King will say to those on his right: 'Come, blessed
of my Father! Take possession of the kingdom prepared for
you from the beginning of the world. 35 For I was hungry and
you fed me, I was thirsty and you gave me drink. 36 I was a
stranger and you welcomed me into your house. I was naked
and you clothed me. I was sick and you visited me. I was in
prison and you came to see me.'

37 —Then the good people will ask him: 'Lord, when did we
see you hungry and give you food; thirsty and give you drink,
38 or a stranger and welcome you, or naked and clothe you?
39 When did we see you sick or in prison and go to see you?'
40 The King will answer, 'Truly, I say to you: whenever you did
this to these little ones who are my brothers and sisters, you
did it to me.'

41 —Then he will say to those on his left: 'Go, cursed people, out of my sight into the eternal fire which has been prepared for the devil and his angels! 42 For I was hungry and you
did not give me anything to eat, I was thirsty and you gave me

nothing to drink; [43] I was a stranger and you did not welcome
me into your house; I was naked and you did not clothe me; I
was sick and in prison and you did not visit me.'

[44] —They, too, will ask: 'Lord, when did we see you hungry,
thirsty, naked or a stranger, sick or in prison, and did not help
you?' [45] The King will answer them: 'Truly, I say to you: whatever you did not do for one of these little ones, you did not do
for me.'

[46] —And these will go into eternal punishment, but the just
to eternal life.

Plot to kill Jesus

26 [1] When Jesus had finished all he wanted to say, he told
his disciples:

[2] —You know that in two days' time it will be the Passover
and the Son of Man will be handed over to be crucified.

[3] Then the chief priests and the Jewish authorities gathered
together at the palace of the High Priest whose name was
Caiaphas, [4] and they agreed to trap Jesus and kill him. [5] But
they said among themselves: 'Not during the feast, lest there
be an uprising among the people.'

Anointing at Bethany

[14] Then one of the Twelve, who was called Judas Iscariot,
went off to the chief priests and said:

[15] —How much will you give me if I hand him over to you?
They promised to give him thirty pieces of silver, [16] and from
then on he kept looking for the best way to hand him over to
them.

Passover and Eucharist

[17] On the first day of the Festival of the Unleavened Bread,
the disciples came to Jesus and said to him:

—Where do you want us to prepare the Passover meal for you?

18 Jesus answered:

—Go into the city, to the house of a certain man, and tell him: 'The Master says: My hour is near, and I will celebrate the Passover with my disciples in your house.

19 The disciples did as Jesus had ordered and prepared the Passover meal.

26 While they were eating, Jesus took bread, said a blessing and broke it, and gave it to his disciples saying:

—Take and eat; this is my body.

27 Then he took a cup and gave thanks, and passed it to them saying:

—Drink this, all of you, 28 for this is my blood, the blood of
the Covenant, which is poured out for many for the forgiveness of sins.

31 Then Jesus said to them:

—You will falter tonight because of me, and all will fall. For
the Scripture says: *I will strike the shepherd and the sheep will be*
scattered. 32 But after my resurrection I will go ahead of you to
Galilee.

33 Peter responded:

—Even though all doubt you and fall, I will never fall.
34 Jesus replied:

—Truly, I say to you: this very night before the cock crows, you will deny me three times.

35 Peter said:

—Though I have to die with you, I will never deny you. And all the disciples said the same.

Jesus before the Sanhedrin

57 Those who had arrested Jesus brought him to the house of the High Priest Caiaphas, where the teachers of the Law and the Jewish authorities were assembled.

58 Peter followed him at a distance as far as the courtyard of

the High Priest; he entered and sat with the guards, waiting to see the end. [59]The chief priests and the whole Supreme Council needed some false evidence against Jesus, so that they might put him to death. [60]But they were unable to find any, even though false witnesses came forward. [61]At last, two men came up and declared, 'This man said: I am able to destroy the temple of God and rebuild it in three days.'

[62]The High Priest then stood up and asked Jesus:

—Have you no answer at all? What is this evidence against you?

[63]But Jesus kept silent.

So the High Priest said to him:

—In the name of the living God, I command you to tell us: Are you the Messiah, the Son of God?

[64]Jesus answered:

—It is just as you say. I tell you more: from now on, you will see *the Son of Man seated at the right hand of the Most Powerful God and coming on the clouds of heaven.*

[65]Then the High Priest tore his clothes, saying:

—He has blasphemed. What more evidence do we need? You have just heard these blasphemous words. [66]What is your decision?

They answered:

—He must die!

Jesus before Pilate

27 [11]Jesus stood before the governor who questioned him:

—Are you the King of the Jews?

Jesus answered:

—You say so.

[12]The chief priests and the Elders accused him, but he made no answer. [13]Pilate said to him:

—Do you hear all the charges they bring against you? [14]But he did not answer even a single question, so that the governor wondered.

The scorn of soldiers

27 The Roman soldiers took Jesus into the palace of the governor and the whole troop gathered around him. 28 They stripped him and dressed him in a purple military cloak. 29 Then, twisting a crown of thorns, they forced it onto his head, and placed a reed in his right hand. They knelt before Jesus and mocked him, saying:

—Long life to the King of the Jews!

30 They spat on him, took the reed from his hand and struck him on the head with it.

31 When they had finished mocking him, they pulled off the purple cloak and dressed him in his own clothes again, and led him out to be crucified.

Death of Jesus

32 On the way they met a man from Cyrene called Simon, and forced him to carry the cross of Jesus. 33 When they reached the place called Golgotha (or Calvary) which means *the Skull,* 34 they offered him wine mixed with gall. Jesus tasted it but would not take it.

35 There they crucified him and divided his clothes among themselves, casting lots to decide what each should take. 36 Then they sat down to guard him. 37 The statement of his offense was displayed above his head and it read: 'This is Jesus, the King of the Jews.' 39 People passing by shook their heads and insulted him, 40 saying:

—Aha! So you will destroy the Temple and build it up again in three days. Now save yourself and come down from the cross, if you are Son of God.

41 In the same way the chief priests, the Elders and the teachers of the Law mocked him. 42 They said:

—The man who saved others cannot save himself. Let the King of Israel now come down from his cross and we will believe in him. 43 He trusted in God; let God rescue him if God wants to, since he himself said: I am the Son of God.

44 Even the robbers who were crucified with him insulted
him.

45 From midday darkness fell over the whole land until
mid-afternoon. 46 At about three o'clock, Jesus cried out in a
loud voice, *'Eloi, Eloi, lamma Sabbacthani?'* which means: My
God, my God, why have you forsaken me? 47 As soon as they
heard this, some of the bystanders said:

—He is calling for Elijah.

54 The captain and the soldiers who guarded Jesus were
greatly terrified when they saw the earthquake and all that
had happened, and said:

—Truly, this man was a Son of God.

Burial of Jesus

57 It was now evening and there arrived a wealthy man
from Arimathea, named Joseph, who was also a disciple of
Jesus. 58 He went to Pilate and asked for the body of Jesus, and
the governor ordered that the body be given him. 59 So Joseph
took the body of Jesus, wrapped it in a clean linen sheet 60 and
laid it in his own new tomb which had been cut out of the
rock. Then he rolled a huge stone across the entrance of the
tomb and left.

62 On the following day (the day after the Preparation for
the Passover), the chief priests and the Pharisees went to
Pilate 63 and said to him:

—Sir, we remember that when that impostor was still alive,
he said: I will rise after three days. 64 Therefore, have his tomb
secured until the third day, lest his disciples come and steal
the body and say to the people: He was raised from the dead.
This would be a worse lie than the first.

65 Pilate answered them:

—You have soldiers, go and take all the necessary precautions.

66 So they went to the tomb and secured it, sealing the stone
and placing it under guard.

Resurrection

28 [1] After the Sabbath, at the dawn of the first day of the week, Mary Magdalene and the other Mary went to visit the tomb. [5] The angel said to the women:

—Do not be afraid, for I know that you are looking for Jesus who was crucified. [6] He is not here, for he is risen as he said. Come, see the place where they laid him; [7] then go at once and tell his disciples that he is risen from the dead and is going ahead of you to Galilee. You will see him there. This is my message for you.

[8] They left the tomb at once in holy fear, yet with great joy, and they ran to tell the news to the disciples.

[9] Suddenly, Jesus met them on the way and said:

—Peace.

The women approached him, embraced his feet and worshiped him. [10] But Jesus said to them:

—Do not be afraid. Go and tell my brothers to set out for Galilee; there they will see me.

Mission of the disciples

[16] As for the Eleven disciples, they went to Galilee, to the mountain where Jesus had told them to go. [17] When they saw Jesus, they bowed before him, although some doubted.

[18] Then Jesus approached them and said:

—I have been given all authority in heaven and on earth. [19] Go, therefore, and make disciples from all nations. Baptize them in the Name of the Father and of the Son and of the Holy Spirit, [20] and teach them to fulfill all that I have commanded you. I am with you always until the end of this world.

The other gospels have their own interpretation of these events and have their own particularities as well. We have chosen the most representative of each one, and in the passages that are common we have chosen those that have a special characteristic.

THE GOSPEL ACCORDING TO MARK

Introduction

The theme of the gospel of Mark is the person of Jesus more than his teaching: the mystery of Jesus, the mysterious Jesus. A perspective that dims out leading to a dramatic confrontation. Jesus teaches but his followers do not understand him. Jesus is the Messiah that has to suffer. By the time of the final triumph, Mark is again bare: the confession of the centurion contrasting with the fearful silence of the women.

It seems that Mark writes for a pagan or mixed community; probably a poor and persecuted community. A very old tradition asserts that Mark writes his gospel in Rome, putting in writing the preaching of Peter.

Mark invites for an easy, superficial reading, but the challenge is to read Mark in depth.

1 21 They went into the town of Capernaum and Jesus began
to teach in the synagogue during the sabbath assemblies. 22 The
people were astonished at the way he taught, for he spoke as
one having authority and not like the teachers of the Law.

23 It happened that a man with an evil spirit was in their
synagogue 24 and he shouted:

—What do you want with us, Jesus of Nazareth? Have you come to destroy us? I know who you are: You are the Holy One of God.

25 Then Jesus faced him and said with authority:
—Be silent and come out of this man!
26 The evil spirit shook the man violently and, with a loud
shriek, came out of him.
27 All the people were astonished and they wondered:
'What is this? With what authority he preaches! He even
orders evil spirits and they obey him!' 28 And Jesus' fame
spread throughout all the country of Galilee.

Healings

29 On leaving the synagogue, Jesus went to the home of
Simon and Andrew with James and John. 30 As Simon's mother-in-law was sick in bed with fever, they immediately told
him about her. 31 Jesus went to her and taking her by the hand,
raised her up. The fever left her and she began to wait on
them.

Election of the Twelve

3 13 Then Jesus went up into the hill country and called
those he wanted and they came to him. 14 So he appointed
twelve to be with him; and he called them apostles. He wanted to send them out to preach, 15 and he gave them authority
to drive out demons.
16 These are the Twelve: Simon, to whom he gave the name
Peter; 17 James, son of Zebedee, and John his brother, to whom
he gave the name Boanerges, which means 'men of thunder;'
18 Andrew, Philip, Bartholomew, Matthew, Thomas, James son
of Alpheus, Thaddeus, Simon the Cananean 19 and Judas
Iscariot, the one who betrayed him.

In the synagogue of Nazareth

6 1 Leaving that place, Jesus returned to his own country,
and his disciples followed him. 2 When the Sabbath came, he

began teaching in the synagogue, and most of those who heard him were astonished. They commented:

—How did this come to him? What kind of wisdom has been given to him that he also performs such miracles? 3 Who is he but the carpenter, the son of Mary and the brother of James and Joset and Judas and Simon? His sisters, too, are they not here among us?

So they took offense at him.

4 And Jesus said to them:

—Prophets are despised only in their own country, among their relatives and in their own family.

5 And he could work no miracles there, but only healed a
few sick people by laying his hands on them. 6 Jesus himself
was astounded at their unbelief. Jesus then went around the
villages teaching.

Against ambition

10 35 James and John, the sons of Zebedee, came to Jesus and said to him:

—Master, we want you to grant us what we are going to ask of you.

36 And he said:

—What do you want me to do for you?

37 They answered:

—Grant us to sit one at your right and one at your left when you come in your glory.

38 But Jesus said to them:

—You don't know what you are asking. Can you drink the cup that I drink or be baptized in the way I am baptized?
39 They answered:

—We can.

And Jesus told them:

—The cup that I drink you will drink, and you will be baptized in the way I am baptized. 40 But to sit at my right or at my
left is not mine to grant. It has been prepared for others.

41 On hearing this, the other ten were angry with James and
John; 42 Jesus then called them to him and said:

—As you know, the so-called rulers of the nations act as
tyrants and their great ones oppress them. 43 But it shall not be
so among you; whoever would be great among you must be
your servant, 44 and whoever would be first among you shall
make himself slave of all. 45 Think of the Son of Man who has
not come to be served but to serve and to give his life to
redeem many.

The widow's offering

12 41 Jesus sat down opposite the Temple treasury and
watched the people dropping money into the treasury box;
and many rich people put in large offerings. 42 But a poor
widow also came and dropped in two small coins.

43 Then Jesus called his disciples and said to them:

—Truly I say to you, this poor widow put in more than all
those who gave offerings. 44 For all of them gave from their
plenty, but she gave from her poverty and put in everything
she had, her very living.

The Gospel According to Luke

Introduction

The book of Luke has many things in common with Mark and Matthew. He addresses his writing to a non-Jewish community; his message is more immediately accessible to pagan readers. He wants to write as a historian and presents himself as a historian in the Greek style.

His gospel is the first part of a more extended work that continues with the Acts of the Apostles. In this, his gospel is positioned between the announcement and preparation of the Old Testament, and the time of the Church, beginning at Pentecost.

Luke interweaves his writing with dates taken from the historical happening of the time. He retells the origins of Jesus, the life of Jesus starting with his infancy.

His gospel has a strong ethical and social agenda, in favor of the poor and oppressed. Of primary importance is his message on mercy and the teaching about prayer. He gives particular attention to the role of women.

The old tradition has identified the author with the medical doctor Luke of Colossians 4:14.

The announcement of the birth of John

1 5 In the days of Herod, king of Judea, there lived a priest
named Zechariah, belonging to the priestly clan of Abiah.

Elizabeth, Zechariah's wife, also belonged to a priestly family.
6 Both of them were upright in the eyes of God and lived
blamelessly in accordance with all the laws and commands of
the Lord, 7 but they had no child. Elizabeth could not have any
and now they were both very old.

8 Now, while Zechariah and those with him were fulfilling
their office, 9 it fell to him by lot, according to the custom of the
priests, to enter the sanctuary of the Lord and burn incense.
10 At the time of offering incense all the people were praying
outside; 11 it was then that an angel of the Lord appeared to
him, standing on the right side of the altar of incense. 12 On
seeing the angel, Zechariah was deeply troubled and fear took
hold of him.

13 But the angel said to him:

—Don't be afraid, Zechariah, be assured that your prayer
has been heard. Your wife Elizabeth will bear you a son and
you shall name him John. 14 He will bring joy and gladness to
you and many will rejoice at his birth. 15 This son of yours will
be great in the eyes of the Lord. Listen: he shall never drink
wine or strong drink, but he will be filled with holy spirit even
from his mother's womb. 16 Through him many of the people
of Israel will turn to the Lord their God. 17 He himself will
open the way to the Lord with the spirit and power of the
prophet Elijah; he will reconcile fathers and children, and lead
the disobedient to wisdom and righteousness, in order to
make ready for the Lord a people prepared.

18 Zechariah said to the angel:

—How can I believe this? I am an old man and my wife is
elderly, too.

19 The angel replied:

—I am Gabriel, who stands before God, and I am the one
sent to speak to you and bring you this good news! My words
will come true in their time. 20 But you would not believe and
now you will be silent and unable to speak until this has happened.

21 Meanwhile the people waited for Zechariah, and they
were surprised that he delayed so long in the sanctuary.
22 When he finally appeared, he could not speak to them and
they realized that he had seen a vision in the sanctuary. He
remained dumb and made signs to them.

23 When his time of service was completed, Zechariah
returned home 24 and some time later Elizabeth became pregnant. For five months she kept to herself, remaining at home,
and thinking:

25 —What is the Lord doing for me! This is his time for
mercy and for taking away my public disgrace.

The announcement of the birth of Jesus

26 In the sixth month, the angel Gabriel was sent from God
to a town of Galilee called Nazareth. He was sent 27 to a young
virgin who was betrothed to a man named Joseph, of the family of David; and the virgin's name was Mary.

28 The angel came to her and said:

—Rejoice, full of grace, the Lord is with you.

29 Mary was troubled at these words, wondering what this
greeting could mean.

30 But the angel said:

—Do not fear, Mary, for God has looked kindly on you.
31 You shall conceive and bear a son and you shall call him
Jesus. 32 He will be great and shall rightly be called Son of
the Most High. The Lord God will give him the kingdom of
David, his ancestor; he will rule over the people of Jacob forever 33 and his reign shall have no end.

34 Then Mary said to the angel:

—How can this be if I am a virgin?

35 And the angel said to her:

—The Holy Spirit will come upon you and the power of the
Most High will overshadow you; therefore, the holy child to
be born shall be called Son of God. 36 Even your relative
Elizabeth is expecting a son in her old age, although she was
unable to have a child, and she is now in her sixth month. 37
With God nothing is impossible.

38 Then Mary said:

—I am the handmaid of the Lord, let it be done to me as
you have said.

And the angel left her.

Mary visits Elizabeth

[39] Mary then set out for a town in the Hills of Judah. [40] She
entered the house of Zechariah and greeted Elizabeth. [41] When
Elizabeth heard Mary's greeting, the baby leapt in her womb.
Elizabeth was filled with holy spirit, and [42] giving a loud cry,
said:

—You are most blessed among women and blessed is the
fruit of your womb! [43] How is it that the mother of my Lord
comes to me? [44] The moment your greeting sounded in my
ears, the baby within me suddenly leapt for joy. [45] Blessed are
you who believed that the Lord's word would come true!

[46] And Mary said:
—My soul proclaims the greatness of the Lord,
[47] my spirit exults in God my savior!
[48] He has looked upon his servant in her lowliness,
and people forever will call me blessed.
[49] The Mighty One has done great things for me,
Holy is his Name!
[50] From age to age his mercy extends
to those who live in his presence.
[51] He has acted with power and done wonders,
and scattered the proud with their plans.
[52] He has put down the mighty from their thrones
and lifted up those who are downtrodden.
[53] He has filled the hungry with good things
but has sent the rich away empty.
[54] He held out his hand to Israel, his servant,
for he remembered his mercy,
[55] even as he promised our fathers,
Abraham and his descendants forever.

[56] Mary remained with Elizabeth about three months and
then returned home.

Birth of John

[57] When the time came for Elizabeth, she gave birth to a son.
[58] Her neighbors and relatives heard that the merciful Lord
had done a wonderful thing for her and they rejoiced with her.

59 When on the eighth day they came to attend the circumcision of the child, they wanted to name him Zechariah after
his father. 60 But his mother said:

—Not so; he shall be called John.

61 They said to her:

—No one in your family has that name.

62 And they asked the father by means of signs for the name
he wanted to give. 63 Zechariah asked for a writing tablet and
wrote on it, 'His name is John,' and they were very surprised.
64 Immediately Zechariah could speak again and his first
words were in praise of God.

65 A holy fear came on all in the neighborhood, and
throughout the Hills of Judea the people talked about these
events. 66 All who heard of it pondered in their minds and
wondered, 'What will this child be?' For they understood that
the hand of the Lord was with him.

67 Zechariah, filled with holy spirit, sang this canticle:

68 —Blessed be the Lord God of Israel,
for he has come and redeemed his people.
69 He has raised up for us a victorious Savior
in the house of David his servant,
70 as he promised through his prophets of old,
71 salvation from our enemies
and from the hand of our foes.
72 He has shown mercy to our fathers
and remembered his holy covenant,
73 the oath he swore to Abraham, our father,
74 to deliver us from the enemy,
75 that we might serve him fearlessly
as a holy and righteous people
all the days of our lives.
76 And you, my child,
shall be called prophet of the Most High,
for you shall go before the Lord
to prepare the way for him
77 and enable his people to know of their salvation
when he comes to forgive their sins.
78 This is the work of the mercy of our God,
who comes from on high as a rising sun
79 shining on those who live in darkness

and in the shadow of death,
and guiding our feet into the way of peace.

80 As the child grew up, he was seen to be strong in the Spirit; he lived in the desert till the day when he appeared openly in Israel.

Birth of Jesus

2 1 At that time the emperor issued a decree for a census of
the whole empire to be taken. 2 This first census was taken
while Quirinus was governor of Syria. 3 Everyone had to be

registered in his own town. So everyone set out for his own city; [4]Joseph too set out from Nazareth of Galilee. As he belonged to the family of David, being a descendant of his, he went to Judea to David's town of Bethlehem [5]to be registered with Mary, his wife, who was with child. [6]They were in Bethlehem when the time came for her to have her child, [7]and she gave birth to a son, her firstborn. She wrapped him in swaddling clothes and laid him in the manger, because there was no place for them in the living room.

[8]There were shepherds camping in the countryside, taking turns to watch over their flocks by night. [9]Suddenly an angel of the Lord appeared to them, with the Glory of the Lord shining around them. As they were terrified, [10]the angel said to them:

—Don't be afraid; I am here to give you good news, great joy for all the people. [11]Today a Savior has been born to you in David's town; he is the Messiah and the Lord. [12]Let this be a sign to you: you will find a baby wrapped in swaddling clothes and lying in a manger.

[13]Suddenly the angel was surrounded by many more heavenly spirits, praising God and saying:

14—Glory to God in the highest; peace on earth for God is
blessing humankind.

15 When the angels had left them and gone back to heaven,
the shepherds said to one another:

—Let us go as far as Bethlehem and see what the Lord has
made known to us.

16 So they came hurriedly and found Mary and Joseph with
the baby lying in the manger. 17 On seeing this they related
what they had been told about the child, 18 and all were astonished on hearing the shepherds. 19 As for Mary, she treasured
all these messages and continually pondered over them.
20 The shepherds then returned giving glory and praise to
God for all they had heard and seen, just as the angels had
told them.

Circumcision and presentation

21 On the eighth day the circumcision of the baby had to be
performed; he was named Jesus, the name the angel had given
him before he was conceived.

The boy Jesus at the Temple

41 Every year the parents of Jesus went to Jerusalem for the
Feast of the Passover, as was customary. 42 And when Jesus
was twelve years old, he went up with them according to the
custom for this feast. 43 After the festival was over, they returned, but the boy Jesus remained in Jerusalem and his parents did not know it.

44 They thought he was in the company and after walking
the whole day they looked for him among their relatives and
friends. 45 As they did not find him, they went back to
Jerusalem searching for him, 46 and on the third day they
found him in the Temple, sitting among the teachers, listening
to them and asking questions. 47 And all the people were
amazed at his understanding and his answers.

48 His parents were very surprised when they saw him and
his mother said to him:

—Son, why have you done this to us? Your father and I
were very worried while searching for you.

49 Then he said to them:

—Why were you looking for me? Do you not know that I
must be in my Father's house?

50 But they did not understand this answer. 51 Jesus went
down with them, returning to Nazareth, and he continued to
be subject to them. As for his mother, she kept all these things
in her heart. 52 And Jesus increased in wisdom and age, and in
divine and human favor.

In the synagogue of Nazareth

4 14 Jesus acted with the power of the Spirit, and on his
return to Galilee the news about him spread throughout all
that territory. 15 He began teaching in the synagogues of the
Jews and everyone praised him.

16 When Jesus came to Nazareth where he had been
brought up, he entered the synagogue on the Sabbath as
he usually did. 17 He stood up to read and they handed him
the book of the prophet Isaiah. Jesus then unrolled the
scroll and found the place where it is written: 18 *'The Spirit
of the Lord is upon me. He has anointed me to bring good news
to the poor, to proclaim liberty to captives and new sight to the
blind; to free the oppressed* 19 *and announce the Lord's year of
mercy.'*

20 Jesus then rolled up the scroll, gave it to the attendant
and sat down, while the eyes of all in the synagogue were
fixed on him. 21 Then he said to them:

—Today these prophetic words come true even as you listen.

22 All agreed with him and were lost in wonder, while he
kept on speaking of the grace of God. Nevertheless they
asked:

—Who is this but Joseph's son?

Calling of the first disciples

5 1 One day, as Jesus stood by the Lake of Gennesaret, with
a crowd gathered around him listening to the word of God,
2 he caught sight of two boats left at the water's edge by the
fishermen now washing their nets. 3 He got into one of the
boats, the one belonging to Simon, and asked him to pull out
a little from the shore. There he sat and continued to teach the
crowd.

4 When he had finished speaking he said to Simon:

—Put out into deep water and lower your nets for a catch.

5 Simon replied:

—Master, we worked hard all night and caught nothing.
But if you say so, I will lower the nets.

6 This they did and caught such a large number of fish that
their nets began to break. 7 They signaled their partners in the
other boat to come and help them. They came and filled both
boats almost to the point of sinking. 8 Upon seeing this, Simon
Peter fell at Jesus' knees, saying:

—Leave me, Lord, for I am a sinful man!

9 For he and his companions were amazed at the catch they
had made 10 and so were Simon's partners, James and John,
Zebedee's sons.

Jesus said to Simon:

—Do not be afraid. You will catch people from now on.

11 So they brought their boats to land and followed him,
leaving everything.

Healing of a paralytic

17 One day Jesus was teaching and many Pharisees and
teachers of the Law had come from every part of Galilee and
Judea and even from Jerusalem. They were sitting there while
the power of the Lord was at work to heal the sick. 18 Then
some men brought a paralyzed man who lay on his mat. They
tried to enter the house to place him before Jesus, 19 but they
couldn't find a way through the crowd. So they went up on

the roof and, removing the tiles, they lowered him on his mat into the middle of the crowd, in front of Jesus.

[20] When Jesus saw their faith, he said to the man:

—My friend, your sins are forgiven.

[21] At once the teachers of the Law and the Pharisees began to wonder:

—This man insults God! Who can forgive sins but only God?

[22] But Jesus knew their thoughts and asked them:

—Why are you reacting like this? [23] Which is easier to say: 'Your sins are forgiven,' or: 'Get up and walk?' [24] Now you shall know that the Son of Man has authority on earth to forgive sins.

And Jesus said to the paralyzed man:

—Get up, take your mat and go home.

[25] At once the man stood before them. He took up the mat he had been lying on and went home praising God.

[26] Amazement seized the people and they praised God. They were filled with a holy fear and said:

—What wonderful things we have seen today!

Forgives a woman sinner

7 [36] One of the Pharisees asked Jesus to share his meal, so he went to the Pharisee's home and as usual reclined on the

sofa to eat. 37 And it happened that a woman of this town, who
was known as a sinner, heard that he was in the Pharisee's
house. She brought a precious jar of perfume 38 and stood
behind him at his feet, weeping. She wet his feet with tears,
she dried them with her hair and kissed his feet and poured
the perfume on them.

39 The Pharisee who had invited Jesus was watching and
thought:

—If this man were a prophet, he would know what sort of person is touching him; isn't this woman a sinner?

40 Then Jesus spoke to the Pharisee and said:

—Simon, I have something to ask you.

He answered:

—Speak, master.

And Jesus said:

41 —Two people were in debt to the same creditor. One
owed him five hundred silver coins, and the other fifty. 42 As
they were unable to pay him back, he graciously canceled the
debts of both. Now, which of them will love him more?

43 Simon answered:

—The one, I suppose, who was forgiven more.

And Jesus said:

—You are right.

44 And turning toward the woman, he said to Simon:

—Do you see this woman? 45 You gave me no water for
my feet when I entered your house, but she has washed my
feet with her tears and dried them with her hair. You didn't
welcome me with a kiss, but she has not stopped kissing
my feet since she came in. 46 You provided no oil for my
head, but she has poured perfume on my feet. 47 This is why,
I tell you, her sins, her many sins, are forgiven, because of
her great love. But the one who is forgiven little, has little
love.

48 Then Jesus said to the woman:

—Your sins are forgiven.

49 The others sitting with him at the table began to wonder:

—Now this man claims to forgive sins!

50 But Jesus again spoke to the woman:

—Your faith has saved you, go in peace.

Transfiguration

9 28 About eight days after Jesus had said all this, he took
Peter, John and James and went up the mountain to pray.
29 And while he was praying, the aspect of his face was
changed and his clothing became dazzling white. 30 Two men
were talking with Jesus: Moses and Elijah. 31 They had just
appeared in heavenly glory and were telling him about his
departure that had to take place in Jerusalem.

32 Peter and his companions had fallen asleep, but they
awoke suddenly and saw Jesus' Glory and the two men standing with him. 33 As Moses and Elijah were about to leave, Peter
said to him:

—Master, how good it is for us to be here for we can make three tents, one for you, one for Moses and one for Elijah.

For Peter didn't know what to say. 34 And no sooner had he
spoken than a cloud appeared and covered them; and the disciples were afraid as they entered the cloud. 35 Then these
words came from the cloud:

—This is my Son, my Chosen one, listen to him.

36 And after the voice had spoken, Jesus was there alone.

The disciples kept this to themselves at the time, telling no one of anything they had seen.

The Good Samaritan

10 25 Then a teacher of the Law came and began putting
Jesus to the test. And he said:

—Master, what shall I do to receive eternal life? 26 Jesus
replied:

—What is written in the Scripture? How do you understand it?

27 The man answered:

—It is written: *You shall love the Lord your God with all your heart, with all your soul, with all your strength* and with all your mind. And *you shall love your neighbor as yourself.*

28 Jesus replied:

—What a good answer! Do this and you shall live.

29 The man wanted to keep up appearances, so he replied:

—Who is my neighbor?

30 Jesus then said:

—"There was a man going down from Jerusalem to Jericho, and he fell into the hands of robbers. They stripped him, beat him and went off leaving him half-dead.

31 "It happened that a priest was going along that road and
saw the man, but passed by on the other side. 32 Likewise a
Levite saw the man and passed by on the other side. 33 But a
Samaritan, too, was going that way, and when he came upon
the man, he was moved with compassion. 34 He went over to
him and treated his wounds with oil and wine and wrapped
them with bandages. Then he put him on his own mount and
brought him to an inn where he took care of him.

35 "The next day he had to set off, but he gave two silver coins to the innkeeper and told him: 'Take care of him and whatever you spend on him, I will repay when I come back.'"

36 Jesus then asked:

—Which of these three, do you think, made himself neighbor to the man who fell into the hands of robbers?
37 The
teacher of the Law answered:

—The one who had mercy on him.

And Jesus said:

—Go then and do the same.

Parable of the banquet's guests

14 15 Upon hearing these words, one of those at the table said to Jesus:

—Happy are those who eat at the banquet in the kingdom of God!

16 Jesus replied:

—A man once gave a feast and invited many guests.
17 When it was time for the feast he sent his servant to tell
those he had invited to come, for everything was ready. 18 But
all alike began to make excuses. The first said: 'Please excuse
me. I must go and see the piece of land I have just bought.'
19 Another said: 'I am sorry, but I am on my way to try out the
five yoke of oxen I have just bought.' 20 Still another said,
'How can I come when I have just married?'

21 —The servant returned alone and reported this to his
master. Upon hearing the account, the master of the house
flew into a rage and ordered his servant: 'Go out quickly into
the streets and alleys of the town and bring in the poor, the
crippled, the blind and the lame.'

22 —The servant reported after a while: 'Sir, your orders
have been carried out, but there is still room.' 23 The master
said: 'Go out to the highways and country lanes and force people to come in, to make sure my house is full. 24 I tell you, none
of those invited will have a morsel of my feast.'

The lost sheep and the lost coin

15 1 Tax collectors and sinners were seeking the company
of Jesus, all of them eager to hear what he had to say. 2 But the
Pharisees and the scribes frowned at this, muttering:

—This man welcomes sinners and eats with them.

3 So Jesus told them this parable:

4 —Who among you, having a hundred sheep and losing
one of them, will not leave the ninety-nine in the wilderness
and seek out the lost one till he finds it? 5 And finding it,
will he not joyfully carry it home on his shoulders? 6 Then he
will call his friends and neighbors together and say:
'Celebrate with me for I have found my lost sheep.' 7 I tell
you, just so, there will be more rejoicing in heaven over one
repentant sinner than over ninety-nine upright who do not
need to repent.

The prodigal son

11 Jesus continued:

—There was a man with two sons. 12 The younger said to his father: 'Give me my share of the estate.' So the father divided his property between them.

13—Some days later, the younger son gathered all his belongings and started off for a distant land where he squandered his wealth in loose living. 14 Having spent everything, he was hard pressed when a severe famine broke out in that land. 15 So he hired himself out to a well-to-do citizen of that place and was sent to work on a pig farm. 16 So famished was he that he longed to fill his stomach even with the food given to the pigs, but no one offered him anything.

17—Finally coming to his senses, he said: 'How many of my father's hired workers have food to spare, and here I am starving to death! 18 I will get up and go back to my father and say to him: Father, I have sinned against God and before you. 19 I no longer deserve to be called your son. Treat me then as one of your hired servants.' With that thought in mind he set off for his father's house.

20—He was still a long way off when his father caught sight of him. His father was so deeply moved with compassion that he ran out to meet him, threw his arms around his neck and kissed him. 21 The son said: 'Father, I have sinned against Heaven and before you. I no longer deserve to be called your son.'

22—But the father turned to his servants: 'Quick! Bring out the finest robe and put it on him. Put a ring on his finger and sandals on his feet. 23 Take the fattened calf and kill it. We shall celebrate and have a feast, 24 for this son of mine was dead and has come back to life. He was lost and is found.' And the celebration began.

25—Meanwhile, the elder son had been working in the fields. As he returned and was near the house, he heard the sound of music and dancing. 26 He called one of the servants and asked what it was all about. 27 The servant answered: 'Your brother has come home safe and sound, and your father is so happy about it that he has ordered this celebration and killed the fattened calf.'

[28]—The elder son became angry and refused to go in. His
father came out and pleaded with him. [29]The indignant son
said: 'Look, I have slaved for you all these years. Never have
I disobeyed your orders. Yet you have never given me even a
young goat to celebrate with my friends. [30]Then when this son
of yours returns after squandering your property with loose
women, you kill the fattened calf for him.'

[31]—The father said: 'My son, you are always with me, and
everything I have is yours. [32]But this brother of yours was
dead, and has come back to life. He was lost and is found. And
for that we had to rejoice and be glad.'

The coming of the kingdom of God

17 [20]The Pharisees asked Jesus when the kingdom of
God was to come. He answered:

—The kingdom of God is not like something you can
observe [21]and say of it: 'Look, here it is! There it is!' See, the
kingdom of God is among you.

The Pharisee and the tax collector

18 [9]Jesus told another parable to some persons fully convinced of their own righteousness, who looked down on others:

[10]—Two men went up to the Temple to pray; one was a
Pharisee and the other a tax collector. [11]The Pharisee stood by
himself and said: 'I thank you, God, that I am not like other
people, grasping, crooked, adulterous, or even like this tax
collector. [12]I fast twice a week and give the tenth of all my
income to the Temple.'

[13]—In the meantime the tax collector, standing far off,
would not even lift his eyes to heaven, but beat his breast saying: 'O God, be merciful to me, a sinner.'

[14]—I tell you, when this man went down to his house, he
had been set right with God, but not the other. For whoever
makes himself out to be great will be humbled, and whoever
humbles himself will be raised.

Jesus and Zacheus

19 1 When Jesus entered Jericho and was going through
the city, 2 a man named Zaccheus was there. He was a tax collector and a wealthy man. 3 He wanted to see what Jesus was
like, but he was a short man and could not see because of the
crowd. 4 So he ran ahead and climbed up a sycamore tree.
From there he would be able to see Jesus who had to pass that
way. 5 When Jesus came to the place, he looked up and said to
him:

—Zaccheus, come down quickly for I must stay at your house today.

6 So Zaccheus hurried down and received him joyfully.

7 All the people who saw it began to grumble and said:

—He has gone to the house of a sinner as a guest.

8 But Zaccheus spoke to Jesus:

—The half of my goods, Lord, I give to the poor, and if I have cheated anyone, I will pay him back four times as much.

9 Looking at him Jesus said:

—Salvation has come to this house today, for he is also a
true son of Abraham. 10 The Son of Man has come to seek and
to save the lost.

Prayer in the garden

22 39 After this Jesus left to go as usual to Mount Olives
and the disciples followed him. 40 When he came to the place,
he told them:

—Pray that you may not be put to the test.

41 Then he went a little further, about a stone's throw, and kneeling down he prayed:

42 —Father, if it is your will, remove this cup from me; still not my will but yours be done.

43 And an angel from heaven appeared to give him strength.

44 As he was in agony, he prayed even more earnestly and great drops of blood formed like sweat and fell to the ground.

45 When he rose from prayer, he went to his disciples but found them worn out with grief, and asleep. 46 And he said to them:

—Why do you sleep? Get up and pray, so that you may not be put to the test.

The seize

47 Jesus was still speaking when a group appeared and the man named Judas, one of the Twelve, was leading them. He drew near to Jesus to kiss him, 48 and Jesus said to him:

—Did you need this kiss to betray the Son of Man?

49 Those with Jesus seeing what would happen, said to him:

—Master, shall we use the sword?

50 And one of them struck the High Priest's servant and cut off his right ear. 51 But Jesus stopped him:

—No more of this.

He touched the man's ear and healed him.

52 Then Jesus spoke to those coming against him, the chief priests, officers of the Temple and elders and he said to them:

—Did you really set out against a robber? Do you need swords and clubs to arrest me? 53 Day after day I was among you teaching in the Temple and you did not arrest me. But this is the hour of the power of darkness; this is your hour.

Peter's denial

54 Then they seized him and took him away, bringing him to the High Priest's house. Peter followed at a distance.

55 A fire was kindled in the middle of the courtyard where people gathered, and Peter sat among them. 56 A maidservant noticed him. Looking at him intently in the light of the fire, she exclaimed:

—This man also was with him!

57 But he denied it, saying:

—Woman, I do not know him.

58 A little later someone who saw him said:

—You are also one of them!

Peter replied:

—My friend, I am not!

59 After about an hour another asserted:

—Surely this man was with him, for he is a Galilean.

60 Again Peter denied:

—My friend, I don't know what you are talking about.

He had not finished saying this when a cock crowed. 61 The
Lord turned around and looked at Peter and he remembered
the word that the Lord had spoken: 'Before the cock crows
today you will have denied me three times.' 62 Peter went outside, weeping bitterly.

Crucifixion

23 33 There at the place called The Skull he was crucified
together with the criminals—one on his right and another on
his left. 34 Jesus said:

—Father, forgive them for they do not know what they do.

39 One of the criminals hanging with Jesus insulted him:

—So you are the Messiah? Save yourself and us as well!
40 But the other rebuked him, saying:

—Have you no fear of God, you who received the same
sentence as he did? 41 For us it is just: this is payment for what
we have done. But this man has done nothing wrong.

[42] And he said:

—Jesus, remember me when you come into your kingdom.
[43] Jesus replied:

—Truly, you will be with me today in paradise.

Death of Jesus

[44] It was now about noon. [45] The sun was hidden and darkness came over the whole land until mid-afternoon; and at
that time the curtain of the Sanctuary was torn in two. [46] Then
Jesus gave a loud cry:

—Father, into your hands I commend my spirit.

And saying that, he gave up his spirit.

The road to Emmaus

24 [13] That same day, two of them were going to Emmaus,
a village seven miles from Jerusalem, [14] and they talked about
what had happened. [15] While they were talking and wondering, Jesus came up and walked with them, [16] but their eyes
were held and they did not recognize him.

[17] He asked:

—What is this you are talking about?

The two stood still, looking sad. [18] Then one named Cleophas answered:

—Why, it seems you are the only traveler in Jerusalem who doesn't know what has happened there these past few days.

[19] And he asked:

—What is it?

They replied:

—It is about Jesus of Nazareth. He was a prophet, you
know, mighty in word and deed before God and the people.
[20] But the chief priests and our rulers sentenced him to death.
They handed him over to be crucified. [21] We had hoped that he
would redeem Israel. It is now the third day since all this took
place. [22] It is true that some women of our group have dis-

turbed us. When they went to the tomb at dawn, [23] they did not find his body; they came to tell us that they had seen a vision of angels who told them that Jesus was alive. [24] Some friends of our group went to the tomb and found everything just as the women had said, but they did not see him.

[25] He said to them:

—How dull you are, how slow of understanding! You fail to believe the message of the prophets. [26] Is it not written that the Christ should suffer all this and then enter his glory?

[27] Then, starting with Moses and going through the prophets, he explained to them everything in the Scriptures concerning himself.

[28] As they drew near the village they were heading for, Jesus made as if to go farther. [29] But they prevailed upon him:

—Stay with us, for night comes quickly. The day is now almost over.

So he went in to stay with them. [30] When they were at table, he took the bread, said a blessing, broke it and gave each a piece.

[31] Then their eyes were opened, and they recognized him; but he vanished out of their sight. [32] And they said to each other:

—Were not our hearts filled with ardent yearning when he was talking to us on the road and explaining the Scriptures?

[33] They immediately set out and returned to Jerusalem. There they found the Eleven and their companions gathered together. [34] They were greeted by these words:

—Yes, it is true, the Lord is risen! He has appeared to Simon!

[35] Then the two told what had happened on the road and how Jesus made himself known when he broke bread with them.

Apparition to the disciples

[50] Jesus led them almost as far as Bethany; then he lifted up his hands and blessed them. [51] And as he blessed them, he

withdrew (and was taken to heaven. They worshiped him).
52 They returned to Jerusalem full of joy and 53 were continually in the Temple praising God.

The Gospel According to John

Introduction

The book of John is very original; it is also a gospel but very different from the other three. It is written quite late, at the end of the Century: the Christian communities most probably already knew the other gospels. The author does not want to repeat them, instead he makes a profound theological reflection about Jesus, although without completely abandoning the aspect of "retelling the sayings and deeds of the Master." But the deeds are very few, just enough to give support to doctrine. And the doctrine is not the original one of Jesus, the parables, but long discourses where this doctrine is explained as a theological reflection.

The author presents himself as witness, and many events present in his gospel appear as told by a "personal witness". But most of what is being said is full of symbolisms, many of them taken from the Old Testament. The sacraments of the first Christian communities also appear here, baptism and the eucharist, being Jesus himself the one who makes reference to them.

We feel transported to another world while reading this gospel: the direct, simple style of the Synoptic gospels allowing us to understand them as a chronicle of Jesus' life, here becomes solemn, theological, and symbolic.

A very old tradition identifies the author with the apostle John, son of Zebedee. It is very possible that John's preaching be at the origin of this gospel. But its writing, as we have it today, is without doubt work of his disciples, some of whom were also called John.

Among the many famous fragments of this gospel we single out the splendid Prologue, being the proclamation and announcement of the whole message: Who is Jesus, the incarnate Word; and what is the human drama: to accept Jesus or to take refuge in darkness.

1 1 In the beginning was the Word.
And the Word was with God
and the Word was God;
2 he was in the beginning with God.
3 All things were made through him
and without him nothing came to be.
Whatever has come to be, 4 found life in him,
life which for humans was also light.
5 Light that shines in the dark:
light that darkness could not overcome.
9 For the Light was coming into the world,
the true Light that enlightens everyone.
10 He was already in the world
and through him the world was made,
the very world that did not know him.
11 He came to his own,
yet his own people did not receive him;
12 but all who have received him
he empowers to become children of God
for they believe in his Name.
13 These are born, but without seed
or carnal desire or will of man:
they are born of God.
14 And the Word was made flesh;
he had his tent pitched among us,
and we have seen his Glory,
the Glory of the only Son
coming from the Father:
fullness of truth and loving-kindness.

The first disciples

35 On the following day John was standing there again with two of his disciples. 36 As Jesus walked by, John looked at him and said:

—There is the Lamb of God.

37 On hearing this, the two disciples followed Jesus. 38 He
turned and saw them following, and he said to them:

—What are you looking for?

They answered:

—Rabbi (which means *Master*), where are you staying?

39 Jesus said:

—Come and see.

So they went and saw where he stayed and spent the rest of that day with him. It was about four o'clock in the afternoon.

40 Andrew, the brother of Simon Peter, was one of the two
who heard what John had said and followed Jesus. 41 Early the
next morning he found his brother Simon and said to him:

—We have found the Messiah (which means *the Christ*).

42 And he brought Simon to Jesus. Jesus looked at him and said:

—You are Simon, son of John, but you shall be called Cephas (which means *Rock*).

43 The next day, Jesus decided to set off for Galilee. He found Philip and said to him:

—Follow me.

44 Philip was from Bethsaida, the town of Andrew and
Peter. 45 Philip found Nathanael and said to him:

—We have found the one that Moses wrote about in the Law, and the prophets as well: he is Jesus, son of Joseph, from Nazareth.

46 Nathanael replied:

—Can anything good come from Nazareth?

Philip said to him:

—Come and see.

47 When Jesus saw Nathanael coming, he said of him:

—Here comes an Israelite, a true one; there is nothing false in him.

48 Nathanael asked him:

—How do you know me?

And Jesus said to him:

—Before Philip called you, you were under the fig tree and I saw you.

49 Nathanael answered:

—Master, you are the Son of God! You are the King of Israel!

50 But Jesus replied:

—You believe because I said: 'I saw you under the fig tree.'
But you will see greater things than that. 51 Truly, I say to you,
you will see the heavens opened and the angels of God ascending and descending upon the Son of Man.

The wedding at Cana

2 1 Three days later there was a wedding at Cana in
Galilee and the mother of Jesus was there. 2 Jesus was also
invited to the wedding with his disciples. 3 When all the wine
provided for the celebration had been served and they had run out of wine, the mother of Jesus said to him:

—They have no wine.

4 Jesus replied:

—Woman, what concern is that to you and me? My hour has not yet come.

5 However his mother said to the servants:

—Do whatever he tells you.

6 Nearby were six stone water jars meant for the ritual washing as practiced by the Jews; each jar could hold twenty
or thirty gallons. 7 Jesus said to the servants:

—Fill the jars with water.

And they filled them to the brim. 8 Then Jesus said:

—Now draw some out and take it to the steward.

So they did. 9 The steward tasted the water that had become wine, without knowing from where it had come; for only the servants who had drawn the water knew. So, he called the
bridegroom 10 to tell him:

—Everyone serves the best wine first and when people have drunk enough, he serves that which is ordinary. Instead you have kept the best wine until the end.

11 This miraculous sign was the first, and Jesus performed it at Cana in Galilee. In this way he let his Glory appear and his disciples believed in him.

12 After this, Jesus went down to Capernaum with his mother, his brothers and his disciples; and they stayed there for a few days.

Jesus and the Samaritan woman

4 Jesus 4 had to cross Samaria.

5 He came to a Samaritan town called Sychar, near the land
that Jacob had given to his son Joseph. 6 Jacob's well is there.
Tired from his journey, Jesus sat down by the well; it was
about noon. 7 Now a Samaritan woman came to draw water
and Jesus said to her:

—Give me a drink.

8 His disciples had just gone into town to buy some food.

9 The Samaritan woman said to him:

—How is it that you, a Jew, ask me, a Samaritan and a woman, for a drink? (For Jews, in fact, have no dealings with Samaritans)

10 Jesus replied:

—If you only knew the Gift of God! If you knew who it is that asks you for a drink, you yourself would have asked me and I would have given you living water.

11 The woman answered:

—Sir, you have no bucket and this well is deep; where is
your living water? 12 Are you greater than our ancestor Jacob,
who gave us this well after he drank from it himself, together with his sons and his cattle?

13 Jesus said to her:

—Those who drink of this water will be thirsty again; 14 but
those who drink of the water that I shall give will never be thirsty; for the water that I shall give will become in them a spring of water welling up to eternal life.

15 The woman said to him:

—Give me this water, that I may never be thirsty and never have to come here to draw water.

25 The woman said to him:

—I know that the Messiah, that is the Christ, is coming; when he comes, he will tell us everything.

26 And Jesus said:

—I who am talking to you, I am he.

27 At this point the disciples returned and were surprised that Jesus was speaking with a woman; however, no one said, 'What do you want?' or: 'Why are you talking with her?'

31 In the meantime the disciples urged Jesus:

—Master, eat.

32 But he said to them:

—I have food to eat that you don't know about.

33 And the disciples wondered:

—Has anyone brought him food?

34 Jesus said to them:

—My food is to do the will of the One who sent me and to
carry out his work. 35 You say that in four more months it will
be the harvest; now, I say to you, look up and see the fields
white and ready for harvesting. 36 People who reap the harvest
are paid for their work, and the fruit is gathered for eternal
life, so that sower and reaper may rejoice together. 37 Indeed
the saying holds true: 'One sows and another reaps.' 38 I sent
you to reap where you didn't work or suffer; others have
worked and you are now sharing in their labors.

39 In that town many Samaritans believed in him when they heard the woman who declared:

—He told me everything I did.

40 So, when they came to him, they asked him to stay with
them and Jesus stayed there two days. 41 After that many more
believed because of his own words 42 and they said to the
woman:

—We no longer believe because of what you told us; for we have heard for ourselves and we know that this is the Savior of the world.

43 When the two days were over, Jesus left for Galilee.

The bread of life

6 22 Next day the people who had stayed on the other side realized that only one boat had been there and that Jesus had not entered it with his disciples; rather, the disciples had gone away alone. When they found him on the other side of the lake, they asked him, 30 They then said:

—Show us miraculous signs, that we may see and believe you. What sign do you perform? 31 Our ancestors ate manna in the desert; as Scripture says: *They were given bread from heaven to eat.*

32 Jesus then said to them:

—Truly, I say to you, it was not Moses who gave you the *bread from heaven.* My Father gives you the true *bread from heaven.* 33 The bread God gives is the One who comes from heaven and gives life to the world.

34 And they said to him:

—Give us this bread always.

35 Jesus said to them:

—I am the bread of life; whoever comes to me shall never be hungry, and whoever believes in me shall never be thirsty.
50 But here you have the *bread which comes from heaven* so that
you may eat of it and not die. 51 I am the living *bread which has come from heaven;* whoever eats of this bread will live forever. The bread I shall give is my flesh and I will give it for the life of the world.

54 The one who eats my flesh and drinks my blood lives with eternal life and I will raise him up on the last day.

55 My flesh is really food and my blood is drink. 56 Those who eat my flesh and drink my blood, live in me and I in them.

66 After this many disciples withdrew and no longer followed him. 67 Jesus asked the Twelve:

—Will you also go away?

68 Peter answered him:

—Lord, to whom shall we go? You have the words of eternal life. 69 We now believe and know that you are the Holy One of God.

Forgives the adulteress

8 1 As for Jesus, he went to the Mount of Olives. 2 At day-

break Jesus appeared in the Temple again. All the people came
to him, and he sat down and began to teach them.

3 Then the teachers of the Law and the Pharisees brought in
a woman who had been caught in the act of adultery. They
made her stand in front of everyone.

4 They said:

—Master, this woman has been caught in the act of adultery. 5 Now the Law of Moses orders that such women be
stoned to death; but you, what do you say?

6 They said this to test Jesus, in order to have some charge
against him.

Jesus bent down and started writing on the ground with
his finger. 7 And as they continued to ask him, he straightened
up and said to them:

—Let anyone among you who has no sin be the first to
throw a stone at her.

8 And he bent down again, writing on the ground.

9 As a result of these words, they went away, one by one,
starting with the elders, and Jesus was left alone with the
woman standing before him. 10 Then Jesus stood up and said
to her:

—Woman, where are they? Has no one condemned you?

11 She replied:

—No one.

And Jesus said:

—Neither do I condemn you; go away and don't sin again.

Healing a blind man

9 1 As Jesus walked along, he saw a man who had been
blind from birth. 2 His disciples asked him:

—Master, was he born blind because of a sin of his, or of his
parents?

3 Jesus answered:

—Neither was it for his own sin nor for his parents'. He
was born blind so that God's power might be shown in him.
4 While it is day we must do the work of the One who sent me;

for the night will come when no one can work. [5] As long as I am in the world, I am the light of the world.

[6] As Jesus said this, he made paste with spittle and clay and rubbed it on the eyes of the blind man. [7] Then he said:

—Go and wash in the Pool of Siloam. (This name means *sent*)

So he went and washed and came back able to see. [8] His neighbors and all the people who used to see him begging, wondered. They said:

—Isn't this the beggar who used to sit here?

[9] Some said:

—It's the one.

Others said:

—No, but he looks like him.

But the man himself said:

—I am the one.

[10] Then they asked:

—How is it that your eyes were opened?

[11] And he answered:

—The man called Jesus made a mud paste, put it on my eyes and said to me: 'Go to Siloam and wash.' So I went, and washed, and I could see.

[12] They asked:

—Where is he?

And the man answered:

—I don't know.

[13] The people brought the man who had been blind to the Pharisees. [14] Now it was a sabbath day when Jesus made mud paste and opened his eyes. [15] The Pharisees asked him again:

—How did you recover your sight?

And he said:

—He put paste on my eyes, and I washed, and now I see. [16] Some of the Pharisees said:

—This man is not from God, for he works on the Sabbath. But others wondered:

—How can a sinner perform such miraculous signs?

They were divided [17] and they questioned the blind man again:

—What do you think of this man who opened your eyes? And he answered:

—He is a prophet.

[18] After all this, the Jews refused to believe that the man had been blind and had recovered his sight; so they called his parents [19] and asked them:

—Is this your son? You say that he was born blind, how is it that he now sees?

[20] The parents answered:

—He really is our son and he was born blind; [21] but how it is that he now sees, we don't know, neither do we know who opened his eyes. Ask him, he is old enough. Let him speak for himself.

[22] The parents said this because they feared the Jews who had already agreed that whoever confessed Jesus to be the Christ was to be expelled. [23] Because of this his parents said: 'He is old enough, ask him.'

[24] So a second time the Pharisees called the man who had been blind, and they said to him:

—Tell us the truth; we know that this man is a sinner. [25] He replied:

—I don't know whether he is a sinner or not; I only know that I was blind and now I see.

[26] They said to him:

—What did he do to you? How did he open your eyes?

[27] He replied:

—I have told you already and you would not listen. Why do you want to hear it again? Do you also want to become his disciples?

[28] Then they started to insult him.

—Become his disciple yourself! We are disciples of Moses. [29] We know that God has spoken to Moses, but as for this man we don't know where he comes from.

[30] The man replied:

—It is amazing that you don't know where the man comes

from, and yet he opened my eyes! 31 We know that God does-
n't listen to sinners, but if anyone honors God and does his
will, God listens to him. 32 Never, since the world began, has it
been heard that anyone opened the eyes of a person who was
born blind. 33 If this man were not from God, he could do nothing.

34 They answered him:

—You were born a sinner and now you teach us!

And they expelled him.

35 Jesus heard that they had expelled him. He found him and said:

—Do you believe in the Son of Man?

36 He answered:

—Who is he, that I may believe in him?

37 Jesus said:

—You have seen him and he is speaking to you.

38 He said:

—Lord, I believe.

And he worshiped him.

39 Jesus said:

—I came into this world to carry out a judgment: Those who do not see shall see, and those who see shall become blind.

40 Some Pharisees stood by and asked him:

—So we are blind?

41 And Jesus answered:

—If you were blind, you would not be guilty. Now you say: 'We see'; this is the proof of your sin.

The good shepherd

10 11 —I am the good shepherd. The good shepherd gives
his life for the sheep. 12 Not so the hired hand or any other person who is not the shepherd and to whom the sheep do not
belong. They abandon the sheep as soon as they see the wolf
coming; then the wolf snatches and scatters the sheep. 13 This

is because the hired hand works for pay and cares nothing for
the sheep.
14 —I am the good shepherd. I know my own and my own
know me.

Resurrects Lazarus

11 1 There was a sick man named Lazarus who was from
Bethany, the village of Mary and her sister Martha.
17 When Jesus came, he found that Lazarus had been in the
tomb for four days. 20 When Martha heard that Jesus was coming, she went to meet him while Mary remained sitting in the
house. 21 And she said to Jesus:
—If you had been here, my brother would not have died.
22 But I know that whatever you ask from God, God will give
you.
23 Jesus said:
—Your brother will rise again.
24 Martha replied:
—I know that he will rise in the resurrection, at the last day.
25 But Jesus said to her:
—I am the resurrection; whoever believes in me, though he
die, shall live. 26 Whoever lives and believes in me will never
die. Do you believe this?
27 Martha then answered:
—Yes, *Lord,* I have come to believe that you are the Christ,
the Son of God, he who is coming into the world.
28 After that Martha went and called her sister Mary secretly, saying:
—The Master is here and is calling for you.
29 As soon as Mary heard this, she rose and went to him.
30 Jesus had not yet come into the village, but was still in the
place where Martha had met him. 32 As for Mary, when she
came to the place where Jesus was and saw him, she fell at his
feet and said:
—*Lord,* if you had been here, my brother would not have
died.

33 When Jesus saw her weeping and the Jews also who had come with her, he was moved in the depths of his spirit and troubled. 34 Then he asked:

—Where have you laid him?

They answered:

—*Lord,* come and see.

39 Jesus ordered:

—Take the stone away.

Martha said to him:

—*Lord,* by now he will smell, for this is the fourth day.

40 Jesus replied:

—Have I not told you that if you believe, you will see the glory of God?

41 So they removed the stone.

Jesus lifted up his eyes and 43 cried out in a loud voice:

—Lazarus, come out!

44 The dead man came out, his hands and feet bound with linen strips and his face wrapped in a cloth. So Jesus said to them:

—Untie him and let him go.

47 So the chief priests and the Pharisees called the Sanhedrin Council. They said:

—What are we to do? For this man keeps on giving miraculous signs.

54 Because of this, Jesus no longer moved about freely among the Jews. He withdrew instead to the country near the wilderness and stayed with his disciples in a town called Ephraim.

Washes the disciple's feet

13 1 It was before the feast of the Passover. Jesus realized that his hour had come to pass from this world to the Father, and as he had loved those who were his own in the world, he would love them with perfect love.

[2]They were at supper and the devil had already put into
the mind of Judas, son of Simon Iscariot, to betray. [3]Jesus
knew that the Father had entrusted all things to him, and as
he had come from God, he was going to God. [4]So he got up
from table, removed his garment and taking a towel, wrapped
it around his waist. [5]Then he poured water into a basin and
began to wash the disciples' feet and to wipe them with the
towel he was wearing.

[6]When he came to Simon Peter, Simon said to him:

—Why, *Lord,* you want to wash my feet!

[7]Jesus said:

—What I am doing you cannot understand now, but afterwards you will understand it.

[8]Peter replied:

—You shall never wash my feet.

Jesus answered him:

—If I do not wash you, you can have no part with me.
[9]Then Simon Peter said:

—*Lord,* wash not only my feet, but also my hands and my head!

[10]Jesus replied:

—Whoever has taken a bath does not need to wash (except the feet), for he is clean all over. You are clean, though not all of you.

[11]Jesus knew who was to betray him; because of this he
said, "Not all of you are clean. [12]When Jesus had finished
washing their feet, he put on his garment again, went back to
the table and said to them:

—Do you understand what I have done to you? [13]You call
me Master and *Lord,* and you are right, for so I am. [14]If I, then,
your *Lord* and Master, have washed your feet, you also must
wash one another's feet. [15]I have just given you an example
that as I have done, you also may do. [16]Truly, I say to you, the
servant is not greater than his master, nor is the messenger
greater than he who sent him.

[17]Understand this, and blessed are you if you put it into practice.

Announces the treason

21 After saying this, Jesus was distressed in spirit and said plainly:

—Truly, one of you will betray me.

22 The disciples then looked at one another, wondering who he meant. 23 One of the disciples, the one Jesus loved, was reclining near Jesus; 24 so Simon Peter signaled him to ask Jesus whom he meant. 25 And the disciple who was reclining near Jesus asked him:

—*Lord,* who is it?

26 Jesus answered:

—I shall dip a piece of bread in the dish, and he to whom I give it, is the one.

So Jesus dipped the bread and gave it to Judas Iscariot, the son of Simon. 27 And as Judas took the piece of bread, Satan entered into him. Jesus then said to him:

—What you are going to do, do quickly.

31 When Judas had gone out, Jesus said:

—Now is the Son of Man glorified and God is glorified in him. 34 Now I give you a new commandment: love one another. Just as I have loved you, you also must love one another. 35 By this everyone will know that you are my disciples, if you have love for one another.

Promise of the Spirit

14 25 —I told you all this while I was still with you. 26 From now on the Helper, the Holy Spirit whom the Father will send in my name, will teach you all things and remind you of all that I have told you.

27 Peace be with you; I give you my peace. Not as the world gives peace do I give it to you. Do not be troubled; do not be afraid.

15 12 This is my commandment: love one another as I have loved you. 13 There is no greater love than this, to give

one's life for one's friends; 14 and you are my friends if you do
what I command you.

15 I shall not call you servants any more, because servants
do not know what their master is about. Instead I have called
you friends, since I have made known to you everything I
learned from my Father.

16 You did not choose me; it was I who chose you and sent
you to go and *bear fruit,* fruit that will last. And everything you
ask the Father in my name, he will give you.

17 This is my command, that you love one another.

The work of the Spirit

16 13 —When he, the Spirit of truth comes, he will guide
you into the whole truth.

Condemned to death

19 1 Pilate had Jesus taken away and scourged. 2 The soldiers also twisted thorns into a crown and put it on his head.
They threw a cloak of royal purple around his shoulders 3 and
began coming up to him and saluting him:

—Hail, king of the Jews.

And they struck him on the face.

Crucifixion

25 Near the cross of Jesus stood his mother, his mother's sister Mary, who was the wife of Cleophas, and Mary of
Magdala. 26 When Jesus saw the Mother, and the disciple
whom he loved, he said to the Mother:

—Woman, this is your son.

27 Then he said to the disciple:

—There is your mother.

And from that moment the disciple took her to his own
home.

Death of Jesus

28 With that Jesus knew all was now finished and he said:
—*I am thirsty*
29 A jar full of bitter wine stood there; so, putting a sponge
soaked in the wine on a twig of hyssop, they raised it to his
lips. 30 Jesus took the wine and said:
—It is accomplished.
Then he bowed his head and gave up the spirit.
31 As it was Preparation Day, the Jews did not want the bodies to remain on the cross during the Sabbath, for this Sabbath
was a very solemn day. They asked Pilate to have the legs of the
condemned men broken, so they might take away the bodies.
32 The soldiers came and broke the legs of the first man and of
the other who had been crucified with Jesus. 33 When they came
to Jesus, they saw that he was already dead; so they did not
break his legs. 34 One of the soldiers, however, pierced his side
with a lance and immediately there came out blood and water.
35 The one who has seen here gives his witness so that you
may believe: his witness is true and He knows that he speaks
the truth. 36 All this happened to fulfill the words of Scripture,
Not one of his bones shall be broken. 37 Another text says: *They
shall look on him whom they have pierced.*

Appearance to Mary Magdalene

20 11 Mary stood weeping outside the tomb, and as she
wept she bent down to look inside; 12 she saw two angels in

white sitting where the body of Jesus had been, one at the head, and the other at the feet. 13 They said:

—Woman, why are you weeping?

She answered:

—Because they have taken my *Lord* and I don't know where they have put him.

14 As she said this, she turned around and saw Jesus standing there, but she did not recognize him. 15 Jesus said to her:

—Woman, why are you weeping? Who are you looking for? She thought it was the gardener and answered him:

—*Lord*, if you have taken him away, tell me where you have put him, and I will go and remove him.

16 Jesus said to her:

—Mary!

She turned and said to him:

—Rabboni (which means, *Master).*

17 Jesus said to her:

—Do not cling to me; you see I have not yet ascended to the Father. But go to my brothers and say to them: I am ascending to my Father, who is your Father, to my God, who is your God.

18 So Mary of Magdala went and announced to the disciples:

—I have seen the *Lord,* and this is what he said to me.

Appearance to the disciples

19 On the evening of that day, the first day after the Sabbath, the doors were locked where the disciples were, because of their fear of the Jews, but Jesus came and stood in their midst. He said to them:

—Peace be with you.

20 Then he showed them his hands and his side. The disciples kept looking at the *Lord* and were full of joy.

21 Again Jesus said to them:

—Peace be with you. As the Father has sent me, so I send you.

[22] After saying this he breathed on them and said to them:

—Receive the Holy Spirit; [23] for those whose sins you forgive, they are forgiven; for those whose sins you retain, they are retained.

[24] Thomas, the Twin, one of the Twelve, was not with them
when Jesus came. [25] The other disciples told him:

—We have seen the *Lord.*

But he replied:

—Until I have seen in his hands the print of the nails, and put my finger in the mark of the nails and my hand in his side, I will not believe.

[26] Eight days later, the disciples were inside again and Thomas was with them. Despite the locked doors Jesus came and stood in their midst and said:

—Peace be with you.

[27] Then he said to Thomas:

—Put your finger here and see my hands; stretch out your hand and put it into my side. Resist no longer and be a believer.

[28] Thomas then said:

—You are my *Lord* and my God.

[29] Jesus replied:

—You believe because you see me, don't you? Happy are those who have not seen and believe.

[30] There were many other signs that Jesus gave in the presence of his disciples, but they are not recorded in this book.
[31] These are recorded so that you may believe that Jesus is the Christ, the Son of God; believe and you will have life through his Name.

Appearance by the lake

21 [1] After this Jesus revealed himself to the disciples by
the Lake of Tiberias. He appeared to them in this way. [2] Simon
Peter, Thomas who was called the Twin, Nathanael of Cana in Galilee, the sons of Zebedee and two other disciples were
together; [3] and Simon Peter said to them:

—I'm going fishing.

They replied:

—We will come with you.

And they went out and got into the boat, but they caught nothing that night. [4] When day had already broken, Jesus was standing on the shore, but the disciples did not know that it was Jesus. [5] Jesus called them:

—Children, have you anything to eat?

They answered:

—Nothing.

[6] Then he said to them:

—Throw the net on the right side of the boat and you will find some.

When they had lowered the net, they were not able to pull it in because of the great number of fish.

[7] Then the disciple Jesus loved said to Peter:

—It's the Lord!

At these words, 'It's the Lord,' Simon Peter put on his clothes, for he was stripped for work, and jumped into the water. [8] The other disciples came in the boat dragging the net full of fish; they were not far from land, about a hundred meters.

[9] When they landed, they saw a charcoal fire with fish on it, and some bread. [10] Jesus said to them:

—Bring some of the fish you've just caught.

[11] So Simon Peter climbed into the boat and pulled the net to shore. It was full of big fish—one hundred and fifty-three—but, in spite of this, the net was not torn.

[12] Jesus said to them:

—Come and have breakfast.

And not one of the disciples dared ask him, 'Who are you?' for they knew it was the Lord. [13] Jesus then came and took the bread and gave it to them, and he did the same with the fish.

[14] This was the third time that Jesus revealed himself to his disciples after rising from the dead.

[15] After they had finished breakfast, Jesus said to Simon Peter:

—Simon, son of John, do you love me more than these?

He answered:

—Yes, Lord, you know that I love you.

And Jesus said:

—Feed my lambs.

16 A second time Jesus said to him:

—Simon, son of John, do you love me?

And Peter answered:

—Yes, Lord, you know that I love you.

Jesus said to him:

—Look after my sheep.

17 And a third time he said to him:

—Simon, son of John, do you love me?

Peter was saddened because Jesus asked him a third time, 'Do you love me?' and he said:

—Lord, you know everything; you know that I love you.

Jesus then said:

—Feed my sheep. 18 Truly, I say to you, when you were young you put on your belt and walked where you liked. But when you grow old, you will stretch out your hands and another will put a belt around you and lead you where you do not wish to go.

19 Jesus said this to make known the kind of death by which Peter was to glorify God. And he added:

—Follow me.

20 Peter looked back and saw that the disciple Jesus loved
was following as well, the one who had reclined close to Jesus
at the supper and had asked him, 'Lord, who is to betray you?'
21 On seeing him Peter asked Jesus:

—Lord, what about him?

22 Jesus answered:

—If I want him to remain until I come, does that concern you? Follow me.

23 Because of this the rumor spread in the community that this disciple would not die. Yet Jesus had not said to Peter, 'He will not die,' but 'suppose I want him to remain until I come.'

24 It is this disciple who testifies about the things he has
recorded here and we know that his testimony is true.

Acts of the Apostles

Introduction

The Book of the Acts of the Apostles is the second part of the gospel of Luke. It is a unique work in the New Testament, of great historical value, even though we find elements typical of the time, like the discourses that are literary creation of the author, though reflecting without doubt what was said. History is also idealized: attention centers in the marvelous work of the Spirit in those communities, more than in concrete life. Nevertheless it does not hide the difficulties, and even the mistakes and wrongdoings of the apostles themselves.

Even if it appears that the main actors are the apostles, and even more, all the members of the first communities, the first part of the book centers on Peter, while the second part has Paul as the main protagonist.

This history therefore narrates the marvelous expansion of the church, not simply in its exterior, geographical dimension, but mainly in its interior dimension: how the Spirit works to make the church understand better the message of Jesus. The most salient thesis of the book has to do with one of the main concerns of the followers of Jesus at that time: if the norms of the Old Testament were still applicable or if, on the contrary, what Jesus brought was "new wine", through which the old molds were no longer applicable. The historical circumstance that provoked this controversy was the conversion of many pagans. Paul will be the champion of the independence of Christians in relationship with the Old Law.

Promise of the Holy Spirit

1 [4]Once when he had been eating with them, he told them:

—Do not leave Jerusalem but wait for the fulfillment of the Father's promise about which I have spoken to you: [5]John baptized with water, but you will be baptized with the Holy Spirit within a few days.

Ascension

[9]After Jesus said this, he was taken up before their eyes and a cloud hid him from their sight. [10]While they were still looking up to heaven where he went, suddenly, two men dressed in white stood beside them [11]and said:

—Men of Galilee, why do you stand here looking up at the sky? This Jesus who has been taken from you into heaven, will return in the same way as you have seen him go there.

Election of Matthias

12 Then they returned to Jerusalem from the Mount called
Olives, which is a fifteen-minute walk away. 13 On entering
the city they went to the room upstairs where they were staying. Present there were Peter, John, James and Andrew; Philip
and Thomas, Bartholomew and Matthew, James, son of
Alpheus; Simon the Zealot and Judas son of James. 14 All of
these together gave themselves to constant prayer. With them
were some women and also Mary, the mother of Jesus, and
his brothers.

15 It was during this time that Peter stood up in the midst
of the community—about one hundred and twenty in all—
16 and he said:

—Brothers, it was necessary that the Scriptures referring to
Judas be fulfilled. The Holy Spirit had spoken through David
about the one who would lead the crowd coming to arrest
Jesus. 17 He was one of our number and had been called to
share our common ministry. 21 Therefore we must choose
someone from among those who were with us during all the
time that the Lord Jesus moved about with us, 22 beginning
with John's baptism until the day when Jesus was taken away
from us. One of these has to become, with us, a witness to his
resurrection.

23 Then they proposed two: Joseph, called Barsabbas, also
known as Justus, and Matthias. 24 They prayed:

—You know, Lord, what is in the hearts of all. Show us,
therefore, which of the two you have chosen 25 to replace Judas
in this apostolic ministry which he deserted to go to the place
he deserved.

26 Then they drew lots between the two and the choice fell
on Matthias who was added to the eleven apostles.

Pentecost

2 1 When the day of Pentecost came, they were all together in one place. 2 And suddenly out of the sky came a sound
like a strong rushing wind and it filled the whole house where
they were sitting. There appeared 3 tongues as if of fire which

parted and came to rest upon each one of them. [4] All were filled with Holy Spirit and began to speak other languages, as the Spirit enabled them to speak.

[5] Staying in Jerusalem were religious Jews from every nation under heaven. [6] When they heard this sound, a crowd gathered, all excited because each heard them speaking in his own language. [7] Full of amazement and wonder, they asked:

—Are not all these who are speaking Galileans? [8] How is it that we hear them in our own native language?

[12] They were amazed and greatly confused, and they kept asking one another:

—What does this mean?

[13] But others laughed and said:

—These people are drunk.

[14] Then Peter stood up with the Eleven and, with a loud voice, addressed them:

—Fellow Jews and all foreigners now staying in Jerusalem, listen to what I have to say. [15] These people are not drunk as you suppose, for it is only nine o'clock in the morning. [16] Indeed what the prophet Joel spoke about has happened: [17] *In the last days, God says, I will pour out my Spirit on every mortal. Your sons and daughters will speak through the Holy Spirit; your young men will see visions and your old men will have dreams.*

[18] *In those days I will pour out my Spirit even on my servants, both men and women, and they will be prophets.*

[22] Fellow Israelites, listen to what I am going to tell you about Jesus of Nazareth. God accredited him and through him did powerful deeds and wonders and signs in your midst, as you well know. [23] You delivered him to sinners to be crucified and killed, and in this way the purpose of God from all times was fulfilled. [24] But God raised him to life and released him from the pain of death, because it was impossible for him to be held in the power of death. [32] This Messiah is Jesus and we are all witnesses that God raised him to life. [33] He has been exalted at God's right side and the Father has entrusted the Holy Spirit to him; this Spirit he has just poured upon us as you now see and hear. [36] Let Israel then know for sure that God has made Lord and Christ this Jesus whom you crucified.

41 So those who accepted his word were baptized; some
three thousand persons were added to their number that
day. 42 They were faithful to the teaching of the apostles, the
common life of sharing, the breaking of bread and the prayers.

43 A holy fear came upon all the people, for many wonders
and miraculous signs were done by the apostles. 44 Now all the
believers lived together and shared all their belongings.
45 They would sell their property and all they had and distribute the proceeds to others according to their need. 46 Each day
they met together in the Temple area; they broke bread in their
homes; they shared their food with great joy and simplicity of
heart; 47 they praised God and won the people's favor. And
every day the Lord added to their number those who were
being saved.

The seven deacons

6 1 In those days, as the number of disciples grew, the so-
called *Hellenists* complained against the so-called *Hebrews,*
because their widows were being neglected in the daily distribution. 2 So the Twelve summoned the whole body of disciples
together and said:

—It is not right that we should neglect the word of God to
serve at tables. 3 So, friends, choose from among yourselves
seven respected men full of Spirit and wisdom, that we may
appoint them to this task. 4 As for us, we shall give ourselves
to prayer and to the ministry of the Word.

5 The whole community agreed and they chose Stephen, a
man full of faith and Holy Spirit; Philip, Prochorus, Nicanor,
Timon, Parmenus and Nicolaus of Antioch who was a prose-
lyte. 6 They presented these men to the apostles who first
prayed over them and then laid hands upon them.

Stephen, detained

8 Stephen, full of grace and power, did great wonders and
miraculous signs among the people. 11 As they were unable to
face the truth, they bribed some men to say:

—We heard him speak against Moses and against God.

[12] So they stirred up the people, the elders and the teachers
of the Law; they took him by surprise, seized him and brought
him before the Council. [13] Then they produced false witnesses
who said:

—This man never stops speaking against our Holy Place
and the Law. [14] We even heard him say that Jesus the Nazarean
will destroy our Holy Place and change the customs which
Moses handed down to us

Stephen's discourse

7 [1] So the High Priest asked him:

—Is it true?

He answered:

[51] —You are a stubborn people, you hardened your hearts
and closed your ears. You have always resisted the Holy Spirit
just as your fathers did. [52] Was there a prophet whom your
ancestors did not persecute? They killed those who
announced the coming of the Just One whom you have now
betrayed and murdered, [53] you who received the Law through
the angels but did not fulfill it.

Stephen's death

[54] When they heard this reproach, they were enraged and
they gnashed their teeth against Stephen. [55] But he, full of the
Holy Spirit, fixed his eyes on heaven and saw the glory of God
and Jesus at God's right hand, [56] so he declared:

—I see the heavens open and the Son of Man at the right hand of God.

[57] But they shouted and covered their ears with their hands
and rushed together upon him. [58] They brought him out of the
city and stoned him, and the witnesses laid down their cloaks
at the feet of a young man named Saul. [59] As they were ston-
ing him, Stephen prayed saying:

—Lord Jesus, receive my spirit.

60 Then he knelt down and said in a loud voice:

—Lord, do not hold this sin against them.

And when he had said this, he died

8 1 Saul was there, approving his murder.

Conversion of Saul

9 1 Meanwhile Saul considered nothing but violence and
death for the disciples of the Lord. 2 He went to the High Priest
and asked him for letters to the synagogues of Damascus that
would authorize him to arrest and bring to Jerusalem anyone
he might find, man or woman, belonging to the Way.

3 As he traveled along and was approaching Damascus, a
light from the sky suddenly flashed around him. 4 He fell to
the ground and heard a voice saying to him:

—Saul, Saul! Why do you persecute me?

5 And he asked:

—Who are you, Lord?

The voice replied:

—I am Jesus whom you persecute. 6 Now get up and go
into the city; there you will be told what you are to do.

7 The men who were traveling with him stood there
speechless: they had heard the sound, but could see no one.
8 Saul got up from the ground and, opening his eyes, he could
not see. They took him by the hand and brought him to
Damascus. 9 He was blind and he did not eat or drink for
three days.

10 There was a disciple in Damascus named Ananias, to
whom the Lord called in a vision:

—Ananias!

He answered:

—Here I am, Lord!

11 Then the Lord said to him:

—Go at once to Straight Street and ask, at the house of Judas, for a man of Tarsus named Saul. You will find him praying, 12 for he has just seen in a vision that a man named Ananias has come in and placed his hands upon him, to restore
his sight.

13 Ananias answered:

—Lord, I have heard from many sources about this man
and all the harm he has done to your saints in Jerusalem,
14 and now he is here with authority from the High Priest to
arrest all who call upon your name.

15 But the Lord said to him:

—Go! This man is my chosen instrument to bring my name
to the pagan nations and their kings, and the people of Israel
as well. 16 I myself will show him how much he will have to
suffer for my name.

17 So Ananias left and went to the house. He laid his hands
upon Saul and said:

—Saul, my brother, the Lord Jesus, who appeared to you
on your way here, has sent me to you so that you may receive
your sight and be filled with Holy Spirit. 18 Immediately something like scales fell from his eyes and he could see; he got up
and was baptized. 19 Then he took food and was strengthened.

For several days Saul stayed with the disciples at
Damascus, 20 and he soon began to proclaim in the synagogues that Jesus was the Son of God. 21 All who heard were
astonished and said:

—Is this not the one who cast out in Jerusalem all those calling upon this Name? Did he not come here to bring them bound before the chief priests?

22 But Saul grew more and more powerful, and he confounded the Jews living in Damascus when he proved that Jesus was the Messiah.

23 After a fairly long time, the Jews conspired together to
kill him. 24 But Saul became aware of their plan: Day and night
they kept watch at the city gate in order to kill him. 25 So his
disciples took him one night and let him down from the top of
the wall, lowering him in a basket.

Saul in Jerusalem

26 When Saul came to Jerusalem, he tried to join the disciples there, but they were afraid of him because they could not
believe that he was a disciple. 27 But Barnabas took him and
brought him to the apostles. He recounted to them how Saul had seen the Lord on his way and the words the Lord had spoken to him. He told them also how Saul had preached boldly in the name of Jesus.

31 Meanwhile, the Church had peace. It was building up throughout all Judea and Galilee and Samaria with eyes turned to the Lord and filled with comfort from the Holy Spirit.

Healing and resurrection

32 As Peter traveled around, he went to visit the saints who
lived in Lydda. 33 There he found a man named Aeneas who
was paralyzed, and had been bedridden for eight years.
34 Peter said to him:

—Aeneas, Jesus Christ heals you, get up and make your bed!

And the man got up at once.

42 This became known throughout all of Joppa and many people believed in the Lord because of it.

Peter and Cornelius

10 1 There was in Caesarea a man named Cornelius, captain of what was called the Italian Battalion. 2 He was a religious
and God-fearing man together with his whole household. He
gave generously to the people and constantly prayed to God.

3 One afternoon at about three he had a vision in which he
clearly saw an angel of God coming towards him and calling
him:

—Cornelius!

4 He stared at the vision with awe and said:

—What is it, sir?

And the angel answered:

—Your prayers and your alms have just been recalled
before God. 5 Now send some men to Joppa and summon a
certain Simon also known as Peter; 6 he is the guest of Simon,
a tanner, who lives beside the sea.

7 As soon as the angel who spoke to him departed,
Cornelius called two of his servants and a devout soldier from
among those attached to his service, 8 and after having
explained everything to them, he sent them to Joppa.

9 The next day, while they were on their journey and
approaching the city, Peter went up to the roof at about noon
to pray. 10 He became hungry and wished to eat, but while
they were preparing food, he fell into a trance. 11 The heavens
were opened to him and he saw an object that looked like a
large sheet coming down, until it rested on the ground by its
four corners. 12 In it were all kinds of four-legged animals of
the earth, reptiles and birds.

13 Then a voice said to him:

—Get up, Peter, kill and eat!

14 But Peter replied:

—Certainly not, Lord! I have never eaten any defiled or
unclean creature.

15 And again a second time the voice spoke:

—What God has made clean, you must not call unclean.
16 This happened three times and then the sheet was taken up
again into the sky.

17 While Peter was still puzzling over the meaning of the
vision he had seen, the messengers of Cornelius arrived at the
gate asking for the house of Simon. 18 They called out to
inquire whether Simon, also known as Peter, was staying
there. 19 At that moment, as Peter continued pondering on the
vision, the Spirit spoke to him:

—There are men looking for you; 20 get up and go down-
stairs and follow them without hesitation, for I have sent
them.

21 So Peter went and said to the men:

—I am the one you are looking for. What brings you here?

They answered:

22 —He who sent us is Captain Cornelius. He is an upright
and God-fearing man, well respected by all the Jewish people.
He has been instructed by a holy angel to summon you to his
house, so that he may listen to what you have to say.

23 So Peter invited them in and put them up for the night.
The next day he went off with them and some of the believers
from Joppa accompanied him. 24 The following day, he arrived
in Caesarea where Cornelius was expecting them; he had
called together his relatives and close friends. 25 As Peter was
about to enter, Cornelius went to him, fell on his knees and
bowed low. 26 But Peter lifted him up saying:

—Stand up, for I too am a human being.

Peter's discourse

34 Peter then spoke to them:

—Truly, I realize that God does not show partiality, 35 but in
all nations he listens to everyone who fears God and does
good. 36 And this is the message he has sent to the children of
Israel, the good news of peace he has proclaimed through
Jesus Christ, who is the Lord of all. 37 No doubt you have
heard of the event that occurred throughout the whole country of the Jews, beginning from Galilee, after the baptism John
preached. 38 You know how God anointed Jesus the Nazarean
with Holy Spirit and power. He went about doing good and
healing all who were under the devil's power, because God

was with him; [39] we are witnesses of all that he did throughout the country of the Jews and in Jerusalem itself. Yet they put him to death by hanging him on a wooden cross.

[40] But God raised him to life on the third day and let him manifest himself, [41] not to all the people, but to the witnesses that were chosen beforehand by God—to us who ate and drank with him after his resurrection from death. [42] And he commanded us to preach to the people and to bear witness that he is the one appointed by God to judge the living and the dead.

[44] Peter was still speaking when the Holy Spirit came upon all who listened to the Word. [45] And the believers of Jewish origin who had come with Peter were amazed:

—Why! God gives and pours the Holy Spirit on foreigners also!

[46] For indeed this happened: they heard them speaking in tongues and praising God.

[47] Then Peter declared:

—Can we refuse to baptize with water these people who have received the Holy Spirit, just as we have?

[48] So he had them baptized in the name of Jesus Christ. After that they asked him to remain with them for some days.

The Church of Antioch

11 19 Those who had been scattered because of the persecution over Stephen traveled as far as Phoenicia, Cyprus and
Antioch, telling the message, but only to the Jews. 20 But there
were some natives of Cyprus and Cyrene among them who, on
coming into Antioch, spoke also to the Greeks, giving them the
good news of the Lord Jesus. 21 The hand of the Lord was with
them so that a great number believed and turned to the Lord.

22 News of this reached the ears of the Church in Jerusalem,
so they sent Barnabas to Antioch. 23 When he arrived and saw
the manifest signs of God's favor, he rejoiced and urged them
all to remain firmly faithful to the Lord; 24 for he himself was a
good man filled with Holy Spirit and faith. Thus large crowds
came to know the Lord.

25 Then Barnabas went off to Tarsus to look for Saul 26 and
when he found him, he brought him to Antioch. For a whole
year they had meetings with the Church and instructed many
people. It was in Antioch that the disciples were first called
Christians.

Martyrdom of James. Peter imprisoned

12 1 About that time King Herod decided to persecute
some members of the Church. 2 He had James, the brother of
John, killed with the sword, 3 and when he saw how it pleased
the Jews, he proceeded to arrest Peter also.

This happened during the festival of the Unleavened
Bread. 4 Herod had him seized and thrown into prison with
four squads, each of four soldiers, to guard him. He wanted to
bring him to trial before the people after the Passover feast,
5 but while Peter was kept in prison, the whole Church prayed
earnestly for him.

6 On the very night before Herod was to bring him to trial,
Peter was sleeping between two soldiers, bound by a double
chain, while guards kept watch at the gate of the prison.

7 Suddenly an angel of the Lord stood there and a light
shone in the prison cell. The angel tapped Peter on the side
and woke him saying:

—Get up quickly!

At once the chains fell from Peter's wrists. The angel said:

—Put on your belt and your sandals.

Peter did so, [8] and the angel added:

—Now, put on your cloak and follow me.

[9] Peter followed him out; yet he did not realize that what was happening with the angel was real; he thought he was seeing a vision. [10] They passed the first guard and then the second and they came to the iron door leading out to the city, which opened of itself for them. They went out and made their way down a narrow alley, when suddenly the angel left him.

[11] Then Peter recovered his senses and said:

—Now I know that the Lord has sent his angel and has rescued me from Herod's clutches and from all that the Jews had in store for me.

[12] Peter then found his bearings and came to the house of Mary, the mother of John also known as Mark, where many were gathered together and were praying. [13] When he knocked at the outside door, a maid named Rhoda came to answer it. [14] On recognizing the voice of Peter she was so overcome with joy that, instead of opening the door, she ran in to announce that Peter was at the door. [15] They said to her:

—You are crazy!

And as she insisted, they said:

—It must be his angel.

[16] Meanwhile, Peter continued knocking and, when they finally opened the door, they were amazed to see him. [17] He motioned to them with his hand to be quiet and told them how the Lord had brought him out of prison. And he said to them:

—Report this to James and to the brothers.

Then he left and went to another place.

[18] At daybreak there was a great commotion among the soldiers over what had become of Peter. [19] Herod began a search for him and, not finding him, had the guards questioned and executed. After that, he came down from Judea to Caesarea and stayed there.

Mission of Paul and Barnabas

13 1 There were at Antioch—in the Church which was
there—prophets and teachers: Barnabas, Symeon known as
Niger, Lucius of Cyrene, Manaen who had been brought up
with Herod, and Saul. 2 On one occasion while they were cel-
ebrating the Lord and fasting, the Holy Spirit said to them:

—Set apart for me Barnabas and Saul to do the work for which I have called them.

3 So, after fasting and praying, they laid their hands on them and sent them off.

4 These then, sent by the Holy Spirit, went down to the port
of Seleucia and from there sailed to Cyprus. 5 Upon their
arrival in Salamis they proclaimed the word of God in the Jewish synagogue; John was with them as an assistant.

6 They traveled over the whole island as far as Paphos where they met a certain magician named Bar-Jesus, a Jewish false prophet.

11 At once a misty darkness came upon him, and he groped
about for someone to lead him by the hand. 12 The governor
saw what had happened; he believed, and was deeply impressed by the teaching about the Lord.

Antioch in Pisidia

13 From Paphos, Paul and his companions set sail and came to Perga in Pamphylia. There John left them and returned to
Jerusalem 14 while they went on from Perga and came to
Antioch in Pisidia. On the Sabbath day they entered the synagogue and sat down.

Paul's vision

16 9 There one night Paul had a vision. A Macedonian stood before him and begged him:

—Come over to Macedonia and help us!

10 When he awoke, he told us of this vision and we under-

stood that the Lord was calling us to give the Good News to the Macedonian people.

11 So we put out to sea from Troas and sailed straight across to Samothrace Island, and the next day to Neapolis. 12 From there we went inland to Philippi, the leading city of the district of Macedonia, and a Roman colony. We spent some days in that city.

13 On the sabbath we went outside the city gate to the bank of the river where we thought the Jews would gather to pray. We sat down and began speaking to the women who were gathering there. 14 One of them was a God-fearing woman named Lydia from Thyatira City, a dealer in purple cloth.

As she listened, the Lord opened her heart to respond to what Paul was saying. 15 After she had been baptized together with her household, she invited us to her house, "If you think I am faithful to the Lord, come and stay at my house." And she persuaded us to accept her invitation.

17 15 Paul was taken as far as Athens by his escort, who then returned to Beroea with instructions for Silas and Timothy to come to him as soon as possible.

In Athens

16 While Paul was waiting for them in Athens, he felt very uneasy at the sight of a city full of idols. 17 He held discussions in the synagogue with the Jews and the God-fearing people, as well as daily debates in the public square with ordinary passersby.

18 Epicureans and Stoic philosophers debated with him, some of them asking:

—What is this babbler trying to say?

Others commented:

—He sounds like a promoter of foreign gods.

Because he was heard to speak of Jesus and 'the Resurrection.' 19 So they took Paul and led him off to the Areopagus hall, and said:

—We would like to know what this new teaching is that you are talking about. [20] Some of the things we hear you say sound strange to us, and we would like to know what they mean.

[21] Indeed, all Athenian citizens, as well as the foreigners who live there, have as their favorite occupation talking about or listening to the latest news.

[22] Then Paul stood up in the Areopagus hall and said:

—Athenian citizens, I note that in every way you are very religious. [23] As I walked around looking at your shrines, I even discovered an altar with this inscription: *To an unknown God.* Now, what you worship as unknown, I intend to make known to you.

[24] —God, who made the world and all that is in it, does not dwell in sanctuaries made by human hands, being as he is Lord of heaven and earth. [25] Nor does his worship depend on anything made by human hands, as if he were in need. Rather it is he who gives life and breath and everything else to everyone.

[30] —But now God prefers to overlook this time of ignorance and he calls on all people to change their ways. [31] He has already set a day on which he will judge the world with justice through a man he has appointed. And, so that all may believe it, he has just given a sign by raising this man from the dead.

[32] When they heard Paul speak of a resurrection from death, some made fun of him, while others said:

—We must hear you on this topic some other time.

[33] At that point Paul left. [34] But a few did join him, and believed. Among them were Dionysius, a member of the Areopagus court, a woman named Damaris, and some others.

Trip to Jerusalem

21 [15] After this we got ready and went up to Jerusalem. [16] With us were some of the disciples of Caesarea who brought us to the house of a Cypriot where we were to stay. He was called Mnason and was one of the early disciples.

In Jerusalem

17 When we arrived in Jerusalem the brothers welcomed us
warmly. 18 The next day Paul went with us to James' house
where all the elders had gathered. 19 After greeting them, Paul
began telling them in detail everything God had done among
the non-Jews through his ministry.

Arrested in the Temple

27 When the seven days were almost over, some Jews from
Asia, who saw Paul in the Temple, began to stir up the whole
crowd. They seized him 28 shouting:

—Fellow Israelites, help! This is the man who is spreading his teaching everywhere against our people, our law and this Sanctuary. And now he has even brought non-Jews into the Temple area, defiling this Holy Place.

30 Then turmoil spread through the whole city. People came running from all sides. They seized Paul and dragged him outside the Temple. At once the gates were shut.

31 They would have killed him, had not a report reached the
commander of the Roman troops that all of Jerusalem was
rioting. 32 At once the commander took some officers and soldiers and rushed down to the crowd.

On seeing him with the soldiers, the crowd stopped beat-
ing Paul. 33 The commander went over to Paul, arrested him
and ordered him to be bound with two chains; then he
inquired who he was and what he had done. 34 But some in the
crowd shouted one thing and others another. As the commander was unable to find out the facts because of the uproar,
he ordered Paul to be brought to the fortress. 35 When Paul
reached the steps, he actually had to be carried up by the soldiers because of the violence of the mob, 36 for a multitude of
people followed shouting:

—Kill him!

37 Just as he was about to be taken inside, Paul said to the
commander:

—May I say something to you?

He replied:

—So you speak Greek! 38 Are you not the Egyptian, then, who caused a riot some time ago and let a band of four thousand terrorists out into the desert?

Paul answered:

39 —I am a Jew, a citizen of Tarsus, a well-known city in Cilicia. I beg you, let me address these people.

The commander agreed. 40 So Paul standing on the steps, motioned to the people with his hand and, when they were silent, he began to speak to them in Hebrew.

Paul's discourse

22 1 —Brothers and fathers,—listen to what I have to say to you in my defense.

2 When they heard him speaking to them in Hebrew, they became more quiet. So he went on.

3 —I am a Jew, born in Tarsus in Cilicia, but brought up here in this city where I was educated in the school of Gamaliel, according to the strict observance of our Law. And I was dedicated to God's service, as are all of you today. 4 As for this *way*, I persecuted it to the point of death and arrested its followers, both men and women, throwing them into prison.

5 —The High Priest and the whole Council of elders can bear witness to this. From them I received letters for the Jewish brothers in Damascus and I set out to arrest those who were
there and bring them back to Jerusalem for punishment. 6 But as
I was traveling along, nearing Damascus, at about noon a great light from the sky suddenly flashed about me. 7 I fell to the
ground and heard a voice saying to me: 'Saul, Saul, why do you
persecute me?' 8 I answered: 'Who are you, Lord?' And he said
to me: 'I am Jesus the Nazarean whom you persecute.' 9 The
men who were with me saw the light, but they did not understand the voice of the one who was speaking to me. 10 I asked:
'What shall I do, Lord?' And the Lord replied: 'Get up and go to Damascus; there you will be told all that you are destined to
do.' 11 Yet the brightness of that light had blinded me and so I
was led by the hand into Damascus by my companions.

12 —There a certain Ananias came to me. He was a devout observer of the Law and well spoken of by all the Jews who were living there. 13 As he stood by me, he said: 'Brother Saul, recover your sight.' At that moment I could see and I looked at him. 14 He then said, 'The God of our ancestors has chosen you to know his will, to see the Just One and to hear the words from his mouth. 15 From now on you shall be his witness before all the pagan peoples and tell them all that you have seen and heard. 16 And now, why delay? Get up and be baptized and have your sins washed away by calling upon his Name.'

17 —On my return to Jerusalem I was praying in the Temple, when I fell into a trance 18 and saw him. He spoke to me: 'Get ready to leave Jerusalem without delay, because they will not accept your testimony about me.' 19 I answered: 'Lord, they know well that I imprisoned those who believed in you and had them beaten in every synagogue, 20 and while the blood of your witness Stephen was being poured out, I stood by and approved it and even guarded the cloaks of his murderers.' 21 Then he said to me: 'Go, for I am sending you far away to the pagan nations.'

22 Up to this point the crowd listened to Paul, but on hearing the last words, they began to shout:

—Kill him! He does not deserve to live!

23 They were screaming and waving their cloaks and throwing dust into the air. 24 So the commander ordered Paul to be brought inside the fortress and questioned after flogging, to find out why they made such an outcry against him.

25 But when the soldiers had strapped him down, Paul said to the officer standing there:

—Is it legal to flog a Roman citizen without a trial?

26 On hearing this the officer went to the commander and said:

—What are you doing? That man is a Roman citizen.

27 So the commander came and asked him:

—Tell me, are you a Roman citizen?

Paul answered:

—Yes.

28 The commander then said:

—It cost me a large sum of money to become a Roman citizen.

Paul answered:

—I am one by birth.

29 Then those who were about to question him backed away, and the commander himself was alarmed when he realized that he had put a Roman citizen in chains.

Appeal to Caesar

25 1 Three days after Festus arrived in the province, he
went up from Caesarea to Jerusalem. 2 There the chief priests
and the elders accused Paul again. 3 In a very hypocritical way,
they asked as a favor from Festus that Paul be brought to
Jerusalem; but they were planning to kill him on the way.
9 Then Festus, who wanted to please the Jews, asked Paul:

—Do you wish to go up to Jerusalem to be tried before me?

10 Paul answered:

—I am on trial before Caesar's tribunal; here I have to be
tried. I have done no wrong to the Jews: you yourself know
this very well. 11 If I have committed any crime which deserves
death, I accept death. But if I have not done anything of which
they accuse me, no one can give me up to them. I appeal to
Caesar.

12 So Festus, after conferring with his council, answered:

—You have appealed to Caesar. To Caesar you shall go.

Sailing for Rome

27 1 When it was decided that we should sail for Italy,
they handed over Paul and the other prisoners into the care of
an officer of the Augustan battalion, named Julius. 2 We boarded a ship of Adramyttium bound for the Asian coasts, and we
left accompanied by Aristarchus, a Macedonian from the city
of Thessalonica. 7 We sailed slowly for several days, and

arrived with great difficulty at Cnidus. As the wind did not allow us to enter that port, we sailed for the shelter of Crete with the Cape of Salmone within sight. [8] We turned with difficulty and arrived at a place called Good Ports, near the city of Lasea.

[9] Time passed and the crossing began to be dangerous: we had already celebrated the feast of the Fast. [10] Then Paul said to them:

—Friends, I believe that it would not be very wise to proceed with our crossing for we could lose not only the cargo and the ship but also our lives.

[11] But the Roman officer relied more on the ship's captain and the owner of the ship than on the words of Paul. [12] And as the port was not suitable for wintering, the majority agreed to set out from there in the hope of reaching the harbor of Crete called Phoenix, overlooking Africa and Choros.

Storm

[13] Then the south wind began to blow and they thought that they had gained their purpose; they weighed anchor and sailed along the island of Crete. [14] But a little later, a strong wind called 'the northeaster' swept down on them, from across the island.

[21] As we had not eaten for days, Paul stood up among them and said: "Friends, if you had followed my advice when I told you not to set sail from Crete, we would not be in such danger now, and we could have avoided this loss. [22] But now I invite you to regain courage for no one among you shall die; only the ship shall be destroyed. [41] But they struck a sandbank and the ship ran aground. The bow stuck and was immovable, while the stern was broken up by the violent waves.

[42] The soldiers then planned to kill the prisoners for fear that some of them might escape by swimming. [43] But the captain, who wished to save Paul, did not allow them to do this. He ordered those who knew how to swim, to be the first to jump into the water and head for the shore, [44] and the rest to hold on to planks or pieces of the ship. So all of us reached land safe and sound.

Malta and Rome

28 1 After being saved, we learned that the island was
called Malta.

11 After three months, we boarded a ship that had spent the
winter at the island. It belonged to an Alexandrian company
and carried the figurehead of Castor and Pollux as insignia.
12 We sailed for Syracuse, staying there for three days 13 and,
after circling the coast, we arrived at Rhegium. On the following day, a south wind began to blow, and at the end of two
days we arrived at Puteoli, 14 where we found some of our
brothers who invited us to stay with them for a week. And
that was how we came to Rome.

16 Upon our arrival in Rome, the captain turned the prisoners over to the military governor but permitted Paul to lodge
in a private house with the soldier who guarded him.

17 After three days, Paul called together the leaders of the
Jews. When they had gathered, he said to them:

—Brothers, though I have not done anything against our
people or against the traditions of our fathers, I was arrested
in Jerusalem and handed over to the Romans. 18 They examined me and wanted to set me free, for they saw nothing in my
case that deserved death. 19 But the Jews objected, so I was
forced to appeal to Caesar without the least intention of bringing any case against my own people. 20 Therefore, I have asked
to see you and speak with you, since it is because of the hope
of Israel that I bear these chains.

21 They answered:

—We have not received any letter about you from Judea,
and none of the brothers who have come from there have
brought any message or said anything against you. 22 But we
wish to hear from you what you think, although we know
already that everywhere people speak against this sect that
you belong to.

23 They set a day for him and came in great numbers to his
lodging. So Paul explained everything he wanted to tell them
regarding the kingdom of God and tried to convince them
concerning Jesus, taking the Law of Moses and the Prophets
as his starting point. This continued from morning till night.

[24] Some were convinced by his words, others were not. [25] Finally the Jews left, still arguing strongly among themselves; and Paul sent them away with this statement:

—What the Holy Spirit said has come true, when he spoke to your ancestors through the prophet Isaiah: [26] *Go to this people and say to them: However much you hear, you will not understand; you will see and see again but not perceive.* [27] *The heart of this people has grown hard; they have covered their ears and closed their eyes, lest they should see with their eyes and hear with their ears, lest their spirit understand, and I should heal them.* [28] Let it be known to you, then, that this salvation of God has been sent to the pagans: they will listen.

[30] Paul stayed for two whole years in a house he himself rented, where he received without any hindrance all those who came to see him. [31] He proclaimed the kingdom of God and taught the truth about Jesus Christ, the Lord, quite openly and without any hindrance.

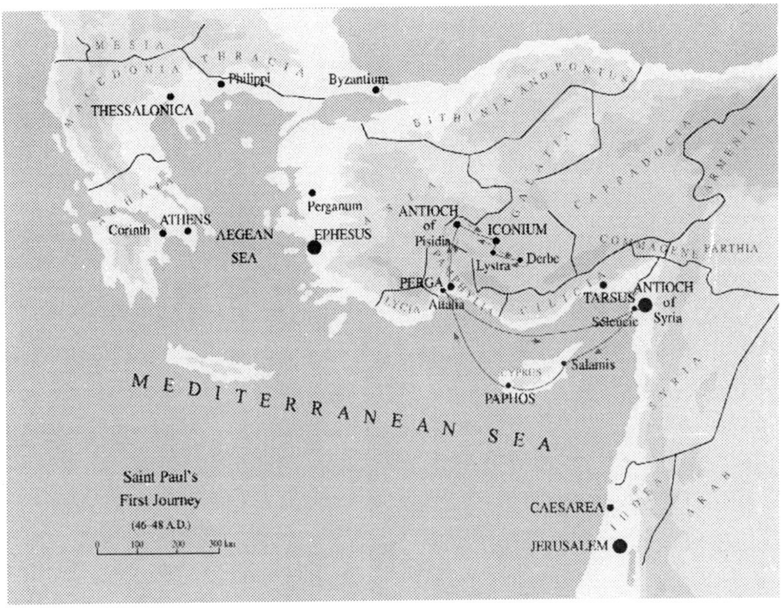
Philippi
Byzantium
THESSALONICA
Pergamum
ANTIOCH
of
Pisidia
ICONIUM
Corinth
ATHENS
AEGEAN
SEA
EPHESUS
Lystra
Derbe
PERGA
Attalia
TARSUS
ANTIOCH
of
Syria
Seleucia
Salamis
PAPHOS
MEDITERRANEAN SEA
PARTHIA
Saint Paul's
First Journey
(46-48 A.D.)
CAESAREA
JERUSALEM

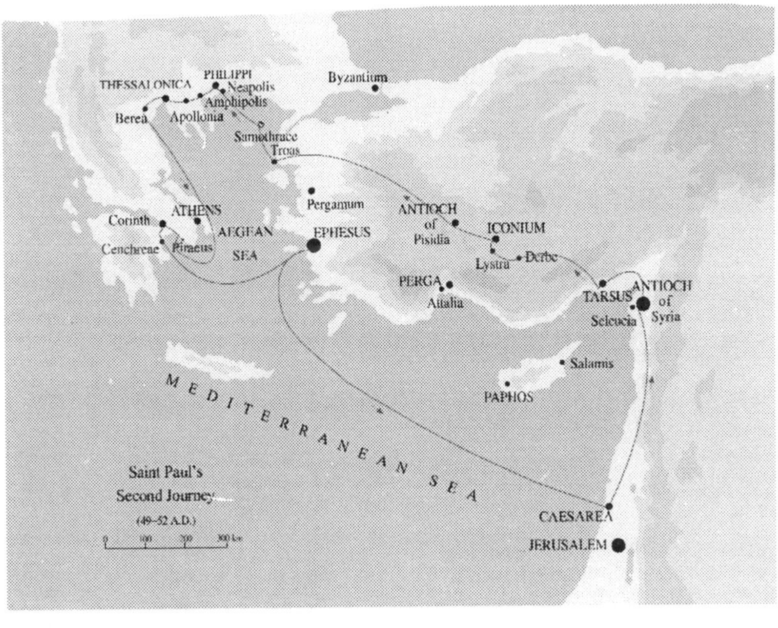
THESSALONICA
PHILIPPI
Neapolis
Amphipolis
Berea
Apollonia
Byzantium
Samothrace
Troas
Pergamum
ANTIOCH
of
Pisidia
ICONIUM
Corinth
ATHENS
AEGEAN
SEA
Cenchreae
Piraeus
EPHESUS
Lystra
Derbe
PERGA
Attalia
TARSUS
ANTIOCH
of
Syria
Seleucia
Salamis
PAPHOS
MEDITERRANEAN SEA
Saint Paul's
Second Journey
(49-52 A.D.)
CAESAREA
JERUSALEM

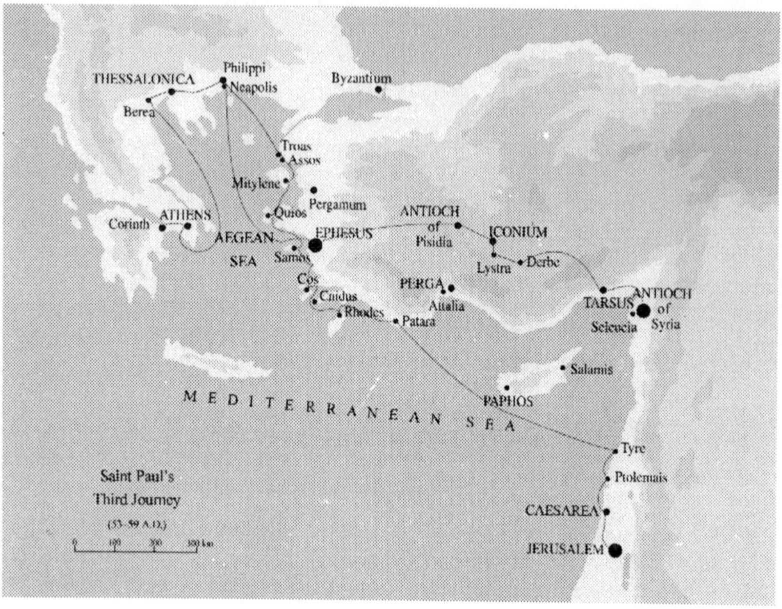
THESSALONICA
Philippi
Neapolis
Byzantium
Berea
Troas
Assos
Mitylene
Pergamum
Quios
Corinth
ATHENS
AEGEAN
SEA
EPHESUS
ANTIOCH
of
Pisidia
ICONIUM
Samos
Lystra
Derbe
Cos
Cnidus
Rhodes
Patara
PERGA
Attalia
TARSUS
ANTIOCH
of
Syria
Seleucia
Salamis
PAPHOS
M E D I T E R R A N E A N S E A
Tyre
Ptolemais
CAESAREA
JERUSALEM
Saint Paul's
Third Journey

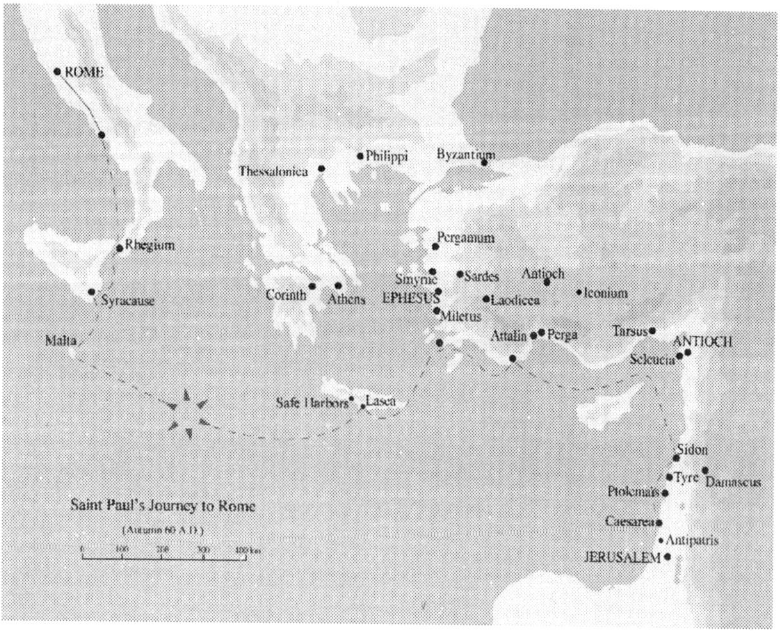
ROME
Philippi
Byzantium
Thessalonica
Rhegium
Pergamum
Sardes
Antioch
Smyrne
Iconium
Syracause
Corinth
Athens
EPHESUS
Laodicea
Miletus
Malta
Attalia
Perga
Tarsus
ANTIOCH
Seleucia
Safe Harbors
Lasea
Sidon
Tyre
Damascus
Ptolemais
Caesarea
Antipatris
JERUSALEM
Saint Paul's Journey to Rome

Letters

Another literary genre of the New Testament are the letters written by some apostles to the first Christian communities.

In these letters they applied the evangelical principles to particular situations or explain controversial points. Of great importance also is the transmission of the gospel message to new cultural categories, creating in this way a theology of faith.

The most known letters are the ones of St. Paul, responsible for embarking towards a new expansion of Christianity.

We select here some of the most known texts of Paul, James and John as they have been used in the liturgy and in Christian tradition.

Letters of Saint Paul

Letter to the Romans

Introduction

Probably at Corinth Paul decides to write and send a letter to the community of Rome.

The letter is a strong, stable and tense structure between two poles: fidelity to Judaism and to the universal vocation. And it presents a capital point of the Christian faith. Some authors call it soteriology or the doctrine about salvation.

The letter to the Romans is one of the documents that have influenced more in the history of the Church

Life of the Spirit

8 14 All those who walk in the Spirit of God are sons and
daughters of God. 15 Then, no more fear: you did not receive
a spirit of slavery, but the Spirit that makes you sons and
daughters and every time we cry, '*Abba!* (that is Dad!)
Father!' 16 the Spirit assures our spirit that we are sons and
daughters of God. 17 If we are children, we are heirs, too.
Ours will be the inheritance of God and we will share it with
Christ; for if we now suffer with him, we will also share
Glory with him.

Norms about Christian life

12 9 Let love be sincere. Hate what is evil and hold to
whatever is good. 10 Love one another and be considerate.
Outdo one another in mutual respect. 11 Be zealous in fulfilling
your duties. Be fervent in the Spirit and serve God.

12 Have hope and be cheerful. Be patient in trials and pray
constantly. 13 Share with other Christians in need. With those
passing by, be ready to receive them.

14 Bless those who persecute you; bless and do not wish evil
on anyone. 15 Rejoice with those who are joyful, and weep
with those who weep. 16 Live in peace with one another. Do
not dream of extraordinary things; be humble and do not hold
yourselves as wise.

17 Do not return evil for evil, but let everyone see your good
will. 18 Do your best to live in peace with everybody.
19 Beloved, do not avenge yourselves, but let God be the one
who punishes, as Scripture says: *Vengeance is mine, I will repay,
says the Lord.* 20 And it adds: *If your enemy is hungry, feed him; if
he is thirsty, give him to drink; by doing this you will heap burning
coals upon his head.* 21 Do not let evil defeat you, but conquer
evil with goodness.

First Letter to the Corinthians

Introduction

In the past Corinth was a cosmopolitan commercial empire. Its two ports, at East and West, opened it up advantageously and made of it a center for cultural communication. Paul founded there a Christian community, composed to a great extent by low class people. The church at Corinth was a prosperous pluralistic community, exposed to the contamination of the pagan environment and undergoing internal tensions.

Starting from concrete life situation, Paul rises up to great principles and Christian vision.

Superior wisdom

2 1 When I came to reveal to you the mystery of God's
plan I did not count on eloquence or on a show of learning. 2 I
was determined not to know anything among you but Jesus,
the Messiah, and a crucified Messiah. 3 I myself came weak,
fearful and trembling; 4 my words and preaching were not
brilliant or clever to win listeners. 5 It was, rather, a demon-
stration of spirit and power, so that your faith might be a matter, not of human wisdom, but of God's power.

Agape and Eucharist

11 23 This is the tradition of the Lord that I received and
that in my turn I have handed on to you; the Lord Jesus, on the
night that he was delivered up, took bread and, 24 after giving
thanks, broke it, saying, 'This is my body which is broken for
you; do this in memory of me.' 25 In the same manner, taking
the cup after the supper, he said, 'This cup is the new
Covenant in my blood. Whenever you drink it, do it in memory of me.' 26 So, then, whenever you eat of this bread and
drink from this cup, you are proclaiming the death of the Lord
until he comes.

27 Therefore, if anyone eats of the bread or drinks from the
cup of the Lord unworthily, he sins against the body and
blood of the Lord.

28 Let each one, then, examine himself before eating of the
bread and drinking from the cup. 29 Otherwise, he eats and
drinks his own condemnation in not recognizing the Body.
34 The other instructions I shall give when I go there.

Charisms

12 12 As the body is one, having many members, and all
the members, while being many, form one body, so it is with
Christ. 13 All of us, whether Jews or Greeks, slaves or free,
have been baptized in one Spirit to form one body and all of
us have been given to drink from the one Spirit.

14 The body has not just one member, but many. 15 If the foot
should say, 'I do not belong to the body for I am not a hand,'
it would be wrong: it is part of the body! 16 Even though the
ear says, 'I do not belong to the body for I am not an eye,' it is
part of the body. 17 If all the body were eye, how would we
hear? And if all the body were ear, how would we smell?

18 God has arranged all the members, placing each part of
the body as he pleased. 19 If all were the same part where
would the body be? 20 But there are many members and one
body. 21 The eye cannot tell the hand, 'I do not need you,' nor
the head tell the feet, 'I do not need you.'

Hymn to Christian love

13 1 If I could speak all the human and angelic tongues,
but had no love, I would only be sounding brass or a clanging
cymbal.

2 If I had the gift of prophecy, knowing secret things with all
kinds of knowledge, and had faith great enough to remove
mountains, but had no love, I would be nothing. 3 If I gave everything I had to the poor, and even give up my body to be
burned, if I am without love, it would be of no value to me.

4 Love is patient, kind, without envy. It is not boastful or
arrogant. It is not ill-mannered nor does it seek its own interest. 5 Love overcomes anger and forgets offenses. 6 It does not
take delight in wrong, but rejoices in truth. 7 Love excuses
everything, believes all things, hopes all things, endures all
things.

8 Love will never end. Prophecies may cease, tongues be
silent and knowledge disappear. 9 For knowledge grasps
something of the truth and prophecy as well. 10 And when
what is perfect comes, everything imperfect will pass away.
11 When I was a child I thought and reasoned like a child, but
when I grew up, I gave up childish ways.

12 Likewise, at present we see dimly as in a mirror, but then
it shall be face to face. Now we know in part, but then I will
know as I am known. 13 Now we have faith, hope and love,
these three, but the greatest of these is love.

Resurrection of the death

15 3 In the first place, I have passed on to you what I
myself received: that Christ died for our sins, as Scripture
says; 4 that he was buried; that he was raised on the third day,
according to the Scriptures; 5 that he appeared to Cephas and
then to the Twelve. 6 Afterwards he appeared to more than
five hundred brothers and sisters together; most of them are
still alive, although some have already gone to rest. 7 Then he
appeared to James and after that to all the apostles. 8 And last
of all, he appeared to the most despicable of them, this is to

me. [11] Now, whether it was I or they, this we preach and this you have believed.

[13] If there is no resurrection of the dead, then Christ has not been raised. [14] And if Christ has not been raised, our preaching is empty and our belief comes to nothing.

[20] But no, Christ has been raised from the dead and he comes before all those who have fallen asleep. [21] A human being brought death; a human being also brings resurrection of the dead. [22] All die for being Adam's, and in Christ all will receive life.

Second Letter to the Corinthians

Introduction

New happenings have appeared in Corinth since the first letter. Some people have arrived questioning Paul's authority. Paul reacts with passion.

In this way the letter becomes a vital treatise about the apostolic mission.

The faith criterion

5 11 So we know the fear of the Lord and we try to convince people while we live openly before God. And I trust that
you know in your conscience what we truly are. 12 Once more,
we do not try to win your esteem; we want to give you a reason to feel proud of us, that you may respond to those who
heed appearances and not the reality. 13 Now, if I have spoken
foolishly, let God alone hear; if what I have said makes sense,
take it for yourselves.

14 Indeed the love of Christ holds us and we realize that if
he died for all, all have died. 15 He died for all so that those
who live may live no longer for themselves, but for him who
died and rose again for them. 16 And so from now on, we do
not regard anyone from a human point of view; and even if
we once knew Christ personally, we should now regard him
in another way.

Boasting about a fake fool

11 18 As some people boast of human advantages, I will do the same. 19 Fortunately you bear rather well with fools, you who are so wise! 21 What a shame that I acted so weakly with you!

But if others are so bold, I shall also dare, although I may speak like a fool. 22 Are they Hebrews? So am I. Are they Israelites? So am I. Are they descendants of Abraham? So am I. 23 Are they ministers of Christ? (I begin to talk like a madman) I am better than they.

Better than they with my numerous labors. Better than they with the time spent in prison. The beatings I received are beyond comparison. How many times have I found myself in danger of death! 24 Five times the Jews sentenced me to thirty-nine lashes. 25 Three times I was beaten with a rod, once I was stoned. Three times I was shipwrecked, and once I spent a night and a day adrift on the high seas.

26 I have been continually in hazards of traveling because of rivers, because of bandits, because of my fellow Jews, or because of the pagans; in danger in the city, in the open country, at sea; in danger from false brothers. 27 I have worked and often labored without sleep, I have been hungry and thirsty and starving, cold and without shelter.

28 Besides these and other things, there was my daily concern for all the churches.

Revelations and shortcomings

12 1 It is useless to boast; but if I have to, I will go on to some visions and revelations of the Lord.

2 I know a certain Christian: fourteen years ago he was taken up to the third heaven. 3 Whether in the body or out of the body, I do not know, God knows. But I know that this man, whether in the body or out of the body—I do not know, God knows—4 was taken up to Paradise where he heard words that cannot be told: things which humans cannot express.

5 Of that man I can indeed boast, but of myself I will not

boast except of my weaknesses. 6 If I wanted to boast, it would
not be foolish of me, for I would speak the truth. 7 However, I
better give up lest somebody think more of me than what is
seen in me or heard from me. Lest I become proud after so
many and extraordinary revelations, I was given a thorn in
my flesh, a true messenger of Satan, to slap me in the face.
8 Three times I prayed to the Lord that it leave me, 9 but he
answered, 'My grace is enough for you; my great strength is
revealed in weakness.'

Gladly, then, will I boast of my weakness that the strength of Christ may be mine.

Letter to the Galatians

Introduction

Paul had preached in the Roman Province of Galatia. There he started some communities of converted pagans. Some time later some judaizers appear there preaching that Christians had to be circumcised and observe certain Mosaic prescriptions.

The letter is a vibrant declaration in favor of Christian freedom, citing autobiographical traits and anecdotes.

Paul's vocation

1 [13] You have heard of my previous activity in the Jewish
community; I furiously persecuted the Church of God and
tried to destroy it. [14] For I was more devoted to the Jewish religion than many fellow Jews of my age, and I defended the traditions of my ancestors more fanatically.

[15] But one day God called me out of his great love, he who
had chosen me from my mother's womb; and he was pleased [16] to
reveal in me his Son, that I might make him known among the
pagan nations. Then I did not seek human advice [17] nor did I
go up to Jerusalem to those who were apostles before me. I
immediately went to Arabia, and from there I returned again
to Damascus. [18] Later, after three years, I went up to Jerusalem
to meet Cephas, and I stayed with him for fifteen days. [19] But
I did not see any other apostle except James, the Lord's brother. [20] On writing this to you, I affirm before God that I am not
lying.

[21] After that I went to Syria and Cilicia. [22] The churches of

Christ in Judea did not know me personally; [23] they had only
heard of me: 'He who once persecuted us is now preaching
the faith he tried to uproot.' [24] And they praised God because
of me.

Paul and the other apostles

2 [1] After fourteen years I again went up to Jerusalem with
Barnabas, and Titus came with us. [2] Following a revelation, I
went to lay before them the Gospel that I am preaching to the
pagans. I had a private meeting with the leaders—lest I
should be working or have worked in a wrong way. [7] They
recognized that I have been entrusted to give the Good News
to the pagan nations, just as Peter has been entrusted to give
it to the Jews. [8] In the same way that God made Peter the apostle of the Jews, he made me the apostle of the pagans. [9] James,
Cephas and John acknowledged the graces God gave me.
Those men who were regarded as the pillars of the Church
stretched out their hand to me and Barnabas as a sign of fellowship; we would go to the pagans and they to the Jews.
[10] We should only keep in mind the poor among them. I have
taken care to do this.

Letter to the Philippians

Introduction

Philippos, a small city with a great aura. Founded by Philip, father of Alexander Magnus, a Roman colony in Greek territory and juncture of communications. It is the first city in European territory evangelized by Paul.

And the highlight: the hymn to Christ, humbled and exalted, model and hope of Christians, and vastly used in the liturgy. We select it as a jewel of Christian tradition.

Christian love and humility of Christ

2 5 Your attitude should be the same as Jesus Christ had:
6 Though he was in the form of God,
he did not regard equality with God
as something to be grasped,
7 but emptied himself,
taking on the nature of a servant,
made in human likeness,
and in his appearance found as a man.
8 He humbled himself by being obedient to death,
death on the cross.
9 That is why God exalted him
and gave him the Name which outshines all names,
10 so that at the Name of Jesus
all knees should bend
in heaven, on earth and among the dead,

11 and all tongues proclaim that Christ Jesus
is the Lord
to the glory of God the Father.

Letter to the Colossians

Introduction

The text is presented as a letter written by Paul, a prisoner in Rome, to the community of Colossos, in Phrygia, Asia Minor. The occasion is a great danger of heresy that threatens that community.

A critical examination of the theme, language and style, suggests that the letter is written by a disciple of Paul, of the next generation, able to imitate well the master and using Paul's authority.

3 12 Clothe yourselves, then, as is fitting for God's chosen
people, holy and beloved of him. Put on compassion, kindness, humility, meekness and patience 13 to bear with one

another and forgive whenever there is any occasion to do so.
As the Lord has forgiven you, forgive one another. 14 Above
all, clothe yourselves with love which binds everything
together in perfect harmony. 15 May the peace of Christ overflow in your hearts; for this end you were called to be one
body. And be thankful.

16 Let the word of God dwell in you in all its richness.
Teach and admonish one another with words of wisdom.
With thankful hearts sing to God psalms, hymns and sponta-
neous praise. 17 And whatever you do or say, do it in the
Name of Jesus, the Lord, giving thanks to God the Father
through him.

Second Letter to Timothy

Introduction

Given the topic and style three writings are gathered together with the title of pastoral letters, because Paul addresses them to persons responsible of a local community, giving them norms of government for their use and of Christian conduct for the community.

The addressees are Timothy and Titus. Timothy was closely united with Paul; he was his companion on trips and mission, a man of trust for important and delicate assignments.

2 8 Remember Christ Jesus, risen from the dead, Jesus, son
of David, as preached in my Gospel.
11 This statement is true:
If we have died with him, we shall also live with him;
12 If we endure with him, we shall reign with him;
If we deny him, he will also deny us;
13 If we are unfaithful, he remains faithful for he cannot
deny himself.

Other Letters

LETTER OF JAMES

Introduction

The heading is proper of a letter. It is sent by James, known as the brother of Lord (Mk 6:3; Gal 1:19), head of the Jerusalem church (Acts 15:13), one of the Twelve.

The letter resembles a wise writing, with ethical topics, and transferred to a Christian context.

1 1 James, a servant of God and of the Lord Jesus Christ,
sends greetings to the twelve tribes scattered among the
nations.

Partiality

2 1 My brothers and sisters, if you truly believe in our glorified Lord, Jesus Christ, you will not discriminate between
persons. 2 Suppose a person enters the synagogue where you
are assembled, dressed magnificently and wearing a gold
ring; at the same time, a poor person enters dressed in rags. 3 If
you focus your attention on the well-dressed and say, 'Come
and sit in the best seat,' while to the poor one you say, "Stay
standing or else sit down at my feet," 5 Listen, my beloved
brothers and sisters, did God not choose the poor of this world
to receive the riches of faith and to inherit the kingdom which
he has promised to those who love him? 6 Yet you despise
them! Is it not the rich who are against you and drag you to
court? 8 If you keep the Law of the Kingdom, according to

Scripture: *Love your neighbor as yourself,* you do well; 9 but if you make distinctions between persons, you break the law and are condemned by the same law. 10 For whoever keeps the whole law but fails in one aspect, is guilty of breaking it all.

Rich and satisfied

5 1 So, now for what concerns the rich! Cry and weep for the misfortunes that are coming upon you. 2 Your riches are rotting and your clothes eaten up by the moths. 3 Your silver and gold have rusted and their rust grows into a witness against you. It will consume your flesh like fire, for having piled up riches in these the last days.

4 You deceived the workers who harvested your fields but now their wages cry out to the heavens. The reapers' complaints have reached the ears of the Lord of hosts. 5 You lived in luxury and pleasure in this world thus fattening yourselves for the day of slaughter. 6 You have easily condemned and killed the innocent since they offered no resistance.

Patience and prayer

13 Are any among you discouraged? They should pray. Are any of you happy? They should sing songs to God. 14 If anyone is sick, let him call on the elders of the Church. They shall pray for him, anointing him with oil in the name of the Lord. 15 The prayer said in faith will save the sick person; the Lord will raise him up and if he has committed any sins, he will be forgiven.

16 There will be healing if you confess your sins to one another and pray for each other. The prayer of the upright man has great power, provided he perseveres.

First Letter of John

Introduction

The authentic Christian is known by several signs: fulfills the commandments, avoids sins and practices justice, confesses Jesus as Messiah and, especially, loves neighbor. God is light, God is love.

The old tradition has attributed this letter to John, the author of the gospel. The similarity between these two writings is obvious.

1 1 This is what has been from the beginning, and what we have heard and have seen with our own eyes, what we have looked at and touched with our hands, I mean the *Word* who is Life…

2 The *Life* made *itself* known, we have seen Eternal Life and we bear witness, and we are telling you of it. It was with the Father and made himself known to us.

3 So we tell you what we have seen and heard, that you may be in fellowship with us, and us, with the Father and with his Son, Jesus Christ.

4 And we write this that our joy may be complete.

Christians and the world

2 12 My dear children, I write this to you: you have
already received the forgiveness of your sins through the
Name of Jesus. 13 Fathers, I write this to you: you know him
who is from the beginning. Young men, I write this to you:

you already know the Father.

14 Fathers, I write to you because you know him who is from the beginning. Young men, I write to you because you are strong and the Word of God lives in you who have indeed overcome the Evil One.

15 Do not love the world or what is in it. If anyone loves the world, the love of the Father is not in him.

16 For everything in the world
—the craving of the flesh,
the greed of eyes
and people boasting of their superiority—
all this belongs to the world, not to the Father.

17 The world passes away with all its craving but those who do the will of God remain for ever.

The commandment of love

3 11 For this is the message taught to you from the beginning: we must love one another. 13 So, be not surprised, brothers if the world hates us; 14 we love our brothers and sisters,
and with this we know that we have passed from death to life.
The one who does not love remains in death.

15 The one who hates his brother is a murderer, and, as you know, eternal life does not remain in the murderer.

16 This is how we have known what love is: he gave his life for us. We, too, ought to give our life for our brothers and sisters.

17 If anyone enjoys the riches of this world, but closes his
heart when he sees his brother or sister in need, how will the
love of God remain in him? 18 My dear children, let us love not
only with words and with our lips, but in truth and in deed.

God is love

4 7 My dear friends, let us love one another for love comes
from God. Everyone who loves is born of God and knows
God. 8 Those who do not love have not known God, for God is

love. 9 How did the love of God appear among us? God sent
his only Son into this world that we might have life through
him.

10 This is love: not that we loved God but that he first loved
us and sent his Son as an atoning sacrifice for our sins.

19 So let us love one another, since he loved us first.

20 If you say, 'I love God,' while you hate your brother or
sister, you are a liar. How can you love God whom you do not
see, if you do not love your brother whom you see? 21 We
received from him this commandment: let those who love
God also love their brothers.

Revelation

Introduction

We find ourselves in front of the last book of the New Testament and indeed of the whole Bible. Its name is already telling us about its content: "revelation", "manifestation" of what is hidden.

Two styles are found in the composition of this book: on the one hand, the prophetic style, as found in the prophets Isaiah, Ezekiel, Zachariah; and on the other, the apocalyptic style as it clearly appears in the book of Daniel and the apocrypha.

In the prophetic part a series of advises are gathered, addressed to the seven Churches of Asia (Ephesus, Smyrna, Pergamum, Thyatira, Sardis, Philadelphia and Laodicea); we could take these as warnings to the universal Church. It praises some of its achievements while at the same time calling attention to some aspects of its life that have to be amended and changed.

The apocalyptic part tells us about the signs at the end of the world (the famous seven seals and the four horsemen of Revelation); later on it presents the great confrontation where "the power and the kingdom of our God" is victorious, concluding with the great final manifestation of "the new heavens and the new earth."

The main character and central figure of this book is the sacrificed and risen Messiah, receiving the emblematic title of "Lamb" as John the Baptist applied it to Jesus describing him as "the lamb of God who takes away the sins of the world."

This powerful, enigmatic and symbolic book has fascinated readers and artists. Unfortunately many did not know how to read and interpret the book, therefore misunderstanding its content and reaching partial and illegitimate interpretations and conclusions.

Formerly it was thought that the author was the apostle John, the writer of the gospel. There are a series of coincidences: the name appearing at the beginning of the book, the mentioning of the island of Patmos seemed to confirm it. Very few today accept this identification. It seems, nevertheless, that the description of difficulties and persecutions mentioned in the book refer to the persecution of Diomitian in the years 81–96 of our era.

Message to the seven Churches

1 4 From John to the seven Churches of Asia: receive grace
and peace from him who is, who was and who is to come, and
from the seven Spirits of God which are before his throne,
5 and from Jesus Christ, the faithful witness, the firstborn of
the dead, the ruler of the kings of the earth.

To him who loves us and has washed away our sins with
his own blood, 6 making us a kingdom and priests for God his
Father, to him be the glory and power for ever and ever.
Amen.

7 See *he comes with the clouds* and everyone will see him,
even *those who pierced him;* on his account *all the nations of the
earth will beat his breast*. Yes. It will be so.

10 On the Lord's day, the Spirit took possession of me and I
heard a voice behind me which sounded like a trumpet,
11 "Write down all that you see, in a book, and send it to the
seven Churches of Ephesus, Smyrna, Pergamum, Thyatira,
Sardis, Philadelphia and Laodicea."

Church of Ephesus

2 1 Write this to the angel of the Church in Ephesus, "Thus
says the one who holds the seven stars in his right hand and
who walks among the seven golden lamp stands:

2 I know your works, your difficulties and your patient suffering. I know you cannot tolerate evildoers but have tested
those who call themselves apostles and have proved them to
be liars. 3 You have persevered and have suffered for my name
without losing heart.

4 Nevertheless, I have this complaint against you: you have

lost your first love. 5 Remember from where you have fallen
and repent, and do what you used to do before. If not, I will
come to you and remove your lampstand from its place; this I
will do, unless you repent.

Church of Smyrna

8 Write this to the angel of the Church in Smyrna, 'Thus
says the First and the Last, he who was dead and returned to
life:

9 I know your trials and your poverty: you are rich indeed.
I know how you are slandered by those who pretend to be
Jews but are not, for they are, in fact, the synagogue of Satan.
10 Do not be afraid of what will happen to you. The devil will
throw some of you into prison to test you and there will be ten
days of trials. Remain faithful even to death and I will give
you the crown of life.

11 Let anyone who has ears listen to what the Spirit says to
the Churches: The victor has nothing to fear from the second
death.'

Church of Pergamum

12 Write this to the angel of the Church in Pergamum, 'Thus
says the one who has the sharp, double-edged sword:

13 I know where you live, where Satan's throne is, but you
cling firmly to my name; you have not renounced me, not
even in the days when Antipas, my faithful witness, was
killed in your place, where Satan lives.

14 Nevertheless, I have a few complaints against you: Some
among you hold the teaching of Balaam, who taught Balak
how to make the Israelites stumble by eating food sacrificed to
idols and comitting adultery. 15 Also, among you some follow
the teaching of the Nicolaitans. 16 Therefore, repent; if not, I
will come to you soon to attack these people with the sword
of my mouth.

17 Let anyone who has ears listen to what the Spirit says to
the Churches: To the victor I will give the hidden manna. And

I will also give a white stone with a new name written on it
which no one knows except the one who receives it.'

Church of Thyatira

18 Write this to the angel of the Church in Thyatira, 'Thus
says the Son of God whose eyes are like flames of fire and
whose feet are like burnished bronze. 19 I know your works:
your love, faith, service, patient endurance and your later
works, greater than the first.

20 Nevertheless, I have a complaint against you: you tolerate your Jezebel, this woman who calls herself a prophetess
and is deceiving my servants; she teaches them prostitution
and the eating of food sacrificed to idols.

26 To the victor who keeps to my ways to the end, *I will give
power over the nations,* 27 *to rule them with an iron rod and shatter
them like earthen pots*; he will be like me, who received this power
from my Father. 28 Moreover, I will give him the Morning Star.

29 Let anyone who has ears listen to what the Spirit says to
the Churches.'

Church of Sardis

3 1 Write this to the angel of the Church in Sardis, 'Thus
says he who holds the seven spirits of God and the seven
stars:

I know your worth: you think you live but you are dead.
2 Wake up and strengthen that which is not already dead. For
I have found your works to be imperfect in the sight of my
God. 3 Remember what you were taught; keep it and change
your ways. If you do not repent I will come upon you like a
thief at an hour you least expect.

4 Yet, there are some left in Sardis who have not soiled their
robes; these will come with me, dressed in white, since they
deserve it. 5 The victor will be dressed in white and I will
never erase his name from the book of life; instead, I will
acknowledge it before my Father and his angels.

6 Let anyone who has ears listen to what the Spirit says to
the Churches.'

Church of Philadelphia

7 Write this to the angel of the Church in Philadelphia, 'Thus
says he who is holy and true, who holds the key of David; if he
opens, nobody shuts and if he shuts nobody opens.

8 I know your worth; I have opened a door before you,
which nobody can close, because you have kept my Word and
not renounced me, in spite of your lack of power. 9 I am giving
you some of the synagogue of Satan who call themselves Jews
but they are only liars. I will make them fall at your feet and
recognize that I have loved you.

10 Because you have kept my words with patient
endurance, I, for my part, will keep you safe in the hour of
trial that is coming upon the whole world, to test the people
of the earth. 11 I am coming soon; hold fast to what you have,
lest anyone take your crown.

12 I will make the victor into a column in the sanctuary of
my God where he will stay forever. I will write on him the
name of my God and the name of the city of my God, the new
Jerusalem, which comes down from my God in heaven, and
my own new name. 13 Let anyone who has ears listen to what
the Spirit says to the Churches.'

Church of Laodicea

14 Write this to the angel of the Church in Laodicea, 'Thus
says the Amen, the faithful and true witness, the beginning of
God's creation:

15 I know your works: you are neither cold nor hot. Would
that you were cold or hot! 16 You are lukewarm, neither hot nor
cold so I will spit you out of my mouth. 17 You think you are
rich and have piled up so much that you need nothing, but
you do not realize that you are wretched and to be pitied,
poor, blind and naked.

18 I advise you to buy from me gold that has been tested by
fire, so that you may be rich, and white clothes to wear so that
your nakedness may not shame you, and ointment for your
eyes that you may see. 19 I reprimand and correct all those I
love. Be earnest and change your ways.

[20] Look, I stand at the door and knock. If you hear my call
and open the door, I will come in to you and have supper with
you, and you with me. [21] I will let the victor sit with me on my
throne just as I was victorious and took my place with my
Father on his throne. [22] Let anyone who has ears listen to what
the Spirit says to the Churches.'

War in heaven

[7] War broke out in heaven with Michael and his angels bat-
tling with the dragon. The dragon fought back with his angels,
[8] but they were defeated and lost their place in heaven. [9] The
great dragon, the ancient serpent known as the devil or Satan,
seducer of the whole world, was thrown out. He was hurled
down to earth, together with his angels.

[10] Then I heard a loud voice from heaven:
Now has salvation come,
with the power and the kingdom of our God,
and the rule of his anointed.
For our brothers' accuser has been cast out,
who accused them night and day, before God.
[11] *They conquered him by the blood of the Lamb*
and by the word of their testimony,
for they gave up their lives going to death.
[12] *Rejoice, therefore, O you heavens*
and you who dwell in them;
but woe to you, earth and sea,
for the devil has come to you in anger
knowing that he has but a little time.

New heaven and new earth

21 [1] Then I saw a new heaven and a new earth. The first
heaven and the first earth had passed away and no longer was
there any sea. [2] I saw the new Jerusalem, the holy city coming
down from God, out of heaven, adorned as a bride prepared
for her husband. [3] A loud voice came from the throne, "Here is
the dwelling of God among mortals: *He will pitch his tent*

among them and they will be his people; he will be God-with-them.

[4]He will *wipe every tear from their eyes*. There shall be no more death or mourning, crying out or pain, for the world that was has passed away. [5]The One seated on the throne said, 'See, I make all things new.'

And then he said to me, "Write these words because they are sure and true."

[6]And he said to me: It is already done! I am the Alpha and the Omega, the Beginning and the End. I myself will give the thirsty to drink without cost from the fountain of living water. [7]Thus the winner will be rewarded: *For him I shall be God and he will be my son*.

[8]As for cowards, traitors, depraved, murderers, adulterers, sorcerers, and idolaters—all those who live in falsehood, their place is the lake of burning sulfur. This is the second death.'

22 [6]Then the angel said to me, 'These words are sure and true; the Lord God who inspires the prophets has sent his angel to show his servants what must happen soon.'

[7]'I am coming soon! Happy are those who keep the prophetic words of this book.'

Come, Lord Jesus

[8]I, John, saw and heard all this. When I had seen and heard them I fell at the feet of the angel who had shown me everything, to worship him. [9]But he said; 'No, I am a fellow servant like you and your brothers, the prophets, and those who heed the words of this book. It is God you must worship.'

[10]He then said to me: 'Do not keep secret the prophetic words of this book because the time is near. [11]'Let the sinner continue to sin and the defiled remain in his defilement; let the righteous continue to do what is right and he who is holy grow holier.'

[12]'I am coming soon, bringing with me the salary I will pay to each one according to his deeds. [13]I am the Alpha and the Omega, the First and the Last, the Beginning and the End.'

14 Happy are those who wash their robes for they will have
free access to the tree of Life and enter the city through the
gates. 15 Outside are the dogs, sorcerers, the immoral, murderers, idolaters and all who take pleasure in falsehood!

16 'I, Jesus, sent my angel to make known to you these revelations concerning the Churches. I am the Shoot and
Offspring of David, the radiant Morning Star.'

20 He who has declared all this says: 'Yes, I am coming
soon.'

Amen! Come, Lord Jesus.

21 May the grace of the Lord Jesus be with you all.

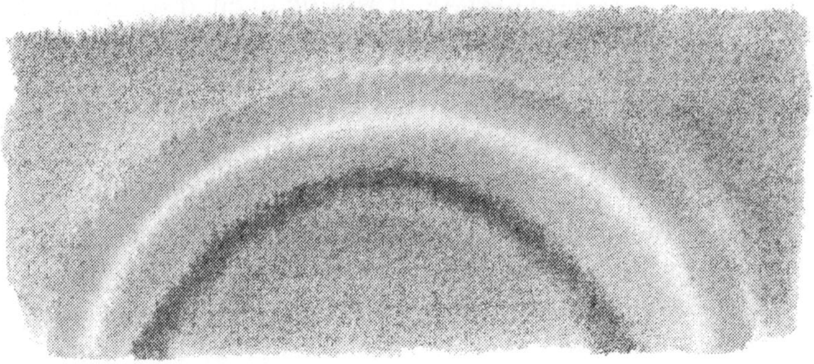

The Last Word...

We are sure you have enjoyed a beautiful tour of the Bible. It is just an introduction, an appetizer! You are now invited to discover the Word in its totality: To open the Bible with faith and hope in your heart and allow it to guide your life.

God will introduce you to the Truth. Search with perseverance: the door will be opened to those who knock. Do not give up if you cannot understand at the beginning, but ask in prayer and you will receive light. To grasp the teaching of God you also have to search for it together with your brothers and sisters as you participate in the Christian community.

The translation of the text of the Bible that you read in this book is taken from the Christian Community Bible, Catholic Pastoral Edition. This Pastoral Bible has already been published in many languages. We encourage you to read the whole Bible... the only Last Word!

If you have comments or questions you can write to us at the Pastoral Bible Foundation or email us at cci@claret.org

We also invite you to visit our web page and consult the Pastoral Bible on line in different languages: www.bible.claret.org

PASTORAL BIBLE FOUNDATION
U.P.P.O.Box 4
Diliman, 1101 Quezon City
Philippines